Getting to The Motley Fool Online!

David and Tom Gardner are cofounders of The Motley Fool, an online forum that can be found on the Web at www.Fool.com and on America Online at keyword: FOOL.

Whether you're looking for additional research on the stocks in your portfolio, new investment ideas, information about your 401(k) plan, daily news updates on the world's most dynamic companies, minute-by-minute stock quotes, or just a place to talk to other investors, Fool.com has all of that and more—available twenty-four hours a day.

You can enjoy additional benefits of being a Fool by registering (for free!) at Fool.com. These benefits include:

- Special discounts on Foolish products
- Your own personalized Fool home page
- The ability to track your portfolio online and compare its performance with the S&P 500
- The opportunity to post messages on our popular discussion boards
- Alerts when there are Fool appearances or events in your neighborhood

Check it all out at www.register.Fool.com.
Get Foolish!

THE
MOTLEY FOOL
INVESTMENT
GUIDE

HOW THE FOOL BEATS
WALL STREET'S WISE MEN
AND HOW YOU CAN TOO
COMPLETELY REVISED
AND EXPANDED

DAVID AND
TOM GARDNER

A FIRESIDE BOOK
PUBLISHED BY SIMON & SCHUSTER

New York • London • Toronto • Tokyo • Singapore

FIRESIDE
Rockefeller Center
1230 Avenue of the Americas
New York, NY 10020

FIRESIDE and colophon are registered trademarks
of Simon & Schuster, Inc.

Designed by Victoria Hartmann
Manufactured in the United States of America

10   9   8   7   6   5   4   3   2   1

Library of Congress Cataloging-in-Publication Data is available.

ISBN 0-7432-0173-6

For Dad

Contents

Foreword

* * * * *

In the spring of 1995, Iomega Corporation (NYSE: IOM) came out with a revolutionary disk drive whose disks held seventy times the capacity of existing floppies.

Between the initial announcement and the debut of its Zip drive, Iomega shares took off, running from $2 to $10 in a matter of months. The rise drew strength from the expectations created by the five-star reviews that computer industry rags lavished upon the new product, praise that was universal and without reservation.

But demand for the drive far outstripped manufacturing capacity, causing skeptics to conclude that little Iomega could never make enough Zips to turn a profit before the big boys showed up sporting copycat whiskers and claiming the market. Supporting the bearish view, Iomega was coming off two consecutive years of losses; it was fair to say then that the company's recent performance had been reminiscent of a young Elvis Presley . . . but without the voice or looks. Could Iomega's single great product justify a market valuation five times what it had been six months before? Some said the stock was going back to $2.

Simultaneously, with far less of a splash, a revolution started.

Unlike many grassroots revolutions, it didn't begin slowly in some rural backwater, or on a stump in a city park. Quite the contrary: Though quiet, it was instant and it was national. In metropolitan centers east to west across the union, private investors started polling their local computer stores, inquiring about their current stock of Zip drives and their backlogged orders for the product. ("So, how far would I be down the waiting list at this point?")

They then signed online to publish this information in a public discussion of Iomega available to anyone Foolish (yes, that's a capital *F*) enough to listen. Concurrently, an anonymous engineer took a simple tour of the plant in Roy, Utah, and observed the Zip manufacturing process. From fifteen minutes of observation, he contributed his own numerical estimates of Iomega's production, apparently doing it so well that company management itself joined the discussion at that point, making a public accusation that he—a complete outsider—had provided inside information! (The charge was later retracted.) Further, another fellow on the East Coast had his parents, who lived an hour away from the factory in Utah, drive to the company's headquarters on a Sunday afternoon in order to report how many cars appeared in the company parking lot. (It was full.)

What resulted from the collection and online publication of these seemingly inconsequential details was a national public conversation of a kind that had never taken place before, that had never been *possible* before. And it created an almost overnight survey of Zip drive sales, one that clearly demonstrated Iomega's success in meeting the demand to an extent far exceeding general expectations.

How well the company was doing—a subject of so much speculation among benighted *offline* investors—had a pretty good answer among enlightened onliners.

The information was provided so quickly and so exhaustively that no Wall Street analyst or firm could ever have pulled it off. (In fact, at the time only one analyst, from a small regional brokerage, was following Iomega.) But within a week, Wall Street institutional traders were gravitating to the discussion; a single spot in cyberspace had become *the* place to go for understanding and valuing Iomega. This was confirmed by a reporter who, in the midst of doing a story on the "Iomega online phenomenon," discovered with surprise that all four of her regular Wall Street sources were getting their information from something called The Motley Fool.

In less than two months, Iomega zoomed from $10 to $30 as brokers, banks, pension funds, and investment newsletters piled in.

We know the story pretty well because we dreamt up, created, and operate The Motley Fool, and we bought Iomega at $15 based almost completely on our readers' research. But cribbing in this case was fair play. You see, through our writings and our online portfolio, we were the ones who had inspired many of those readers to take their financial futures in their own hands in the first place, encouraging them to renounce the mediocrity of their mutual funds in favor of the greater risk and reward of common stocks.

That was and is the revolution, because somewhere in the midst of it we realized that all of a sudden the world had changed, and changed utterly. The lesson of the Iomega story—the power of people working together over a network for new benefit—has been repeated countless times at Fool.com. With free online education, community interaction, and supplemental information coming from investor research via new sites like our own Soapbox.com, it is now little-guy investors—not huge brokerage firms—who hold the most valuable cards.

The Motley Fool Investment Guide will show you offline how to do the same thing that we've been doing online. This book will enable even the rankest novice to invest expertly on his or her own, enjoy the heck out of it, and *beat* the market averages over long periods of time . . . all things that too many people think takes an expert, a Wise man, or a market insider to do—those Foolish enough, that is, to believe that the market can be beaten at all.

Not that every investment will make you rich, or even pay off at all! We'd be fools (with a small f) if we led you to believe that. In fact, Iomega wound up going way above the level listed above, but a few years later it declined so significantly (and the CEO quit) that today it is well below its mid-1990s high. Fortunately, even before that we had purchased America Online, aiming to capitalize on the explosive growth of the Internet. Our investments in Iomega and AOL both started as huge successes, but then took wildly disparate paths. Their stories are recounted in "Appendix C. A Tale of Two Stocks." The ultimate lesson is that by practicing patient investing, one's successes should more than compensate for the inevitable failures in every investor's portfolio.

If you harbor the faintest intellectual curiosity, relish—not wilt from—risk and challenge, instinctively enjoy taking responsibility for your own future, and can get online, today's investment environment is for you.

So fish out your jester's cap and get ready to stake your own claim on America's great businesses!

PART I

WHO, WHAT, WHY, AND HOW

·1·

"Fool"?

· · · · ·

Take heed. . . . The wise may be instructed by a fool. . . .
You know how by the advice and counsel and prediction
of fools, many kings, princes, states, and commonwealths
have been preserved, several battles gained, and divers
doubts of a most perplexed intricacy resolved.

—*Rabelais*

Fool?

Not a very *wise* choice for a name when you're trying to ply your trade in the investment world. For decades financial professionals have done their best to sell customers on their Wisdom. Whether it's the pinstripe suit, the avuncular smile, the firm handshake, or the advertising jingle ("Rock Solid, Market Wise" comes to mind), your typical broker, money manager, or financial planner has striven for an image that smacks of success, intelligence, experience, respectability—in a word, Wisdom.

And for years they've all been making a fair amount of money off fools. You know about fools. You may even have been one yourself at some point. Ever listened to a salesman on the other end of a phone long enough that the voice-activated vacuum cleaner he was trying to sell you began to make sense? You were being foolish. Ever bought a stock on your dentist's recommendation without even looking to see if it was listed? How very foolish of you. Or what about when you snapped up shares of International Dashed Hopes Load Fund just because your broker said it was the top performer in its category last year? Terribly, terribly foolish.

Basking in the excesses brought about by this folly, the financial establishment hadn't banked on one thing—that one day the tables might turn when some Fools (and that's a capital *F,* maestro) actually showed up.

The Wise would have you believe that "a Fool and his money are soon parted." But in a world where more than 80 percent of all *professional* mutual fund managers lose to the market averages, year in and year out, how Wise should one aspire to be? In what other realms could such a compelling paradox exist, that the paid professional can do no better than—in fact, cannot even do as well as—dumb luck? And this general ineptitude has been made more ironic by the appurtenances that typically attend the Wise: expensive suits and gold cuff links (to impress their clients), Swiss watches (to convey the importance of their time), mahogany desks (to rest at between rounds of golf), and other similar displays designed to impress and intimidate their customers. Ah, the many-splendored totems of those who were paid too much to make too little.

In fact, we got to thinking after a while that we should just go ahead and call ourselves Fools, since our attitudes and approach to life were so radically different from what was being passed off as Wisdom all around us. So we launched our original *Motley Fool,* taking the name from a nondescript quotation from Shakespeare's *As You Like It:* "A fool, a fool! I met a fool i' the forest, a motley fool." We'd always loved Shakespeare's Fools . . . they amused as they instructed, and were the only members of society who could tell the truth to the king or queen without having their heads lopped off. *The Motley Fool* began as a monthly newsletter, then transformed into a daily feature on a national online service, then became one of the premier financial destinations on the World Wide Web. And among other things, of course, it is also a series of books (of which this is the second, following *The Motley Fool You Have More Than You Think*), all containing as much Foolishness as we can pack into them.

Our goal was and is very simple: Beat the market and show others how to do it—the more novice, the better. In our brief Foolish history, we've enabled thousands of average people who didn't previously know a dividend from a divining rod to invest their own money without the help of Armani suits, and *crush* Wall Street at its own game.

Our approach is best characterized by its hostility to conventional wisdom. For example, the Wise will tell you just to invest your money in loaded mutual funds. (This "double dip" enables them to charge you for that advice *and* then charge you on an annual basis for the funds' management fees.) We, on the other hand, are telling you to buy stocks. They'll tell you, "All right, take on the risk of buying stocks. But if you're going to do that, just buy the safest ones and hold on." Or alternatively, some brokers will try to sell you a variety of rinky-dink shares of penny stocks, dubious entities with an even more dubious likelihood of ever paying off. We say poppycock, in both cases. We're telling you to sprinkle some more volatile growth stocks in with your blue-chips to improve your returns. And avoid penny stocks altogether! We're also educating you—horror of horrors—about *shorting* stocks, a devilishly fun attempt to profit off the *decline* of a stock, rather than its rise. To the Wise, there is no more risky, bad-faith investment decision than shorting stocks. To us, if you're an advanced investor for whom the stock market is more than a passing fancy, we believe you should at least consider the potential advantages of shorting. And the outrageous list goes on. It is topped off by the very idea that you would even manage your own money yourself. To many segments of the financial services industry today, and portions of the press, this idea remains well-nigh taboo.

In what follows, we therefore hope to teach you, to amuse you, and ultimately to make you good money at the same time.

But first we should introduce ourselves.

Who We Are, by Way of Explaining
What This Book Ain't Going to Do

We're David and Tom Gardner, brothers, and the original editors of *The Motley Fool*. We hope that you have already gotten to know us through our first book in The Motley Fool trilogy, *The Motley Fool You Have More Than You Think,* but in case you haven't, let's mention again how we started. Yep, we originally began investing simply because, upon turning eighteen, we took over stock portfolios that our parents had started for us at our birth.

It takes some casual investors a lifetime to wean themselves off the numbing teat of mutual funds; we never knew the temptation. Our very first purchase was shares in a trucker called Leaseway Transportation (since acquired by a larger company). One hot summer we watched it go from $26 to $42, where we took our profit. The stock had been culled, using a few elementary measures, from the pages of *Value Line,* that redoubtable seven-inch-thick investment research monstrosity that we rarely use anymore because online resources are so much more powerful and timely. We cannot remember the exact rationale for the purchase of Leaseway, so it can't be listed among our most inspired investments. There is an enduring lesson here, however. If you're willing to take a risk and you're open to continuous learning about the world around you, you can succeed wonderfully in the stock market without paying the Wise for the privilege.

In this book we're going to break down into their primary components the reams of writing that we offer on a daily basis in cyberspace. The idea, as the Man says, is not just to hand you a Twinkie . . . rather, we're going to teach you how to locate your own Twinkies, so that you'll learn to feed yourself for years and years . . . prior to dying of a massive heart attack.

We want to help you help yourself make money. This was our intention back in 1993, when we launched *The Motley Fool* as an investment newsletter. Ye Olde Printed Foole—as we fondly refer to it—contained our stock picks, one monthly investment article, and a patchwork quilt of content in keeping with our motley interests. We mailed out unsolicited copies to a few thousand unsuspecting people and wound up our first month with exactly thirty-eight subscribers. Did the world care this little about getting educated about the stock market? We were depressed.

What we needed was visibility. So we decided to start a conversation about stocks on what at that point was a small but fast-growing national online service—America Online.

Through the power and beauty of el cheapo modems, we connected to America Online over local phone lines and started typing. We offered our investment opinions and advice in response to requests from complete strangers, doing our best to provide them with as much information about their own holdings as they could handle. In so doing, we discovered some wonderful things (like how many people were willing to volunteer their own investment research for the benefit of many) and some bad things too (see Appendix D, "Zeigletics"). But what we mainly did was acquire new subscribers. Within a few months, our little gabfest had grown into the most popular financial discussion on America Online. The company approached us about opening up an actual business on its service, where we could get paid for doing interactively, on a daily basis, many of the same things we were doing just once a month, noninteractively, with Ye Olde Printed Foole. Even better.

Throwing away printing and mailing costs forever, we went into the electronic-publishing business.

By December, the word had started to get around, helped by a brief feature in the *New Yorker*. Soon we were AOL's most frequented service in Personal Finance. Why? Well, it didn't hurt that our Fool Portfolio, a real-money portfolio invested exclusively in stocks (now known as the Rule Breaker Portfolio), rose 11 percent in our first few months online, while the Standard & Poor's 500 (the index used most frequently to track money managers, also known as the S&P 500) stood flat. We closed out our first year up 59 percent, almost 40 percentage points ahead of the market. Lots of people were signing into our area to find out what was up.

What was up was that our stock-picking technique, founded in community involvement, was working. The better it worked, the more Fools came to the forum. And generally, that itself led to better performance. Today, a few million customers visit Fool.com to talk, share information, plan retirement, get out of debt, and discover new opportunities. Fools are helping Fools (and themselves) make money.

Folly

• • • • •

Foolery, sir, does walk about the orb
like the sun; it shines everywhere.
—*Shakespeare*

The too-earnest reader will no doubt wish at this point that the moneymaking grub be served. This isn't that sort of book. If you're interested in fast cash, you can find many other books to sate your appetite. Books with titles like *How to Make $1,000,000 Automatically in the Stock Market* no doubt contain the magical formula that will enable you to become rich beyond your wildest dreams faster than you ever could have imagined. And you can do it, it seems, without using your brain!

This book, dear reader, is written for those who drop—not slam—their token in the bus meter, who remain seated when the FASTEN SEAT BELTS sign turns off, who walk down to the final car of the subway train because it's the one with the fewest people. In short, we write for those who aren't in a hurry, those who think before they act, those who actually enjoy exercising their brains. And to stay in character, we really should begin the book by talking about Folly. It's what we're actually all about once you get past the juggling balls, the pointy caps, and the red-and-green checkered panty hose.

The True Wisdom: Go Against Your Instincts

Foolishness is not a luxury. It is a necessity; it attacks conventional wisdom. Folly is particularly crucial today because, through the miracle of modern communication, more bad thinking now circles the globe quicker than ever before. "For every 10 bytes of value online there seem to be 10,000 bytes of drivel," writes technology commentator Walter Mossberg. Too true. If we're not careful, true wisdom—those proverbial 10 bytes of truly good ideas and approaches—will get lost in the 10,000.

It may take a Fool to notice this, but despite the continual advances in knowledge earned through scientific experiment, archaeological discovery, and globalized computer networking, one thing that has assuredly *not* increased over time is the collective true wisdom (or common sense). So, while modern technology has determined that we'll continue to pile up more and more information, technology has no good mechanism for ensuring that we even maintain our common sense. In fact, it may be leaking away right now! One cannot help but notice that the ancients—Western and Eastern—were far more interested in studying the nature of wisdom and folly than we are, despite the abundant resources of folly in our time. What happens when you combine a rich history of literature and thought on the subject with a modern populace largely ignorant of its substance? Answer: received "truths" that no longer have much truth or meaning behind them but are accepted by wide swaths of the population as conventional wisdom. It is these sorts of situations that put Fools everywhere on red alert.

Good, straight wisdom is a dear commodity. Benjamin Franklin had it, for instance. A glance again through *Poor Richard's Almanack:* "Three may keep a secret if two of them are dead." "He that speaks ill of the Mare will buy her." "He that's content hath enough. He that complains has too much." What makes these aphorisms tokens of true wisdom is the way they contradict our basic instincts. For instance, when we hear that the content man has enough, we naturally assume that the discontent man does *not* have enough. We are told, instead, that he has too much. Our foiled expectations force us to consider this new possibility, and after further reflection on our own experience we recognize that one or another of our grumbling acquaintances does in fact suffer from having too much, not too little.

True wisdom leads to that kind of insight by challenging our preconceived notions or expectations. A Fool has no quarrel with this wisdom. It is a universal good, beloved by all.

In the end, every great investment method succeeds not because of its numerical gizmos, magical formulas, or other assorted whizbangs. Rather, it succeeds by using some of the very commonsense wisdom we're talking about. Good investment practices can almost be called studies in good character. Warren Buffett's investment career, for instance, is not so much about balance-sheet analysis as about Buffett's own humility, patience, and diligence. Peter Lynch's approach is not so much about price-to-earnings ratios as it is about perceptiveness, optimism, and self-effacing humor. The greatest investors are often outstanding human beings, insofar as they exemplify the highest achievement in one or more human characteristics like patience, diligence, perceptiveness, and common sense.

Remember: Dealing in money, the investor constantly must avoid his own *instinctive temptation* toward fear and greed. Fear and greed will ruin your investment returns. It is perhaps an underappreciated trait of great investors that in putting up consistently superb investment returns, they are demonstrating their relative imperviousness to many of the less optimistic aspects of human nature.

This, then, is the true wisdom: to resist one's baser instincts. "Do every day one or two things for no other reason than that you would rather not do them. Thus, when the hour of darkness comes, it will not find you unprepared." So wrote the psychologist William James, another fellow who was more concerned with character than with the minutiae of his respective discipline. James knew that in order to succeed we must vigilantly toil against our own wills.

Resist to subsist.

The Conventional Wisdom: "Go with Your Instincts"

Having set forth true wisdom, we are now left to examine its bastardizations. To revisit an earlier point: True wisdom, or common sense, may be not much more than a husk in our present age, with so few having awareness of or appreciation for its rich history. Another form of wisdom, however, is alive and well: conventional wisdom. It is this counterfeit and useless form of wisdom—the conventional, or worldly, wisdom—masquerading as the real thing, that has roused Fools throughout the ages in a call to arms.

For—say it again—the be-all and end-all of Folly is its attack on conventional wisdom.

We can best summarize the present-day conventional wisdom in this way: We live in a world that does its level best to convince us to follow our own instincts. "Follow your instincts," "Just do it," and "Because you deserve the very best" have been among our most popular advertising slogans. A fashionable Yuletide ad jingle these days urges us to treat ourselves to a gift; this, in the season whose whole meaning—even its secular one—is supposed to be about giving to *others*.

Even more disheartening, the means for the distribution of conventional wisdom are more powerful than ever before, thanks to the mass media. That's because *mass* media, by its very definition, has the power to broadcast to the masses. Never in the history of the world has any tool had the power to create so many like minds as has television. This is obvious, a commonplace. What is not immediately so obvious is how bad so much of the thinking being inculcated in the minds of Americans is. The investment world alone is full of it. Over financial television and in magazines and newspapers, we are constantly exposed to "experts" who are actually there to tell us where the market is headed. As if! This has become so regular and frequent that many take it in stride today, almost as if we believed such prestidigitation possible. And yet no one has ever consistently accurately predicted the direction of the stock market. We have a hunch the average American doesn't realize that—hence the clogging of the mass media with market forecasts, market timing, market predictions.

If journalists held these experts accountable by going back and revisiting their past predictions, we, the audience, would quickly see through the transparent hocus-pocus, see the conventional wisdom for what it is.

If.

Anyway, what results is a large segment of the population that is extremely receptive to the repetitive, conventional pabulum that the mass media features because they believe that conventional wisdom is wise. That's why for market researchers and brokers and financial planners, these people are the easiest (and the most profitable) game in town.

One can learn a great deal from the Wise, though. In fact, the careful investor can learn so much through a brief analysis of common human error that we can't resist putting it right here up front, in the beginning of our book. We'll close our chapter on Folly by examining the two brightest pots of gold that marketers try to convince us we will find at the end of the rainbow if we'll only "just do it . . . follow our instincts . . . because we deserve the very best." Both can be poison for your brokerage account, and they are opposite but deadly investment mistakes. We're talking about the two idols Wealth and Security.

Wealth

Let's take Wealth first. Everyone wants to be just a *little* bit richer, right? We've just about never met anyone who thought he had enough, whether we're talking about billionaires or mendicants. In the investment game, this leads people to take stupid gambles.

Most of the time, these people are younger; the race for Wealth remains one run most fervently by greenhorns. (Security, as we shall see, is quite the opposite.) Unsophisticated first-time investors often almost instinctively swing for the fences. They've heard about that IBM stock their grandfather once bought and unloaded a few decades later for forty-five times his money. They figure the fastest way to make ten times their initial investment is to buy a stock at $5 that might go to $50, rather than one bought at $50 that would have to hit $500. In fact, perhaps one of the few negative side effects of Peter Lynch's excellent book *One Up on Wall Street* is that he induced a generation of readers to shoot for his fabled "ten-bagger" (a stock that makes an investor ten times her original money). Many people shooting for ten-baggers wind up buying pathetic penny stocks sold to them by people who don't have their best interest at heart, even though Lynch is the last one who'd ever advocate such a decision.

We started a wonderful discussion in our discussion boards at Fool.com entitled My Dumbest Investment. In it, we encourage readers to provide a brief story of the worst investment they've ever made and to tell what they've learned from it. Since the day we started it, My Dumbest Investment has been one of our service's best offerings. We've learned a lot.

Take the dentist from Illinois who wrote of the year 1986, when he was a young, happy-go-lucky investor getting ready to invest in a company called Microsoft. But just then, *RINNNNNGGGGGG!* He got a call at work from an investment banker claiming to have just bought an expensive car with the money made off an investment in (whispered) *platinum*. The poor and self-admittedly naive dentist was convinced by this fellow to put his money into platinum on *margin,* which means that he effectively borrowed extra money, beyond what he had, in order to heighten his stack of chips on the table. "A few days later my first margin call came in as the bottom dropped out. I had to put several thousand dollars on my credit card to cover my losses." The lesson learned from his Dumbest Investment was an excellent moral to learn so early in his investing life.

Or take the screenwriter from Los Angeles who noticed in an issue of *Smart Money* magazine that a recent recommendation in its pages had dropped from $2 to just 25 cents per share in value. Excited, he didn't even bother to check out what the company, Memorex-Telex, did. "Now, imagine this," he goes on. "I thought if I had bought it at $2, I would now be down, what, 87 percent or so? But what a deal it was now! A mere quarter! If they thought it was a good buy at two, it must be outta this world at 25 cents!!!"

"When a few months later I received the notice of the company's bankruptcy from my broker, I ruefully rubbed my chin, downed a Manhattan, and considered searching for a tall building." With the characteristic good wit that pervades the Dumbest Investment discussion, the writer concluded, "But I have a family. And, fortunately, I didn't throw away our nest egg. No, I saved that for some other dogs that maybe I'll write about later on."

The stories go on and on, as they will forever. There was the high school student doing a summer framing job for an oil tycoon. The tycoon was praising a company traded on Canada's penny-laden, corruption-ridden Vancouver Exchange. Only problem was, the kid didn't know the exchange's reputation, or anything about money, in fact, except that this tycoon had made a lot of it. So the kid bought New Dolly Varden Minerals at $2.25, just before it dropped to $1.25. He then doubled his holding. It dropped to 25 cents. Having lost 90 percent, he told us he was just hanging on to the thing, since it would "cost more to sell than just to keep."

There was the fellow who kept adding to a stock holding in a since-failed consumer electronics company even as it kept dropping further and further. His wish: "May Crazy Eddie rot in jail for years to come."

There was the guy who, enticed by expectations of big returns, was convinced by his financial planner to make a large investment in a real estate limited partnership in the mid-eighties. He lost it all. "To add insult to injury, I actually paid this guy for his advice, plus invested the rest of my savings in his 5 percent load funds that did a whole lot worse than a simple Vanguard Index no-load." (For more information about mutual funds and what the heck "no-load" means, see "Part II, Mutual Funds: Love 'Em, or Leave 'Em?")

And finally there was the photographer who, "completely ignorant" about managing money, got to talking with his father's broker at his father's funeral (no joke). Soon after, he'd opened up a margin account so his broker could trade currencies for him: Swiss francs, yen, German marks, Eurodollars. "Five months later, the 'new' broker handling my account (never *did* find out where the original broker went, all my calls were never answered) called to tell me I should close out what remained of the account, or write a *new* check to continue trading. I closed: 88 percent loss."

The point of these stories is not that brokers and financial planners are evil. Not at all. Some are very good. Some are good, and just plain wrong sometimes. Every investment entails a measure of risk. The only point we're making is that in every case, the correspondent was taking on stupid risk—because of either having done no research or having been baited by a sales pitch, or both. Why? In order to achieve get-rich-quick returns, in the chase for Wealth.

The lessons are probably self-explanatory: Don't invest in anything you don't understand. Manage your own money if you have the time and instinct. Don't fall in love with (and keep adding to) any given investment. Lots of other people do stupid things too.

The overarching point is that it's those very get-rich-quick returns that will always remain attractive to our human nature. We will be tempted by the conventional wisdom to shoot for the big bucks by "going with our instincts," sometimes on our own initiative, sometimes at the urging of others (who may see us only as so much fodder). Our natural human instinct is toward Greed. It is this very instinct that one *must* resist in order to become a good investor.

Fortunately, you now have some Fools on your side who are aiming to help you do just that.

Security

Opposite Wealth, however, is another bête noire, another gorgon from which to avert one's gaze: Security. This one seems on the face of it to be far less threatening or objectionable than the impulsive chase for Wealth, better known as Greed. How can we seriously advocate that a desire for safety be placed in the same circle of hell as one of medieval Christendom's seven deadly sins?

Easy . . . we're now talking about the two biggest threats to your (or your family's) long-term investment survival. Chasing Wealth, you may run headlong into Madame la Guillotine. But chasing Security is no less deadly a pursuit, akin to inhaling carbon monoxide in sufficient quantity to bring about your eternal rest.

In our first-ever issue of Ye Olde Printed Foole, we printed this contrarian line, to which we still very much subscribe: "The least-mentioned, biggest risk of all is not taking enough risk."

Portions of the investment community today are infatuated with "risk avoidance" (or "risk aversion"). The primary aim of investing, these Wise tell us, is Safety—holding on to your precious dollars. Whatever happens, you *don't* want to lose what you've already earned through the sweat of your labors. Now, a perfect Fool might point out that you are *constantly* losing what you've earned, since even the low inflation of the present day is continuously eroding the value of cash. In fact, a dollar invested in Treasury bills (the *Safest* investment of all) in 1926 increased in real value to $1.53 by 1997, according to a study by Ibbotson Associates. In seventy-one years! That same dollar, had it been put in large-company stocks (the S&P 500 and its predecessors), would have assumed a real value of $154.95! Now of course, with Treasury bills you were ostensibly up every year, and indeed some years you thanked your lucky stars that you avoided going down 20 percent in stocks. But here you are at the end of your investment lifetime tearing out whatever's left of your hair over the Grand Mistake you've made, all to appease the local deity Safety (who for all those years had such an alluring smile—flossed regularly).

The possibility that one might actually make good money sometimes does not seem to enter Wall Street's thinking—among the more respectable element, anyway. And to be sure, most business schools today teach the Efficient Markets Theory, which, when you boil it right down, says that no one can consistently outperform the market over time. (Note: Please keep your eyes closed and pay no attention to those who are outperforming the market. And don't bother telling the profs, either . . . they're probably in league with the mediocre fund managers.)

The cynic may step right in and suggest that many investment "pros" never *will* consistently or impressively beat the market, due to various handicaps, which include the requirement to diversify large portfolios, timidity, a lack of imagination, the inability to short the market, and graduate study at business school. Given this, why *not* make Safety the sine qua non? Like the wastebasket by your desk, it's an easy target. And it seems to keep the customers happy . . . those who don't know what they're doing, anyway.

Speaking of which, we have heard money managers musingly opine, "You know, if the market goes up 25 percent one year, and I go up 15 percent for my clients, no complaints. If the market goes up 5 percent one year and I go *down* 5 percent, I get all sorts of calls." This is quite true to the experience of many money managers, and is a perfect illustration of our point. In both situations, of course, the money manager has underperformed the market averages by 10 percentage points . . . which, to Fools, is the most relevant year-to-year consideration. But in one situation the manager is humored (possibly even complimented), while in the other he's berated.

So, if *you* were an investment professional in this environment, wouldn't you (further evidence) make the sine qua non Safety? The pieces of this puzzle interlock quite snugly.

Now, since we advise whole-hog investing in the stock market for long-term investors, we do need to propound two things about playing it safe Foolishly. First is, invest money that you can afford to wait on. The stock market is risky. We like that very much; it helps us make money, because you almost *never* get something for nothing. But over a given period of time, your stocks could get mashed. Just over seventy years ago, thousands of people lost most of what they had by investing in the market. So, if you get melted down on Meltdown Day, we want you still to have something left to slap back down on the table. Invest money that you plan on keeping in the market for at least five years. (We recommend a lifetime.)

Second, we invest in good companies. We buy stock in companies that dominate their industry, companies that have a sustainable advantage over their competition, companies featuring honest and efficient management and a bunch of other yardsticks offered later in the book.

And that's about it. Beyond the two points about Security just covered, we advise staring down your nose at this slovenly creature, or at the financial adviser who reflexively strikes the low-risk Safety gong. Yuck. With low risk come low returns . . . the numbers shown above regarding Treasury bills are not much better for low-risk mutual funds; their performance as a group is abysmal. The whole point of buying this book is to educate yourself profitably. We expect that even at this early point, you've already graduated beyond much of the rest of the world; much of the rest of the world is going with its instincts, and blaming someone else when it fails.

Now, before we close the curtain on Folly's chapter, we need to stick in a word about people who require income and high degrees of safety. These are typically older people. Just as chasing Wealth attracts the young in huge numbers, chasing Security can be a fervent hobby among the advanced. We've heard before from readers of our service, "Hey, the Fool investment approach may work for younger people who can take some risk. But I'm seventy-six years old. What about somebody in my situation?"

Well, we certainly advocate, first of all, that you get to know your own situation very well and act accordingly. If you don't feel competent to analyze your own situation, hire a financial planner to help. (Though we have faith in you!) If your money is tied up in an annuity and you expect to need its every interest payment over the five additional years you expect to live, you should let that money stay put. On the other hand, if your situation is one that requires some income but allows you to contemplate risk in search of greater investment rewards, we think you're crazy to be just sitting in high-interest-bearing securities. These securities—whether bonds or mutual funds or preferred stock or what have you—*all* underperform the market historically. So, if you're looking out beyond five years—but with income needs— you're probably going to do much better by staying invested Foolishly (in good stocks) and annually *selling off* a portion of your nest egg to meet your income requirements . . . better than any other single investment approach.

Just to make that clear: If you have a $50,000 annuity paying you a flat annual interest of $3,000 (a 6 percent interest rate), consider that you could instead have that money invested in the stock market (historic average return is about 10 percent), earning on average (therefore) $5,000 a year. Assuming an average year, you can sell $3,000 to provide you your income and still wind up with $2,000 to spare, available for reinvestment, to produce an account value of $52,000 to begin the next year. Sure, some years your stocks will lose money and you'll have to take that $3,000 straight out of capital. But except under the worst market periods in history, which occur very rarely (and from which we have *always* eventually recovered), you'll end up well ahead, even despite the occasional horrible two- or three-year run, because some years will be wonderful.

This is the thinking that has us talking down Security and suggesting that people consider keeping their money in the market for their own good, even—perhaps especially—when keeping their money in the market runs against their native instincts. As has been pointed out by many, the market is the best game going because it pays good stakes and the odds are stacked in your favor. Fear sometimes causes people to lose sight of equity investing's superiority, always (it seems) at the wrong time . . . when the market has just hit bottom. Don't let human nature sway you. Consciously taking on smart risk remains the best way to succeed in investing . . . and in life too.

◆ ◆ ◆

In summarizing our Folly chapter, we hope we have demonstrated that conventional wisdom—what we call capital-*W* Wisdom—provides society with stale half-truths that encourage us to follow our instincts. Folly, an ever-radical force for reformation and enlightenment (and a heck of a lot of fun, too), attacks Wisdom by providing contrary truths that enable us to resist our own base instincts. We've addressed the complementary bugaboos of Wealth and Safety, one of which tempts us to take too much risk, the other to take too little. We've explained who we are and told you what we believe. Now, let us show you why you should join us online if you haven't already.

Get Online!

◆　◆　◆　◆

Computing is not about computers anymore.
It is about living.
—*Nicholas Negroponte*

One of the more radical developments of the late twentieth century was the creation of a new medium: the Internet. New media do not come along every decade; this particular arrival was the biggest thing since TV showed up at the 1939 World's Fair. The online world has been the primary means by which we have spread our Folly; it also happens to be the single greatest tool for the individual investor today. This chapter is written mainly for the 50 percent of U.S. households that have not yet hooked into the new online medium. (Can you believe that number was 90 percent only four years ago, when the first edition of this book came out?) If you're already an experienced "Internaut" (an active explorer of the world's information archive, primarily the Internet), you can just skim this section for jokes.

The Communication—Not Information—Age

A neat thing happened in the early 1990s, and not many people noticed. To this day, many still have not noticed. The neat thing has to do with computers.

Most computer users had originally purchased their machines with the intention of accomplishing certain tasks constituting their daily work assignment. The bread and butter of these computers were standard *applications* (or tools) like word processing, spreadsheet and database analysis, and point-of-sale merchandise management. These applications were designed mainly to help a single user working by himself to get his work done. And not much else.

The neat thing that happened is that people started using computers not as superbrain machines enabling them to plan or run their business, but as *communications* devices. People actually started hooking their machines together in order to gab!

Over the past few years, the population and its gab have increased exponentially, due to both an increased awareness of the benefits of the Internet and an ongoing improvement in the technology. What was once displayed on monochromatic, low-resolution screens at 300 bits per second (bps) now appears as high-resolution video transmitted over cable lines at speeds of three *million* bps and up. More striking than the technological improvements, however, are the ongoing diversification and general improvement of the content available. To a certain extent the online revolution has begun to stratify our society, elevating those who recognize the benefits of gabbing online over those who do not.

Gabbing can sometimes be just gabbing . . . weightless gibberish of no particular relevance or lasting significance exchanged between two or more parties. We will continue to see this as long as there are two people in the world with computers and time on their hands. But anyone who thinks that preteen kids shouting at one another in cyberspace chat rooms represents the sum total of online communication possibilities has been duped. Gabbing can be worth a lot more than that.

Gabbing, for starters, can be fun. As just pure fun, and when done right, good gab can be reason enough to sign online. Hook up your computer and you can find somebody somewhere to talk about anything you want, from alpha particles to zoo jokes, twenty-four hours a day, 365 days a year. Your circle of friends will expand to all fifty states and around the world.

But gabbing can also foster and cement social ties of personal or business benefit, as we discovered when we set about building a staff to support our online service. Within four months, we had taken on more than fifty talented volunteers from all across America to execute various responsibilities on a daily basis (writing, editing, managing, and so forth). When we later converted into a corporation, many of these went on to become full-time or part-time employees, and now, years later, we still note that as of this writing a majority of our employees were hired due to their contributions to, and knowledge of, our online area. In several cases in the past, we have not met new employees face-to-face until months after we've hired them. We were amply aware of their competence, however, through their online contributions. In this brave new world (positive Shakespearean connotation intended), they were our employees, and we've built a wonderful business with their help.

The possibilities of good gab are not limited to online publishing companies, of course. Classified ads, auctions, book and CD reviews posted by individuals to the Internet are among its most popular offerings . . . and they're free. And in niches across the online world—some hidden, others out in the open—professionals consult on a daily basis about issues and topics related to their fields. They *network* in the truest sense of the word.

If you've never been online, imagine reading a magazine or the *New York Times* and, instead of just reading articles, being able to talk with other readers at the same time. Imagine the new opportunities for understanding, discussion, and friendship that would create. One-way publishing and broadcasting is yielding to two-way interactivity, and the world will never be the same.

The most exciting, most dynamic, most mass-market-driven use for computers today is communication. Many people, whom we'll continue to refer to as the Wise, still don't recognize this . . . to their detriment.

Benefits to Investors

Perhaps the first true benefit of being online that we ever encountered was the ability to type in our own trades in our own brokerage account. Discount brokers like Charles Schwab championed this drive to introduce hands-on tools for the individual investor. (Deep-discounters like Datek and Ameritrade soon drove commission rates down below $10 per trade, while American Express and others began offering free trades for clients who maintained a minimum balance.) Suddenly, the power for initiating trade executions was in our hands, and our broker was "paying" us to do it. How novel! Our interest in the online world had begun.

Supplementing online trading is real-time investment information, including stock quotes and company news. Many services now provide this information, some of them for free, but of varying quality. (Some of it is so well presented that even those who have zero experience with computers can begin understanding and using it within minutes, so long as they have their minds set on learning.) You can find delayed quotes and company press releases instantly available on Yahoo! The Motley Fool itself offers quotes, company data, and unique Fool News, which brings the most important and interesting financial information to readers well before their morning paper ever arrives . . . assuming they still subscribe to one. We're using the power of real-time information and the power of disseminating that information on a national basis at the mere click of a button.

Another great thing about the data available online is that good services update their research data (earnings estimates, fundamental financial statistics, and so on) every day, putting it right at your fingertips. The result is a net gain for individual investors: more data, coming faster, better organized for retrieval, and costing progressively less over time. An excellent example is afforded us in the evolution of the encyclopedia.

Starting out as huge, shelf-long, multivolume sets, encyclopedias generated good business for decades because repeat customers came back every five or ten years to buy updated versions, while libraries generally purchased the most up-to-date. But the additional expense of buying supplements or (God forbid) a whole additional twenty-three-volume set put many people off. With the recent development of CD-ROM, encyclopedia publishers have now managed to put their entire opus on a single searchable CD-ROM *and* improve the offering by incorporating animation and sound. But even CD-ROMs have to be updated and repurchased from time to time, and even the storage capacity of a CD hampers publishers looking to integrate more memory-eating video into their offerings. So, enter the online world. Now publishers can update their encyclopedias on a *daily* basis and can house truly massive amounts of data on big computer servers that exceed a single CD-ROM's storage as much as the population of China exceeds that of the block on which you live. And they do it all for free: the *Encyclopaedia Britannica* (www.britannica.com) will give you complete and up-to-date information without charging you a penny.

The same is happening, and will continue to happen, with financial information. The most timely info no longer appears in your printed monthly or the Friday-night stock recap on *Wall Street Week*. Nope. It's all going online, and most of it is free.

But in the end, the most compelling reason for investors to explore the Internet is the opportunity to learn in ways more efficient and entertaining than ever before. Our experience has demonstrated that *group education* succeeds wildly online (so long as you pick a good group). In recent years, American educators have tried to bring students together to learn cooperatively in teams, attempting to get away from the more individualistic learning dynamic that prevailed earlier in the century. They need only turn to cyberspace to see it actually working on a grand scale (see the Foreword on Iomega) among people who in many cases will never even meet one another.

Again, here's how it works, roughly. As an investor interested in stocks or funds, by tapping into something like www.Fool.com (AOL keyword: FOOL) you can, with the help of your fellow investors, stay as current on your own holdings as you desire—daily, weekly, or every hour on the hour. Let's say you own some stock in Apple Computer. You can sign online and locate a discussion board expressly dedicated to Apple stock. This is a public discussion, often followed by hundreds or thousands of readers, completely based upon these readers voluntarily providing the latest on the company's news and products, news on its competitors that may affect Apple, and general investment advice, with maybe a decent Silicon Valley joke or two thrown in. Whether you live in Georgia, Minnesota, or Hawaii, you'll be crossing paths with people who actually happen to work for Apple, fund managers, industry insiders, and a swarm of fellow individual investors (some of whom are extremely savvy). You'll probably find that when the printed financial dailies report news on Apple, your discussion board correspondents will already have posted it. They may even have been anticipating it for weeks. And it's all brought about by a group of strangers. They are investors—bulls and bears—who become a sort of community unto themselves, with distinct personalities, shared interests, and a common history based on the news developments and price fluctuations of Apple and its stock.

In fact, the opportunity to stay informed about your investments, while at the same time learning more and more about investing in general, so far surpasses anything previously available that it's not unlike comparing our current picture of the universe with those days when everyone was sure that the sun circled the earth. Typifying the sort of messages that come in to Fool HQ every week, one of our readers wrote: "I have a hard time just trying to keep my usage from going over two hours a day. I am not complaining too much, though, since I have seen a 25 percent rise in both my investment account and IRA account [over the past five months], versus a *decline* in the previous 12 months. And it's no accident either. The free flow of data, news, ideas, opinions, and even rumors helps me make my investment decisions."

We've seen this process repeat itself over and over with thousands of people; and truth be told, the same thing has happened to us.

Once you're online, we doubt you'll ever turn back.

The Comeback of the Word

To digress for a moment: One of the beauties of the online world is actually its widespread use of text. The medium in its present incarnation is helping to restore the power of the written word. In fact, those who are reaching the most prominence in the new medium are, at heart, writers. But so is everyone else online. People communicate online today most frequently by typing back and forth to each other . . . it's a constant pas de deux of reading and writing.

Like many media mavens and education experts, we believe that while a picture may be worth a thousand words, the right thousand words can change the world. You want that in technical terms? *Text-based learning works better than image-based learning.* Our online materials—the stuff that can help you make money—are words, sentences, and paragraphs, not pictures, not videos, though we may use images or audio to decorate our prose. And we're *not* sorry, because we think that words work better.

Television has presumed to inform us through the exclusive use of sound and images, at the expense of written words. This just won't work. Imagine if art historians seriously claimed that we could learn a tremendous amount about Renaissance Italy by gazing at the *Mona Lisa;* we may learn a lot about art there, but not much history. We may, likewise, learn a lot about television itself when watching it, but we collectively come away without understanding what the fuss is really all about.

Fortunately for the next generation—the one that hasn't even hit first grade yet—a new educational force is at work, and it has the potential to dominate. It combines the surefire efficacy of traditional book learning with the dynamism and attraction of video and animation. It's called the Internet. And it's getting better every day.

What the Online World *Doesn't* Do Too Well

After that rousing exhortatory speech, we feel it incumbent upon our Foolish selves to point out something that computers and the online world do *not* do well. The online world has still not come up with a pleasing way to present a book-length work. That's why we're publishing this in traditional book format. You still can't beat it. In fact, we have yet to meet a single person who derives gratification from rocking back in a lounge chair and reading his laptop computer a few hours at a time. And it's certainly not comfy to do at the beach (or even possible, given laptops' dim screens) . . . and, hey, if you can't read it at the beach, it ain't for readin'. In his fine book *Being Digital* (1995), Nicholas Negroponte speculates that designing a computer that looks, feels, even *smells* exactly like a book is just a matter of time. "Multimedia will become more book-like, something with which you can curl up in bed and either have a conversation or be told a story. Multimedia will someday be as subtle and rich as the feel of paper and the smell of leather." The current generation of e-books starts us down this path, but they are a far sight short of the real thing. Maybe they will move closer to replicating the experience. We shall see.

Now that you know where to go and how to get there, let's begin at the beginning and talk a little about (gasp!) mutual funds.

PART II

MUTUAL FUNDS: LOVE 'EM, OR LEAVE 'EM?

·4·

Hey, Maybe You *Should* Just Buy Mutual Funds

· · · · ·

Life is constantly providing us with new funds.
—*Henry Miller*

As we entered into the twenty-first century, mutual funds—the showpiece of the hour—were growing at a phenomenal rate. In 1980 over $145 billion was invested in mutual funds. At the end of 1999, U.S. income, equity, and bond funds held almost $7 trillion in assets, an annual increase of 23 percent, twice the industrial growth rate per year over the same period. And total assets held in mutual funds had doubled in three years. Unbelievable!

But why do Americans choose mutual funds? Why aren't they falling for the latest round of penny-ante pyramid schemes: wireless cable start-ups, futures contracts, ostrich farms, Vancouver Exchange stocks? Why? Because mutual funds seem safe, understandable, trackable, and well marketed. The larger fund families—Fidelity, Vanguard, and others—provide far more consistent returns than the speculative investments that sank Orange County, California, in 1994 and Long-Term Capital Management in 1998. And funds can be held accountable. They can be monitored daily, weekly, monthly, and annually against the market's average performance. You'd have to be very foolish not to recognize the comfort in lumping your money together with that of thousands of other investors, passing it to select managers whose performance can be measured, and going on with daily life.

Contentedness and confidence in the long-term profitability of your savings—those are the cornerstones to investing Foolishly. And mutual funds, which sprang up in an industry that had previously been doing a poor job of providing reassurance, have filled the void. There are really three overriding reasons why mutual funds have blossomed into a multitrillion-dollar industry today. Let's spend the rest of this chapter learning them.

Why Buy Funds? The Broker Made Me Do It

Many investors just plunge their savings into mutual funds in order to avoid one of the financial world's less pleasant relationships, that between the full-service broker and the individual investor. Invest your money in a mutual fund with clearly defined costs and you need fret no more over fair commission rates, or whether your broker is overactively trading your account, or how your portfolio is stacking up against the competition. Full-service brokering of stocks is responsible for all of these ambiguities, possibly designed to bewilder individuals into accepting "standard" fee scales.

Any Fool, however much bewildered, knows that most brokers are rewarded for activity, not productivity—for how often they trade, not how well. It's a bit like motivating an employee to *do* things rather than to *get them done*. It's a preposterous model and the chief reason that Americans will continue to move money away from investment firms into no-load mutual funds in the coming years.

No-load mutual funds are those that can be bought for no additional commission, or *load*. No-loads contrast with loaded funds, which brokers or fund representatives are paid a commission for selling. Because there is no difference in overall performance between the two, the future obviously lies with no-loads; most people would rather avoid situations like the following.

Consider this scenario: A broker calls you during dinner for the fifth time this month, pushing Huge Fruit Inc. (ticker: HUGE), a little-known California outfit involved in "agribusiness biotechnology." HUGE is trading around $3.25 a share and the cold-calling broker is cocksure that the company's LemonLarger engineering system will soon be a smash success. "Got any idea how many gallons of lemonade can be squeezed out of a fifteen-pound citrus?"

You don't, but you figure it's an awful lot.

You've been mulling over this recommendation for weeks now, and you're about ready to take the plunge. A stock that's selling at $3.25 a stub seems appetizing; you'll be able to gobble up more shares. And if in the coming years neighborhoods across the nation are to be serviced by giant-fruit stands, God only knows how much money you'll make. Meanwhile, the broker keeps pushing proofs over the phone to you: "Hey, once they've successfully engineered the oversized pineapple, for example, a multibillion-dollar fruiting operation like Dole either crumbles internally or buys Huge Fruit out at a premium. That's what technology is: cannibalization. Companies like Huge Fruit swallow their slower-moving competitors going forward. Thirty bucks a share isn't out of reach in the next eighteen months, and that's just the beginning. But you've got to get in early to profit."

A *$30 stock,* did he say? At $3.25 per share today, 1,000 shares would cost you $3,250. You multiply 1,000 shares times the projected price of $30. Wow! That's $30,000, for a gain of $26,750—over eight times your original investment. Not bad for a Fool. And it'll be damned fun cheering for a man-sized grape.

What you may not have realized in between your hesitation and the word "Buy!" is that you'll pay the broker exactly the same amount of money whether Huge Fruit Inc. goes to $30 per share or goes under, taking your $3,250 investment down with it. Anyone who's watched $3 biotechnology stocks come down the pike and get truck-squashed knows the amount of risk you're shouldering with Huge Fruit. But your broker isn't taking on *any* risk. In fact, because commission scales can be variable, the excitement that he's generated over HUGE may well have opened the door to charge you a bit more for his efforts. If he's shrewd enough to have sold you on a company whose financial statements you've never seen, whose business you're not familiar with, then he's got to be shrewd enough to see that he can ratchet up his fees on you.

One Fool we know claims it wasn't until he dug diligently through the morass of poorly fashioned monthly brokerage statements that he realized he was paying his broker $400 per trade while for years dramatically underperforming the market's average annual performance. He wrote us: "I didn't have any idea then that I should be setting expectations, and comparing them to the S&P 500's performance. I had no clue whether five percent per year, ten percent, twenty percent per year was reasonable, nor what I should pay a broker in commissions to garner those returns. But now, Fools, *now* I know!"

Most fully served individual investors neither have any idea, nor ought to, whether commissions on a trade like that in Huge Fruit Inc. should sit at $50, $150, $450 . . . or $0—the preference of a Fool who doesn't trade nickel-and-dime stocks! As with all hard selling, the fair price is whatever a customer is willing to pay. Not surprisingly, some brokers make small fortunes persuading customers that those two-bit fruit enlargers, diamond miners, and international oil drillers are going to swallow up the market giants tomorrow. After all, if the stock's going to rocket up ten times in the next year, what's the big deal if you over-pay a hundred bucks on the launching pad?

What has most damaged the reputation of the full-service brokering industry is that incentives are tied only to a broker's deftness in getting you to buy and sell stock. Payment has *nothing* to do with the thor-oughness of his research, the soundness of his logic, or, most important, his performance. This isn't to say that there aren't thousands of terrific brokers who do a stand-up job of outperforming year after year while teaching their clients how to understand stocks. The problem lies in a system that protects the countless many who neither outperform the market nor have any vested interest in doing so.

Fools may be forgiven for wondering whether the full-service bro-kering of stocks in its present form—absent performance incentives—will outlast even the VCR-tape-rental industry. It'll be fun to watch. The middlemen who survive will be those who broker information, exper-tise, and bottom-line accountability. And the majority of individual investors will continue to rush their savings into no-load mutual funds—investment vehicles that they can hold accountable. They won't stand for anything less.

Why Buy Funds? High-Volatility Heartache

Imagine yourself holding on tightly to those shares of Huge Fruit Inc. as it bounds between $5 and $2 every few months. When it trends up to $5, your $3,500 investment at $3.25 (you paid $250 in commissions, ouch) blips up to $5,000, and you can't keep quiet about your winning investment at cocktail parties. "*Yep, m'broker says it's going to $30,*" you trumpet from one corner of the soiree to the next. But then, when HUGE bends back below $2 and your investment contracts to less than $2,000, you can't tell whether it's your liver, kidney, small intestines, gallbladder, or all of them, but something's hurting. Stock volatility, rela-tive to its ebb and flow, can transform modesty into pomposity and di-gestion into heartburn.

Mutual funds are often the tranquilizing alternative. By virtue of their diversification, they're perceived to be less volatile than the average eq-uities portfolio of a private investor. It's calming to know that you sit alongside thousands of other investors owning minute positions in hundreds of companies. That's participating in America's robust corpo-rate growth going forward and sharing the risk. If the weather gets worse, we'll all pop open umbrellas together! And you could only profitably duplicate that diversity using stocks if you had a couple of hundred million dollars in the coffers. (Hey, if you do, put this book down.)

To appreciate better this overdiversification, consider Fidelity's mammoth Magellan Fund, which recently surpassed $100 billion in size. As of September 30, 1999, its biggest holding was General Electric, representing 4.7 percent of the fund's value. If an investor had plunked $3,000 into Magellan then, she'd own only $141 worth of GE, roughly 1 share. A grand total of $36 would be divided among six aerospace and defense companies (such as Boeing and Raytheon), and $138 would be divided among thirteen "electronics" companies (such as Intel and Motorola). When you're invested in hundreds of companies, if some of them do very well, their impact is diluted by the many less-stellar performances.

Essentially what a Fool notes here is that the larger mutual funds, by virtue of their reach and dimension, *are* the market. And since most investors are content to just shadow the market indices, these funds serve their purpose.

What exactly is a market index? you ask. The Dow Jones Industrial Average and the Standard & Poor's 500 Index (also known as the S&P 500) are the two primary indices against which investors compare their investment returns. The Dow is a compilation of thirty huge American companies: Coca-Cola, Disney, McDonald's, Wal-Mart, American Express, ExxonMobil, to name a few. The S&P 500 tracks five hundred industrial, transportation, financial, and utility stocks (for example, semiconductor, trucking, insurance, and heating companies), weighting companies to account for their relative size. AT&T, Apple, Ford, Intel, FedEx, Pepsi, and Nike are among the more familiar issues in the S&P group, some of which are also Dow stocks.

Regardless of their compositional differences, the S&P 500 and the Dow have put up very similar annualized performance since 1925; they have compounded average annualized growth of 11.2 and 10.6 percent per year, respectively. Quite similar, yes—looks like no big difference, right? But if you've read *The Motley Fool You Have More Than You Think,* the first book in this series, you now know the power of compound interest, and you'll have a healthy respect for what a 0.6 percentage point annual difference becomes, compounded over seventy-five years. Yep, $1,000 invested in the Dow in 1925 (the equivalent of about $10,000 in today's dollars) would be worth some $1.9 million in 2000. If you'd put that money in the S&P 500 instead, you'd have almost $2.9 million!

But the overall point is that it turns out you didn't have to be a railroad baron to prepare for the future of your great-grandchildren, eh? The magic of compounding interest takes care of those who trust in its power.

In that spirit, the Foolish approach to investing rests firmly on the belief that your portfolio ought never to keep you up at night. Were the market to collapse, dipping 30 percent in six months and pulling your holdings underground, you shouldn't lose a minute of sleep over it. To illustrate our point, let's consider the best recent example of a market meltdown. Over twenty-one cruel months from early 1973 to mid-1974, the S&P 500 fell from 119.6 to 63.38. That's a 47 percent devaluation! The market was cut in half. *Biff, bam, POW!*

Look at your own investment portfolio today and ask yourself what would happen to your life if, over the next two years, *your* savings got cut in half. How much do you have? $800? It's now $400. $25,000? You're down to $12,500. $3.6 million? Nope, $1.8 million. Could you bear it enough to hold tight even while money managers were throwing themselves in front of bicycles, jumping off one-story buildings, and chomping down Flintstones chewable vitamins hand over fist?

If you couldn't, either your money isn't invested logically or you shouldn't be holding your savings in the stock market. Because if you sell at the market's darkest hour in decades, when what was once whole is now grimly half, you're going to lose a little fortune. Composed investors held on tight through the early 1970s, and today, when you look at the market's growth from 1970 to 2000 (including that 47 percent gutting between '73 and '74), you still find that the S&P 500 has grown 13.5 percent annually with dividends reinvested, better than the average growth that the market has seen over the past seventy-five years . . . the same vehicle that turned $1,000 just sitting there into $2.9 million. Our offer stands: If the S&P 500 isn't up at least 10 percent compounded annually from today's perch, take the Fools by the arm forty years from now on Space Station *Harold* and demand from us a free Tang spritzer.

By buying into the bigger families of funds, you essentially guarantee that you'll be able to participate in America's robust corporate growth in the decades ahead—the growth in companies like Harley-Davidson, Dell Computer, Microsoft, the Gap, General Electric, and yes, Viacom, beloved original owner of this text. And you'll be able to sleep late and peacefully on Sunday morning. The household-name mutual funds virtually guarantee you long-term portfolio stability, low volatility, limited risk, and unscathed stomach lining.

And that's the second reason mutual funds are so popular.

Why Buy Mutual Funds? So Little Time . . .

You didn't see it? You didn't catch the news? You're not tuned in to the stock market twenty-four hours a day? You have a fully developed life outside the financial markets? Well, then you missed the Huge Fruit Inc. news story that crossed the wires earlier this afternoon.

> RIVERSIDE, CAL.—(THE DAILY NEWS WIRE)—Jan. 1, 2001—Huge Fruit Inc. (ticker: HUGE) announced that the Food and Drug Administration (FDA), at a meeting yesterday afternoon to consider the Lemon-Larger® application, recommended rejection of the company's En-Gene technology™ used in the genetic engineering of enlarged fruits and vegetables. After further review of additional materials provided by the company, the FDA cited widespread spinal dissolution in laboratory rats exposed to Huge Fruit's altered lemons. In heavy late-afternoon activity, Huge Fruit Inc. is trading at $0.69, down $2.25, or 76 percent on the day.

One thing you probably didn't realize when you threw some "play money" into Huge Fruit Inc. is that unfamiliar ventures pushed on you by a broker over the telephone demand *more* research time on your part, *not less*. Imagining a glass of lemonade in every hand at Yankee Stadium, all pressed from a single immense lemon, is entertaining; unfortunately, it doesn't count as research in the Fool's School.

You wonder: *What possibly could have helped me dodge this lemon? Risk comes with the territory, no? What could I have done?* Those are fair questions. While the swift and sharp decline in the value of HUGE shares might not have seemed inevitable initially, more research may have made it so. Did Huge Fruit Inc. have other genetic engineering plans brewing in the backhouse? Were alternative streams of revenue being developed? Did the company have a load of cash on the balance sheet and negligible long-term debt?

Given the market's reaction to the announcement—the 76 percent loss of value in a single afternoon—the answer to all of the above questions was probably "Nope." That's a real shame, too. Those are issues that your broker should've addressed in detail over the phone. It would've taken you or him less than an hour of work to uncover. A Fool knows, though, that what often gets lost in dealings with salesmen *is* the research.

Assuming that you don't have the time outside your work and family life to scrutinize dozens of stocks, mutual funds have to look pretty darned enticing. When you join throngs of individual investors who've turned their money over to "professional" management, you've freed up time, eluded the bogeyman, and absolved yourself of the responsibility to research the stock market. A sigh of great relief is in order here. Sigh, Fool, *sigh*.

On a recent train trip to New York, we overheard a retired father confess to his middle-aged son, "I don't know how my funds are doing, but I know they're up, and the money's safe. Somebody told me one of them is up 14 percent, but does that mean for the last year, or since January first, or for the year to come? I don't know. But the money's safe."

Never underestimate the beauty of delegating the management of your assets to a trained professional at a reasonable price. The right mutual funds bring security, profitability, and independence. By passing on the responsibility of money management to the pros, you can get back to your own business, or your walking tour across Montana, or your child's Little League games.

When you put all that in the context of the bankruptcies of Orange County and Barings or the Long-Term Capital Management fiasco, with "traders" forfeiting some or much of what they had—and of what others had invested in them—via currency fandangles, option bloopers, and the latest beast, the derivative, you no doubt understand why individuals are casually plunging their money into pooled, sleepy investment vehicles without checking back on them but once or twice a year. After all, there's nothing wrong with moderate annual portfolio growth on top of moderate annual salary growth. It beats the hell out of Huge Fruit.

◆　◆　◆

Of the options we've discussed so far, the best alternative to sitting through brokerage cold calls during dinner and spending weekends digging into financial statements, and suffering $3 stocks that turn nest eggs into eggshells . . . so far, the best alternative is the mutual fund. Large, popular mutual fund families have historical returns that are clear, risk levels that are estimable, and future returns that can be tracked every day against the S&P 500's performance. Going forward, counting in decades, you can bet that by buying a few of the popular equity funds, you're going to outperform virtually every other nonstock investment vehicle, and the $1,000 of today most likely will be $2.9 million in the savings account of your great-grandchild.

But if you're still going to invest through a friendly full-service broker, be certain that you're at least getting the same treatment as mutual funds afford. Are you on the receiving end of:

- historical returns that are clearly reported?
- risk levels that are estimable?
- future returns that can be tracked against the S&P 500?
- a portfolio that is guaranteed to do no worse than mirror the market's average annual returns?

If your load of savings isn't at least mimicking the S&P 500's performance (after the deduction of all costs), you've blundered as an investor. And it is on that note that we move forward into Chapter 5 and what must seem like unlikely advice, given our above treatment of mutual funds.

Maybe You Should Avoid Mutual Funds

* * * * *

Probably the only place where a man can feel
really secure is in a maximum security prison,
except for the imminent threat of release.
—*Germaine Greer*

Why Avoid Funds? Market Underperformance

It's the most damning statistic in the world of finance: Lipper, Inc., reports that over 80 percent of all mutual funds underperform the market's average return each year. Whether you're looking at five-, ten-, fifteen-, or twenty-year periods, open-end equity funds can't break that 80 percent underperformance barrier. Keep in mind that the statistics actually make the industry look even better than it deserves because of *survivorship bias,* which means that they don't reflect those funds that folded because of their perpetual paucity of profits. Consider, too, that the results don't count the short- and long-term capital gains taxes that mutual funds foist off on their customers every year as they churn their portfolios. (That's not small potatoes, since Morningstar reports that the average domestic-stock mutual fund has an annual turnover rate over 80 percent and rising.) Nor do those results count any load that funds often charge for the privilege of managed mediocrity. In fact, "mediocrity" is too generous: The tags "professional investor" and "institutional investor" have become forever associated with the word "submediocrity" in the minds of Fools.

Imagine that—all those oft-quoted professionals in wing-tipped shoes, with hundreds of millions or billions of dollars to invest, losing to the market average year after year after year. It's like finding out that 80 percent of America's English professors would underperform their students on the Graduate Record Exams. Who's teaching whom here? Who's managing your money?

Think about the effect that a mutual fund's underperformance has on your returns. Say you put $10,000 in a fund that falls 1.2 percentage points short of the S&P's 11.2 percent return every year. Tack on another point for fees and another for taxes. That gives you an annual return of 8 percent. Over thirty years, your mutual fund will be worth just over $100,000. If you'd had an index fund (with its 0.2 percent fees and the current Vanguard turnover of 6 percent), its value would exceed $220,000. Stretch it out another ten years and your mutual fund will have finally gotten to $220,000, but the index fund would have moved up to $650,000.

Given this data, you'll understand why Folly says that all investors in the country must track their annual results against those of an index, like the S&P 500, the Dow Jones Industrial Average, or the Nasdaq composite. Simply stack the total dollar growth of your portfolio against the gains in the indices. That is, if you were to begin investing today, you would track the percentage gains or losses off the current level of the index of your choice against your own bottom-line profits. You can do this easily by tracking your portfolio at Fool.com, where results are automatically compared to the S&P 500.

It's absolutely imperative that you fit your own investment performance into this overall context. Guess what? If you haven't been tracking your investments, don't be surprised to find now that your broker-managed portfolio or your collection of mutual funds has done poorly relative to the indices. Professional investors collectively have been underperforming the market for decades. In fact, they were and are doing it so consistently that to expect better of them is like expecting anyone to knock out George Foreman on fix TV—oops, we mean pay TV.

Say it aloud once more for good measure: Since mutual funds mainstreamed in the early 1970s, over 80 percent of them have regularly underperformed the S&P 500. Consider, then, that every time you drop a dollar of your savings into the pond of mutual funds, there's a four-in-five chance your frog won't o'erleap the stock market's average growth per year. Damned discouraging frog.

Why Do Most Funds Underperform?

As odd as it may seem, some of the challenges money managers face are quite similar to those confronting individual investors, namely a lack of time and a willingness to accept humdrum, average returns. If you're of the mind that mildly below-average returns on your own investments are bearable, given how little time you have to dedicate to portfolio management, rest assured most mutual fund managers probably feel the same way. Fund management teams have *much* else to do besides picking winning stocks. There are accounting tangles, legal matters, advertising plans, corporate development challenges, and these guys are often out on the road peddling their wares; there's an entire business to run *outside* of finding great investments for their shareholders.

Factor in, too, the Securities and Exchange Commission's (SEC) requirement that no single holding in a mutual fund exceed 5 percent of the fund's total assets. A mutual fund manager, therefore, must diversify into at least twenty holdings. Twenty great investment ideas each year? That's about ten more than Warren Buffett believes anyone should be expected to come up with in a lifetime.

Further consider that this accelerated growth in mutual funds over the last few years has driven many of them up into the billion-dollar-asset stratosphere. Managing billions of dollars requires greater diversity of holdings. After all, 5 percent of $10 billion is $500 million, enough to buy a basket of small-capitalization companies outright!

Fund managers also broaden their portfolio base because they know better than to create the impression that their fund is underdiversified. A Fool notes that in the celebrated circles of the Wise, prudence in investing *is* overdiversification. Spread your savings thin and you'll be safe. We may even be to the point today where, if a middle-aged man with no prior investing experience were to don suit and tie, produce and air on CNBC a thirty-second video of himself strutting around a cardboard set, reiterating, "We are Wise, cautious, and prudent money managers," he could be investing a quarter of a billion dollars in less than a year. Just name it the Wisely Diversified Fund.

But the most wondrous and least pardonable form of overdiversification is the common redistribution of large amounts of shareholder money to the fund's management team and outside directors. Over-compensation for management is a laughable example of the laundering of shareholder dollars that goes unchecked. Remember, a $10 billion mutual fund with a standard 1 percent management fee (seems reasonable, doesn't it?) will take in $100 million. That's a lot of money to spread around. The distribution of it to a mutual fund's outside directors, those who by law are not allowed to be involved in the day-to-day management of the business, is just too unthinkable to let slide by here. Each year these people are getting paid hundreds of thousands of dollars to meet for a couple of hours to provide vague expertise in long-term strategic planning and joke about protecting shareholder rights, while getting belly-rubbed in a massage parlor in Tahiti. It's absurd. There just can't be an easier six-figure salary in the United States.

Mind you, a Fool finds nothing improper with paying someone millions of dollars to manage a burgeoning conglomerate that outperforms its industry. Honest success need be rewarded. Does anyone think Michael Jordan was overpaid, given what he did for Nike, Gatorade, the Chicago Bulls, the city of Chicago? There's nothing wrong with paying for performance. It's when fat cats peripheral to the business make loads of money while the operation underperforms the averages—precisely what is happening in the mutual fund business—that a Fool has to get up on his orange crate in the town square.

The final and most entertaining reason that 80 percent of all mutual funds perform sorrily stems from an unusual matter peculiar to the mutual fund industry, called *window dressing*. Window dressing is the quarter-end ritual during which mutual fund managers belatedly window-shop for the best and brightest stocks of the quarter. Why? To make their portfolio look impressive. In March 1995, when Cisco Systems (Nasdaq: CSCO) had risen 45 percent for the quarter, you can be sure that mutual funds were lining up to get a few shares of CSCO on their account statement. Why? To let their shareholders know that they were in on one of the hottest stocks of the quarter. That they took a position after the great run-up and perhaps made nothing on the transaction, or lost money, isn't what matters. What does? Appearance—image is everything. In other words, in this industry it can be as effective to look like you made money as it is actually to have done the deed. Until, that is, some Fool (it could be you) points out that the king (or the fund manager) has no clothes . . . and no profits either.

Why Avoid Funds? So Little Time . . .

When you consider how many publications dedicate themselves to the analysis and tracking of what are primarily lousy investments, you can understand why we have a tough time determining just what are the opportunity costs associated with mutual fund investing. What were the costs for medieval cartographers who spent their lives mapping out a flat Earth when the Greeks had shown the planet was spherical? Can a value be placed on pointlessness?

Look upon mutual funds in this light: Imagine yourself in a university physics exam. The professor passes around copies of the test, then stands in front of the class and announces, "You have two hours. Oh, incidentally, 80 percent of the information in your textbook for this semester was inaccurate. Good luck!"

The same can be said to the reader of any of the hundreds of publications dedicated to the—at last count—over eight thousand mutual funds: 80 percent of your reading is fluff. And no Fool should waste his time trying to determine which minority of it was fruitful. Let us say this again just to be sure you've got it: If you play a game—say the shell game—where four out of five of the choices are losing propositions, then your chances of winning are one in five from the start. Your chances of losing are four in five. Makes you want to find a new game, doesn't it? Well, friends, that's the point.

Strangely enough, you don't hear that sort of talk about the mutual fund industry very often. But then, consider how much money is riding on the profitability of the mutual fund. Newspapers and magazines create advertising-ready pages by doling out mutual fund advice. Among the widely distributed financial magazines today, a single page of advertising can be worth between $25,000 and $75,000. The challenge to an editor, then, is to build up as much material as he can around which to advertise. Ahh, wonderful mutual fund industry, you've doubled the information available to the financial publications of America. No matter if the information is bad, misleading, overoptimistic, or more harmful than helpful; it pays 50 G's per ad page! "Thank you, mighty universe of mutual funds," say the financial retailers coming out of the woodwork to sell funds with front loads, back loads, inter loads, high expense ratios, 12b-1 fees, skylark fees, redemption fees, signature fees—who can keep track of all the related costs? These days salesmen have a hand in every one of your pockets when they sell you a fund, and you'd be a fool to assume that they've done any meaningful research on their recommendation. Incidentally, there's no such thing as an *inter load, skylark fee,* or *signature fee,* but how would most individuals know that?

A Fool must reiterate here that there's nothing wrong with paying for service, creating jobs that handsomely reward hard and profitable work . . . but what about paying handsomely for nothing or, worse, underperformance? With thousands and thousands of funds to research, with brokers selling them on commission, and with many funds sticking their customers with hidden costs, individual investors are really back where they started with Huge Fruit Inc. Namely, weary. They now have to research not simply the investment but the myriad costs associated with it *and* the salesman who's cramming it down their collective throat. Absurd, really.

Why Avoid Funds? Ingredients, Please!

If Fools are to accept the credo "Don't ever invest in something you don't fully understand," then 99 percent of all mutual funds should be crossed off the candidate list. Mutual fund prospectuses feature a wonderfully rich language, Prospectish, that is indecipherable, uninformative, and legalistic. And the idea that you can ever get a serious grip on a fund through the fundamental analysis of its individual holdings is bunk. You'd be analyzing stocks till the next appearance of Halley's comet.

Sad to say, sometimes even the most scholarly fund investors among us, those who willingly forgo summer barbecues to huddle over investment tomes, get backhanded by fund managers who take extra risk on the sly, deviating from their proposed course. What!?! You didn't know that your mutual fund was dabbling in derivatives? You weren't aware that management was experimenting with some option trading this quarter? You didn't hear that Joe, the new intern at Strategic Diversified Wisdom Fund, decided to try his luck at some "currency swapping"?

Pity those well-read mutual fund investors who found out back in the first quarter of 1995 that, while the S&P 500 was racing to new highs, their large-cap, blue-chip, stodgy, old-money mutual fund collapsed because the fund deviated from its proposed course and plunged headlong into Mexican investments. Have sympathy on your neighbors who, after combing through dozens of mutual fund prospectuses, settled on one that decided to—*aww*, what the hell—*go for it* in derivatives. The Fool can name names: Fidelity's Asset Manager Fund wins the bobo prize for being a *non*-emerging-market, conservative fund that got walloped for testing the Latin American waters in 1993. That's right, ladies, gents, and Fools, a *non*-emerging-market fund. Manager Bob Beckwitt increased his exposure to Mexico subsequent to the signing of NAFTA. By year's end the fund was 20 percent invested in Mexico (!)—half in bonds and the remainder in stocks and peso-denominated cash. An additional 5 percent of the fund was exposed to the Argentinian austral and similar Latin American currencies. A *non*-emerging-market fund.

Beckwitt's fund lost 6 percent for the year in 1994. His Asset Manager Growth Fund fared even worse, posting a year-end loss of 9 percent. A 6 percent loss, a 9 percent loss, that's not so terrible . . . right?

During that year, the S&P 500 *rose* 1.32 percent and beat those funds by 7 percentage points and 10 percentage points, respectively. For investors Foolish enough to compare their holdings to the S&P 500, *that* hurt!

But if that looks bad, consider the Piper Jaffray Institutional Government Income Fund. Hands down, it won Bonehead Derivatives Move of the Year in 1994. The fund supposedly sought current income consistent with "*preservation of capital,*" proposing to invest in U.S. Treasury bills, notes, and bonds "*guaranteed as to payment and interest by the U.S government.*" Sounds pretty conservative. But then, head manager of the fund Worth Bruntjen went ahead and bought an array of long-mortgage derivatives, including inverse floaters and principal-only (PO) securities. ("Definitions, please!" You don't need 'em.) Bruntjen also had the fund fully leveraged, keeping it 150 percent invested in 1994. Versus S&P 500 gains of 1.32 percent, the Piper Jaffray Institutional Government Income Fund lost a heartrending 28.5 percent. In a single year. At that rate, the fund would turn $1 million into less than $1,500 in twenty years. Now *that's* investing.

Therein lies a primary reason to avoid mutual funds. You can't see the *business* in which you're investing. And when you can't see what's going on with your money, it doesn't matter how wise or Foolish you are, you can't evaluate a fund's holdings or its strategy. You can only pay your money and take your chances.

And what tool for fairly valuing mutual funds has replaced the good old homegrown fundamental analyses that turned enormous profits in stocks for the great investors of the past? Price studies. The most popular and least meaningful technique used to value mutual funds today is an eyeballing of their one-, three-, and five-year records. Compare it to a baseball game, a Baltimore Orioles–Cleveland Indians game. Disregard whether the game is being played at Camden Yards or Jacobs Field, who's pitching, whether any players are injured; in fact, disregard altogether who's on the teams. Now pull out your Elias Sports Bureau manual and find out how many games each team has won over the past five years. Whichever team has won more, price studies suggest, should win the game. It's ludicrous.

Oh, but before putting money down on that analysis, *do* check to see if the Orioles pitching staff is into inverse-floating derivatives.

Running Historical Numbers

Let's look at some of the numbers together to paint a prettier picture of what happens to our dollars when we hold them in the light of compounded returns. We'll work off a base of $10,000, showing pretax profits and including short-term capital gains that mutual funds pass on every year.

Year/Vehicle	Growth Rate	$10,000 Becomes . . .
I. 20-Year Period		
Huge Fruit Inc.	−95.6%	$0
Crapola Fund	−25%	$32
Treasury Bills	4%	$21,911
Bonds	6%	$32,071
Average Mutual Fund	8%	$46,609
S&P 500	11%	$80,623
II. 40-Year Period		
Crapola Fund	−25%	$0
Treasury Bills	4%	$48,010
Bonds	6%	$102,857
Average Mutual Fund	8%	$217,245
S&P 500	11%	$650,008
III. 60-Year Period		
Treasury Bills	4%	$105,196
Bonds	6%	$329,877
Average Mutual Fund	8%	$1,012,571
S&P 500	11%	$5,240,572

That's the sort of chart that should be stamped on the inside of every investment text published; it oughta be drilled into the minds of business school students and memorized alongside Frost poems in grade school: $10,000 in Treasury bills for sixty years is worth half as much as $10,000 in mutual funds for forty years.

But most astonishing of all is the sixty-year performance of the S&P 500 versus your average mutual fund. The former easily clears $5 million, while the latter struggles to reach $1 million. Pretty damning evidence for an industry that spends billions of dollars each year selling itself to individual investors.

Fools don't while away many hours wondering whether Wall Street is right when it tells us that we ought have our money broadly diversified in mutual funds, bonds, gold, and T-bills. Fools already know that all of these have underperformed the S&P 500 year after year after year. Seventy-five years of history is sufficiently convincing proof for bonds, gold, and T-bills, and the last twenty years have convinced us that mutual funds are an investment opportunity that isn't one.

We close this chapter by calling on all mutual fund managers to waive management fees every year that they underperform the S&P 500 by more than, say, 1 percentage point . . . that they underperform the S&P 500 . . . the S&P 500 . . . 500 . . . 500 . . . echo . . . echo . . . echo.

We didn't think they would listen!

But in the next chapter, we'll prove that being average is really quite simple.

The S&P 500 Index Portfolio

• • • • •

Averageness is a quality we must put up with.
Men march toward civilization in column formation,
and by the time the van has learned to admire the masters
the rear is drawing reluctantly away
from the totem pole.
—Frank Moore Colby

Imagine a single mutual fund whose eminently trackable performance virtually matches market-average growth year after year, whose holdings are clearly outlined for you in advance, and that demands virtually no research. Imagine no more. Your dream is real and available in a variety of index funds. The biggest and best known is Vanguard's 500 Index fund. This *many-trillion*-dollar fund simply duplicates the holdings of the S&P 500 by buying all five hundred stocks in corresponding lots. (The S&P 500 does not weigh each stock equally, but by the size of the company. If Huge Fruit were worth $1 billion and the total worth of the 500 stocks were $10 trillion, then Huge Fruit would make up 0.01 percent of the index.) It is thus able to match (and compound) the index's growth year after year.

When you consider that mutual funds have consistently underperformed the stock market, S&P 500 Index funds really start looking attractive. They demand no research and outperform the majority of funds on the market. For this and the reasons outlined below, we don't really think there's any managed fund out there worth buying.

No Salesmanship

Remember that friendly broker a couple of months back who kept call-ing when you were giving the kids a bath, or working out in the yard, or just sitting down to dinner? You know, the one with that biotechnology stock that was going to radically alter the way we live? Yes, you know, the one who kept calling and calling and calling, getting increasingly impatient as he touted Huge Fruit Inc., the $3.25 stock from the com-pany with only the best of intentions. Remember the hassle? Remem-ber that you lost half your investment? Well, we certainly hope not, since we hope that you've never had any such experience.

Those hazards and hassles don't happen with an index fund. Van-guard and its brethren go a long way toward wiping out the broker and mutual fund world's shoddier practices. With no hard selling, no hid-den fees, and no confusing monthly statements, the index fund truly has been fashioned after the finest of business models: The buyer comes first.

Full Disclosure

Remember that day down at your local bank when they just wouldn't let you out of the building unless you bought into a couple of their fa-vorite heavy-load funds? You know, when they water-pistol-whipped you at the door, tied your feet together, put a sock in your mouth, and forced you to sign sheets of paper against your will. Ah, yes. And how'd those heavy-load mutual funds do—the ones "committed" to only the safest of domestic investment products? Yes, that's right, the ones that instead diversified into Costa Rican corn futures, leveraged options, and a nice load of Canadian penny stocks? Remember, the mutual fund that dropped 29 percent before you limped back into the bank and begged them to free you from the investment? Again, we certainly hope you don't.

The index fund, a no-load fund, doesn't hog-tie you into a lot of in-vestments you hadn't prepared to make while sticking you with a vari-ety of hidden costs down the line. Index funds buy only the five hundred stocks listed on the S&P 500, companies like Coke, AT&T, Pepsi, Colgate Palmolive, Gillette, Toys 'R' Us, Nike. These are all Ameri-can companies that have flourished as industry leaders and that, as a group, will accurately reflect U.S. growth going forward. True, you don't get the excitement of middinner phone calls and bank tellers threatening you at squirt-gunpoint. With an index fund those thrills are gone. What you get in their stead is a mutual fund that paces the most profitable vehicle for investing in the twentieth century: the U.S. stock market.

Hassle-Free Performance

Wouldn't it have been nice if all our dreams of a technological world had turned out as planned, with greater efficiency leaving us more free time? In many ways we've ended up with a professional life that claims as much, more, or far more of our time than it did in the pre-Pong world. In this regard, one of our core Foolish beliefs is that investing ought to be a profitable and timesaving venture: Every step of the way, investors should be evaluating how much of their time they're spending and for how much long-term profit.

When you look out over Wall Street, crowded in now by thousands of mutual funds, doesn't an index fund look ever inviting? You literally have to do no research to participate in America's corporate growth at a moderate pace. Take a look at how some index funds have performed over five and ten years:

Index Funds (as of March 31, 2000)

	5 Years	10 Years
Vanguard 500	26.7%	18.7%
Fidelity Spartan 500	26.4%	18.6%
T. Rowe Price Equity 500	26.4%	18.4%
S&P 500	26.8%	18.8%

You can see that the funds slightly underperform the market, due to the expense of running the fund. However, the annual 0.1 percent shortfall at Vanguard will not have too profound an effect on your returns over time. What you see above is funds that have outperformed most of the competition; but for a second here, look beyond the performance. These funds demand zero research. Zero. And the historical returns of the S&P 500 can be traced back seventy-five years.

When we consider the research responsibilities of mutual fund investing, we can't but conclude that the work is not commensurate with the return. Even if many mutual funds matched the performance of index funds, Fools would still have to sort through the prospectuses, still have to bone up on Prospectish, still have to keep an eye on the operation to be sure that management hadn't fled to warmer climes, still have to be vigilant of the sorts of investments the fund was now making. After all, what's in a name but a name? If management leaves, maybe the Prudent Sage Fund, which had matched market growth for a decade, then collapses under the weight of an overexposure to Moroccan bean futures—a thing you hadn't known existed. There's much to keep your eye on, no?

But in an index fund you find 11 percent growth back-tested seventy-five years, zero research commitment, a full knowledge of what investments the fund is making (weighted long positions in five hundred of America's greatest companies), and—not to be underrated—time to spend on other things.

We know we're repeating ourselves here, but all things considered, how Foolish can you get?

Abiding Expectations

One of the most important investment lessons we hope to illustrate is that you need to set expectations for profit growth.

If you haven't done this already, you now should break out your portfolio's total and compounded growth for the last five years. If you haven't matched or, better yet, outperformed the S&P 500, there's absolutely no reason you shouldn't redistribute all of your savings into an index fund. That's stock market average growth, a beautiful thing stacked up against other investments over time. And all with zero effort, hassle free. It's such a win-win scenario that it hurts us to think of all the money being lost in the Huge Fruits and Wisdom Funds of America. Thankfully, investors are learning. Of the cash poured into mutual funds in 2000, 200 percent more went to index funds than had in 1997. That's a cheerful improvement! (And given that this section was first composed back in the summer of 1995, *expected*.)

Index Shares

There is another way to match index returns that is worth a mention: index shares. The American Stock Exchange offers a variety of stocks that in and of themselves mirror an index. The SPDR (AMEX: SPY) represents the S&P 500; the Diamond (AMEX: DIA) matches the Dow 30; the Nasdaq-100 Tracking Stock (AMEX: QQQ)—well, you can guess what it does. Other offerings track stocks in select sectors or of similar sizes. These stocks don't evade management fees, unfortunately, since each carries an annual expense ratio between 0.1 percent and 0.2 percent. The main advantage of them is that they are very liquid, which means that you can buy and sell them in just a couple of minutes and have the money immediately available for another trade. That makes them an ideal place to stash cash as you look for another investment.

"Whoa!" we hear you cry. "Why would we want to buy and sell our index shares? The index fund is the best investment we've heard about! I thought we were going to hold on to it for our great-grandchildren!"

The Switcheroo!

Surprise!

It's time for the old hidden-ball trick, razzle-dazzle, end around, the hocus-pocus-double-dealing-hoodwink-snooker play. We know it well. Thus far we've done our level best to convince you to invest in stocks and then not to, to convince you to invest in mutual funds and then not to, and most recently, to persuade you to buy the Vanguard Index Trust 500 Portfolio fund and now . . . not to!

We end this chapter by rescinding everything that, up to this point, might be confused with a buy recommendation. Don't buy just any stock because the market does well (for example, Huge Fruit). Don't buy mutual funds because you've lost money in stocks (Wisdom Fund). Don't buy an index fund because your managed funds have been underperforming the market (Vanguard Index Trust 500). Don't buy any of these. Why? Because there are more profitable approaches to investing.

What we have built together, thus far, is the bottom step of the Foolish investing ladder. We ask: Is there any reason to garner less than market-average returns, which have rewarded at the rate of about 11 percent per year for six decades running?

Resoundingly, no!

Step onto that bottom rung and start climbing. Two decades from now you ought to be staring at 11 percent growth (the market average minus 0.2 percent annual expense) compounded on your savings, at the very least. For those with $20,000 to invest, that would grow your portfolio into $161,000 over the next twenty years . . . and more if you were Foolish enough to continue socking away savings there weekly, monthly, quarterly, and annually for your future.

Should you be happy with 11 percent growth per year without carrying out a lick of research? Compared to what's being foisted upon many individual investors by the institutions, most definitely yes, you should be pleased. Investors should not settle for market underperformance over any protracted period of time. And there's nothing at all wrong with 11 percent annual growth, eh? (As we wrote in *The Motley Fool You Have More Than You Think*, most Americans and indeed most people reading our first book will be very well served over the course of their lifetimes by just investing that way, and spending no more time on their investments.)

But what if you actually come to *like* the stock market? What if you think business is interesting? Even more to the point, what if you jangle bells on a cap every so often? What if *you too* have been known occasionally to wear red-and-green checkered panty hose? Then no, dear Fool, you shouldn't be satisfied. Throw away all thoughts of index funds and market-average growth. With some determination and research, we think you can slam past the indices that most money managers lose to each year.

PART III

BUILDING A FOOLISH
INVESTMENT
PORTFOLIO

7

Stepping Away
from Index Funds

• • • • •

The difficult and risky task of meeting
and mastering the new . . . is not undertaken
by the vanguard of society but by its rear.
—*Eric Hoffer*

So now, once again, we opt to pull apart, analyze, and ultimately de-nounce the very things we just celebrated, endeavoring to un-crown King Index, so lately enthroned. That's evolution.

In Chapter 4, we applauded mutual funds for providing a dependable way to turn a profit on your savings. Far more fructiferous than the nickel-and-dime hot and hyped Huge Fruits of "corporate" America, funds give their shareholders diversity, long-term profitability, and com-fort. They're the response to those many cold-calling full-service broker-age firms that haven't yet proved to lowly Fools that they comprehend the notion of *service*.

Service (n): an act of giving assistance and *advantage* to another

Service means putting your customers' well-being, their short- and long-term prosperity, before your own—a pretty good business plan. It's one the industry doesn't always have pegged as its priority, though.

But don't confuse our criticism of poor service in the world of bro-kering for a promotion of the mutual fund construct. Why not? Because the vast majority of mutual funds, while profitable, underperform the market's average return each year. We reiterate that over 80 percent of all mutual funds with a ten-year track record have failed to be just average! So, the next time you find yourself at a shivaree in the company of five fund managers wearing ascots and sipping demon rum with the Wise, ask them if their annual returns have matched those of the S&P 500 over the past five years. Four of them, at least, will hang their heads and sulk. Foolish reader, think how overpaid they are, given that we, any of us, can essentially duplicate the S&P 500's returns without doing a lick of research. Investing in an index fund takes no time, no research, no Pepcid, and puts you out front of 80 percent of the competition.

But now we'll push the ante up once more by thanking-but-no-thanking Mr. Bogle (Vanguard's redoubtable founder) and suggesting that you look beyond his index funds. While no one ought to accept anything less than average returns, if you're able and willing to take risk beyond the index fund, there's a wide, wide world out there. So (remember that soupy 1970s flick *Logan's Run?*) shed your polyester monochromatic jumpsuit and let's escape this sector. Give us an opportunity to demonstrate that with some dedication to your task, you can quite easily outperform Wall Street's well-heeled stewards.

Vanguard Hype: The Efficient Markets Theory

The Efficient Markets Theory (EMT), which backs a very Wise approach to the stock market, is the philosophical underpinning of the Vanguard Group and the index fund industry it spawned. EMT posits that the stock market is an *efficient* thing, wherein all present prices properly reflect the underlying fair market value of stocks. Stocks, EMT theorists tell us, are always fairly priced; the only thing that bumps them up or knocks them down is unforeseeable events—mergers, new partnerships, announcements of new products or services, and so on. The future. Because these price stimulants are *unforeseeable,* the Wise tell us, all future movements on the stock market are therefore random, unpredictable.

The fundamentals of this theory are actually mostly sound. The market's prices at any given moment *do* reflect our collective best guess at a company's stock price, a best guess arrived at by millions of buyers and sellers who are shaking hands over billions of dollars from opposite sides of the table. This is truer and truer the more liquid (commonly held, highly traded) a company's stock is. On the other hand, like most of their species these buyers and sellers are rather a shortsighted lot—especially since so much active trading today is done by people whose attention span rivals that of the common household fly. So you can expect that the market's prices typically aren't looking as far ahead as the Foolish long-term investor. And further, common sense remains of uncommon value when looking at market prices. Is anyone seriously contending that Boston Chicken or Planet Hollywood was ever worth its price even at its initial public offering?

Hmph. You see, the real problem with the Efficient Markets Theory is not with what it says, but rather with what some take it to mean. Some conclude, wrongly, that investing is just guesswork. And because it is guesswork, they say you can't consistently beat the market; it's impossible.

It's unfortunately not surprising that this conclusion has found a home in America's finer, greener universities and business schools, where increasingly the notion of excellence and incentivization has given way to a soft, sleepy relativism. Forces that we can't control determine everything, the Wise tell us. And that being the case, there's no reason to study individual stocks and the businesses behind them, or to prepare, or to aim high, aspiring to outperform. Right? Hey, all stocks at the prices they are today are really just the same! Becoming a part owner of this company over that one is not worth considering. (These are great lessons for our kids, as well.)

It also doesn't amaze a Fool that this jerry-built theory is being inculcated in investors by index fund marketers. Vanguard's promotion of the Efficient Markets Theory is philosophy by convenience, since the "Why bother?" attitude does bolster its multibillion-dollar business. If the best that private investors can do is merely the average, and the worst is unthinkable, Bogle's low-cost index fund looks mighty attractive. How opportune!

But the stock market is not a controlled laboratory experiment, nor does it submit to easy explanations of how much value is in it at any given moment, and how accurately that value is being reflected. The stock market is messy and remains always a little bit wrong in its present estimation, in a charming and sometimes surprising way. Were the market truly efficient—a clean machine—every perfectly valued, publicly traded security would inch forward 0.03 percent per day en route to annual returns of 11 percent . . . *every* market day of *every* market year of *every* market decade. It doesn't happen, and it's the inevitable inefficiencies that have Fools rummaging around looking for market outperformers.

Many have gone before and go with us. The market has been beaten consistently and significantly by the high-profile likes of Philip Fisher, Peter Lynch, and Warren Buffett, to say nothing of tens of thousands of Foolish Everymen, who've done their time in our online forum. And this plays out because the stock market isn't propelled by synergistic forces driving toward greater efficiency, but rather by divergent ones ever generating greater complexity. Pricing in a barter market like the stock exchange isn't the upshot of one mind, one approach, or one analysis, but the consequence of many different attitudes, valuation models, degrees of expertise, and varieties of expectation.

Remember the Intel (Nasdaq: INTC) debacle in the winter of 1994? After rounds of heated argument conducted on the Internet between technologists, investors, and insiders, Intel revealed that its Pentium chip did produce calculative errors at the seventh decimal place. The stock sold off to a low around $56 a share. The questions swirled: Would Intel have to recall and replace all of its Pentium chips? Would Microsoft look to partner with a different supplier? Would the courts bubble over with lawsuits from Pentium users whose businesses relied on flawlessly accurate measurement: engineers, construction companies, chemists, and others? Intel: a brand name forever scarred?

Now consider the myriad reasons why the hundreds of thousands of institutional and individual investors tracking Intel bought and sold this fantastic stock during the upheaval. Some felt the company was in serious trouble; others thought the market had overreacted to the news and that the stock was underpriced; some routinely picked up more INTC shares in their employee stock plan; others cashed out, needing capital to buy a home, a stereo, a Ferrari. Fools recognize that there are an untold number of reasons that stocks are bought and sold at given points in time and at given prices. It's a blooming, chaotic, complex market with few pockets of efficiency—quite a bit like life. And Intel's stock provided a great example of that untidiness of open barter markets; within half a year of the Pentium "disaster" and after few truly significant news items, the stock of the greatest semiconductor chip maker in the world was trading at $115 a share—a clean double. A 100 percent return . . . not bad for six months' time.

In this and countless other instances, the markets' supposed efficiency and the idea that future moves are unpredictable and that every investor in the nation simply ought to buy an index fund and accept market-average returns are all just too simplistic. Vanguard's has been one of the great pitches in the financial industry over the last thirty years, attracting tens of billions of dollars of business. A Fool hopes the logic will be looked through now. The index fund provides a wonderful toehold for most of the world's investors, but it will never ever beat the stock market. And those who suggest this isn't possible do the world a disservice.

Beating the Market Average

We don't want to light into Jack Bogle and the Vanguard index fund mentality too fiercely, though. There's an extraordinarily important and rudimentary lesson that the vast majority of private investors have yet to learn: If you can't beat 'em, join 'em. If you've had trouble historically with your investments, Vanguard is there for you in a way that no other fund company is. For this reason, we consider Jack Bogle a genuine modern-day hero of the individual investor despite our disagreement over the interpretation of the Efficient Markets Theory.

These things said, if you *can* beat 'em, Fool, go ahead and beat 'em! The book would end here if we thought we couldn't direct you to better than average returns in the remaining pages. Now that you know the power of compounded returns, you'll recognize that every extra percentage point we can slap together onto your annualized average return will translate to thousands more dollars down the line. The process can even be relatively painless—nay, downright agreeable—assuming that you enjoy doing some of your own research, and don't mind taking on additional risk and responsibility for your own decision making.

Out of Funds into Stocks

* * * * *

The best servants of the people, like the best valets,
must whisper unpleasant truths in the master's ear.
It is the court fool, not the foolish courtier, whom
the king can least afford to lose.
—*Walter Lippmann*

The remainder of our investment guide is going to concentrate wholly on building investment portfolios that outperform market average. You'll be surprised at just how simple it is for the individual investor to top mutual fund managers, the majority of whom lumber from one investment opportunity to another, follow the herd, are undertrained, underperform the norm, and in many cases end up so because they have tens of millions of dollars to invest. It may seem counterintuitive, but it's true: *You* have the advantage.

But beating Wall Street is going to take some motivation and mobilization. You're going to have to move out of mutual funds, to forget about them altogether, and put your savings into stocks, the most profitable investment over the past six decades, and the previous 140 years as well. Here, from Jeremy J. Siegel's great book *Stocks for the Long Run,* are the total real returns (that is, adjusted for inflation) for $1 invested in popular investment instruments between 1802 and 1997:

Interest-Free Bank Account	$0.07
Gold	$0.84
Short-Term Government Bonds	$275
Long-Term Government Bonds	$803
U.S. Stocks	$558,945

Not much of a contest, is it? Briefly, we'll detail some of the initial challenges you'll encounter and some of the initial steps you'll have to take to begin managing a market-beating portfolio Foolishly.

1. Making the Switch to Stocks

First, we need to hammer home again that our aim is to outdo the 11 percent annual growth that the S&P 500 has compounded over the last seventy-five years. Beating the S&P 500 should be the goal of every institutional investor in stocks on the planet; sadly, for the majority of them, that's nothing more than a pipe dream. Ask any number of fund managers whether they could garner better returns with a $50,000 portfolio or with a $5 billion portfolio; they're fibbing if they don't name the former.

It's no easy road for fund managers, though for the most part they're amply rewarded for poor performance. Why is it tough on them? Not only will they be critiqued weekly with that multihundred-million-dollar portfolio—the chief reason that funds underperform the market—but they'll also find it difficult to invest in the most rewarding operations on the planet: small growth companies on the U.S. market. Try investing $250 million into a company worth $200 million and see what happens. A fair comparison might be managing a million dollars and being forced to invest it all in oranges down at the farmer's market.

The smaller investor can, however, make money on underpriced oranges, or underpriced automobiles, or underpriced land . . . or best of all, underpriced listed stocks. If you're an individual investor with so much money that every time you invest in a small company, you drive the price out of your range, like those oranges and pots of gold above, put down this book. You don't need to walk around being Foolish, and you don't need us! For everyone else, however: Read on. The niches of inefficient pricing on the stock market are so various, so broad, and so exploitable for the individual investor, it's just maddening to see so many substandard returns year after year. Too many investors accept mediocre performance because they think the market indecipherable. Hooey! It's not an exaggeration to say that schoolchildren can beat the market, if provided with a few months of Foolish education on the subject. You can, too.

To start out, you may want to practice. It's easy to set up a series of *mock portfolios* that track different kinds of investments for a few months or a year before setting out on your real investment voyage. This is a great way to start off into the uncharted waters of personal financial management. No money down, no risk, but plenty of rich experience with the art of stock picking, the vagaries of the market, and the beauty of compounding gains! If your straw portfolio turns south, well, you can celebrate your patience as an investor! It's the rarest, most essential investing skill you can have.

2. Your Savings and Your Broker

The first thing you have to do is get your capital over to a discount broker. (In addition to our previous book, which covers discounters in detail, you'll also find more on them in "Appendix A, Stocks 101: A Primer for Those Who'll Admit They Need It.") Discount brokerage firms are businesses that simply take your investment orders and carry them out. You tell them to buy shares of a public company, and they do so promptly. You won't get any advice from discount brokers, and most important, you won't *pay* for any advice—an offering for which financiers have conveniently overcharged decade after decade. Don't be convinced that what they're offering is worth half what they're asking. Your savings are worth more than that.

Now, what sort of money should you put away in the stock market, and how? First of all—Motley Fool investing maxim alert!—invest only money that you can put away for at least five years. And if you can leave it there longer, that's even better. Just look at Warren Buffett: His patience is prodigious! It's the single strongest card that individual investors can play: patience. Stay in front of the eight ball; pick your buy and sell strategies without anxiety; and invest only what you can leave untouched for at least five years.

Once you're ready to tuck away the money, it's time to decide which discount broker to use.

Recognize the differences, first of all, between discount brokers and the so-called deep-discounters. Both take buy and sell orders and promptly execute them; they're large enough that they don't have trouble handling transactions on heavy-volume days. But one way they differ is in their pricing scheme. The discounter charges about $30 per trade, whereas the deep-discounter charges anywhere from $15 to $7, or even nothing for people with a sufficiently high account balance.

Why the big difference? Well, discount brokers dole out more service: They'll send monthly statements, offer trades by phone, provide free IRA accounts and a variety of other twenty-four-hour information services. Deep-discounters often do many of those same things, minus one or two specialty products. For many portfolios, the difference between $30 a trade and $7 a trade may be significant. Run the numbers on your own portfolio, and then determine what sorts of services you'll need to make prudent investment decisions. It will vary from one portfolio to the next. A little shopping might turn up a deep-discounter that provides everything you need.

We're not going to run through the gamut of all discount brokers here; instead, just visit our Discount Brokerage Center at Fool.com (www.fool.com/dbc), where we provide you an easy one-stop shop for making your decision. As it was when we selected you a bank in *The Motley Fool You Have More Than You Think,* so too it is here: The critical tip to making the best decision is to know what you value most. Is your primary need really low commissions (you trader, you), personal service, a good online interface, or what? Do, of course, read through the fine print in every advertisement and brochure upon which you gaze. Yep, they're a bit tedious. Remember, though, that often what looks cheap can have hidden expenses. The advertising in financial newspapers is notoriously slippery, contradictory, and self-promoting. There're some silly-looking sharks in them waters. Read carefully.

3. Accounting Software

You can track the details of your account and determine whether you're outperforming the S&P 500 by setting up a portfolio at Fool.com, but you'll also want to buy some personal finance accounting software to maintain a precise account of your investments. You simply have to know how your investments are performing relative to the stock market; otherwise, "What do you really know?" Stick close to this sort of reasoning:

> When you can measure what you are speaking about, and express it in numbers, you know something about it; but when you cannot measure it, when you cannot express it in numbers, your knowledge is of a meager and unsatisfactory kind: It may be the beginning of knowledge, but you have scarcely, in your thoughts, advanced to the stage of Science.
>
> —*William Thomson*

When you properly account for your portfolio's growth and compare it to market-average growth, you take a giant step toward mastering the art of investing. The most popular accounting programs out there today are Quicken and Microsoft Money. Quicken has dominated the financial applications market, and it makes it pretty easy for you to professionally account for your savings without undue hassle. You can also do this with a spreadsheet, of course. Heck, you can do it all on paper if you like, though we don't recommend it! In time, all of this accounting will probably move to an encrypted Web-based interface, anyway.

Now, it's true that accurate accounting, telling it like it is, can be painful at times. But remember, with an index fund there's no reason to do worse than average. Tap your heels together three times fast and repeat: "There's no reason to do worse than average. There's no reason to do worse than average. There's no reason . . ."

Don't forget: When accounting you'll want to remember to figure in *all* of your research costs as well. Yep, that $500-per-year newsletter/fax service, that $250-per-year financial newspaper, that six-hour phone call with the CFO of Huge Fruit Inc.—all of these should be deducted from portfolio returns. (And many of them are tax deductible as well, so it's profitable to keep close track of them.) If you can't beat the index fund after all costs are deducted, you've blundered.

So, account, account, account!

4. Moving Forward: The Attitude

It is so much in the financial services industry's best interest to race you through trading procedures at their proposed price that Fools may be forgiven occasional bouts of nausea, amusement bordering on mania, or severe *disillusus Wisdomatum*. There's a basic business principle to keep in mind at all times: Let no one rush you.

No one.

Far too many individual investors find themselves thrown out on Wall Street, trading weekly, daily, hourly, juggling a mishmash of investment vehicles, falling behind in their accounting, and leaving out of their lives much of what is inspiring, rejuvenating, fulfilling, and nonfinancial. If you get a chance, drop by the local offices of any of the big discount brokering firms in the nation that provide access to news, the trading desk, and real-time quotes. Therein, you'll often run into bedraggled, wild- and watery-eyed traders—men and women, young and old—with phones on either ear. These are not stock market *investors* but rather bettors, players. Our model, however, is designed for actual investors aiming to prepare for their future, the future of their family, the generations beyond.

Investing Foolishly has you being so daft as to look fully three decades forward and three back. And yet it can enable you to invest without spending lots of time watching daily market movements. Do you believe Warren Buffett when he claims to spend *no* time following the stock market? We do. And we like to contrast his savings account with that of the two-telephone trader.

There is no hurry to investing, and more often than not, there are losses to be had from impatience. *Take your time* locating the best discount broker and practicing investing in mock online portfolios, which will make it very clear how your money is doing relative to the entire stock market. And continue to remember this, above all: *Patience,* mon Fool. Patience above all.

5. What Consequences?

We need to address risk. High-growth stocks—small and large companies alike—can fluctuate by 30 to 50 percent or more in a single quarter, occasionally in any month, week, or even day. Our 1994 investment in then tiny America Online (NYSE: AOL), though astonishingly profitable in our first year, fell more than 25 percent in value twice during that year. Hey, losing 25 percent off the present value of your investment can be daunting. You invest $20,000, it falls to $15,000—*ouch!* You invest $10,000, now it's $7,500—*eesh!* But if you've picked high-quality, highly profitable companies in burgeoning industries, the volatility shouldn't faze you, as long as your company is still fundamentally sound. By the close of our first year (August 1995), America Online had risen more than 260 percent for us, from $14.5 per share to over $52. You can imagine that those two 25 percent drops aren't terribly memorable.

In fact, AOL later lost 75 *percent* of its value in the summer of 1996, which with the passage of time is increasingly less memorable as well. (The investment, as of this writing, was up historically over 5,800 percent.) Your best stocks, if you choose right and remain patient, will often exhibit tremendous volatility—but ultimately volatility to the upside.

The best way to minimize and ultimately absorb the risk associated with equities investing is to carry out research that is thorough, creative, and logical enough that you're well prepared for a variety of scenarios. After all, some stocks fall 25 percent, then fall another 25 percent, then fall through the floor. So, how do we avoid these as we build our Foolish portfolio?

Part of the answer comes down to a minimum time commitment: the time it takes you to track each of your investments quarterly. More mistakes are made, and more money is lost, by investors who become blind or complacent and simply fail to keep up with the public companies they're invested in. All companies are required by the Securities and Exchange Commission to state their financial performance four times a year. The majority of companies run on a December fiscal year, and their quarters end on March 31, June 30, September 30, and December 31. It takes the accountants a few weeks to compile all the information, so you'll find companies typically reporting their quarterly numbers at the end of January, April, July, and October. At the very least, read these reports! Familiarize yourself with what you own. In Chapters 14 and 15 we'll detail what you'll need to concentrate on in those reports; for now, we just emphasize that in the individual stocks that Fools hold, you should at least expect to review the sales, earnings, and cash flow numbers every three months.

Another investment mistake to avoid is the opposite: the temptation to overanalyze your investments. Many people hyperactively trade their own accounts, paying huge amounts in commissions, annual taxes, and (worst of all) their own limited time on this planet. Because many traders do not get to know what they're trading much beyond its ticker symbol, the danger of investing in crummy prospects is high. Don't make this mistake. Remember that more activity in investing does *not* result in more profits. Some investors sketch stock graphs every market day of the year, claiming that price movements tell them more about their investments than the strength and long-term viability of the companies behind them. Over the course of a single day, one of their stocks rises $1, then drops $0.50, then lifts again $0.38, then a further $0.25, then it gives away $1 before the close. So, that hourly analysis is supposed to tell us all something about the value and future direction of these investments? We don't buy it. We've come across no scientific studies showing that short-term price fluctuations are predictable. And even if we did, who would want to live his life this way? Not us. Investment approaches that compel their adherents to track price fluctuations daily or hourly are bad investment ideas, both for investors' bottom line and for their quality of life.

Conversely, having the patience to wait for and wade through quarterly earnings announcements is a discipline that you'll have to master before being dubbed Fool. And even then, sitting through some disappointing quarters (often your best recourse) will demand ever greater self-restraint. If your company comes in with $100 million in sales for the quarter, and Wall Street was expecting $115 million, look out below. More often than not, your investment will take a hit, and oh how you'll be tempted to sell, on a dime. At those times, a Fool digs through the story to see whether the sales letdown was a short-term anomaly or a signal of structural problems symptomatic of some more permanent disorder. Being patient and careful has won—and always will win—on Wall Street.

•9•

How to Find Companies to Invest In

• • • • •

The victorious strategist only seeks battle after the victory
has been won.
—*Sun Tzu*

In Parts V and VI we will soon turn to some of our favorite strategies for identifying outstanding stocks, what to look for in their financial statements, how to value them, where to buy them, and when to sell them. But let's briefly first pretend that you're a complete novice, that you blew off reading (or want a refresher on) *You Have More Than You Think*, that you've read "Appendix A: Stocks 101," and that you want help getting started locating your *first* stock pick. *Where the heck would I find it?* you inevitably wonder. Good question.

Let's begin with where you shouldn't bother searching. In selecting your very first investment, you should *not* pore through your financial newspaper, where you'd be faced with the prospect of looking over some ten thousand stocks listed daily. You should also *not* use the free advice of your neighbor's ex, who at the post office this morning claimed to have overheard rumors of some buyout. Another place *not* to go: financial magazines and newsletters . . . and you can throw out the hot tips revved up on national money-tawk television as well. No, dear reader, neither should you even consult our own Fool.com Web site.

Your first growth stock investment should ideally come directly from your own expertise . . . out of your professional life. One of the fringe benefits to having a job, we've found, is that you get in pretty good touch with what's going on in at least one domestic industry. Take advantage of that, whether you're in automobile manufacturing, housekeeping, natural gas exploration, magazine publishing, parenting, construction, commercial banking, fiber optics—whatever. The public companies working in your industry are playing on your home field. You're employed. You're paying Social Security. Milk it.

Your Industry

If you're waiting tables in a restaurant, order up financial statements from McDonald's (NYSE: MCD); Tricon Global (NYSE: YUM), owner and operator of the Taco Bell, KFC, and Pizza Hut brands; Outback Steakhouse (NYSE: OSI); Darden Restaurants (NYSE: DRI), of Olive Garden and Red Lobster fame; and companies like them. If you're a computer programmer, scour the hundreds of software companies, from BMC Software (Nasdaq: BMCS) to Oracle (Nasdaq: ORCL) to Microsoft (Nasdaq: MSFT) and the like. If you're a lawyer—heck, you needn't worry about investing at all. Just keep inducing your clients to sue other people and take your 3 percent annual growth in CDs.

(Wait, you think we're kidding?)

But can you hear the mating call of employment and investment? In fact, as you, the investor, learn more about your industry—what makes certain outfits better than others, how the companies generate profits, what their prospects are going forward, how much risk there is in the group—then you, the *employee,* become more valuable to your business. Nick Corcodilos, a former headhunter who has contributed lots to The Motley Fool's early understanding of online job hunting, says, "Make yourself more valuable to your business by understanding what drives its profitability and how you can push that forward." Learning about companies in your industry improves the likelihood of your outperforming the S&P 500 *and* will help you maximize your value in the workplace.

Your Interests

The next box to pop open in search of great investments is the one stuffed with your hobbies, interests, and keepsakes. In many instances, the products and services tied to your private life may be nearer and dearer to you than your own career. Name your favorite hobby and you're likely to find a pretty full range of businesses that have developed in support of it. If you love computer games, Electronic Arts (Nasdaq: ERTS) has $1.4 billion in yearly sales. If you love classical music, consider a company like Steinway Musical Instruments (NYSE: LVB), manufacturer of pianos and organs, with annual sales over $300 million. If you love to read, look no further than the consolidation and competition in the publishing industry. Are you a basketball fan? Hmm, doesn't Nike (NYSE: NKE) own that sport?

Pay attention especially to names that everyone knows. *Mindshare* is the most important thing that a business needs to succeed. Quick word association: When we say "fast food," what name comes to mind? Admit it: big red afro, salty fries—McDonald's (NYSE: MCD). How about "motorcycles"? Did a Harley (NYSE: HDI) just ride through your living room? Try this one: "discount retailer." Are visions of Sam Walton's Wal-Mart dancing in your head? It's no accident that these companies have been some of the best investments you could ever have made. The success of a product leads to a familiar brand name; a familiar brand name reinforces the success of a product. The mind share that these companies have created acts like a wall protecting their businesses. You'd have to make a pretty good motorcycle to make people want to buy Joe's Wheels more than they want a Harley.

Wherever you look, there's a public company filling in to serve the market, a public company that might make a wonderful investment. Searching for gems among the places, activities, and services that you prize is about as Foolish as it gets.

Peter Lynch is a great believer in buying stocks in companies whose products you like. As we suggested earlier, some people have taken his advice to an abusive extreme and just bought Sara Lee because they like the croissants, then added on Limited because they buy clothes there, then bought some Starbucks because of a nostalgic feeling regarding a good cup of coffee they once enjoyed after hours . . . all of this without ever doing a lick of homework. Highly un-Foolish. You certainly should take advantage of shared investment ideas with your friends—including companies you've come across both by investment research and by direct exposure to a product—but please, always understand an investment before you undertake it!

Your Insight

The third pathway—hemmed in by giant oaks—en route to that end-of-the-lane whitewashed home shaded by apple trees (and to decent investment returns on your early investments, as well) involves nothing more than looking around yourself: What industries are thriving? What are people talking about? What products and services are your friends hooked on? Everything is fair game, from magazines to Rollerblades to computer networking software, from telecommunications equipment to bowling alleys to pharmaceuticals . . . and you can even splash in some microbrew, too. Every one of us, regardless of his or her present financial condition, comes into contact with extraordinary products and services offered by public companies that would make for fine long-term investments.

The challenge is often just seeing with clear enough eyes. And our online experience has proven that your eyesight can get a lot better when it's backed by the efforts of thousands of *other* eyeballs, all looking to find the best new companies and products. We first heard about a revolutionary company called Celera Genomics (NYSE: CRA) from the online buzz created by those who'd bought it because of its earth-shaking work decoding the human genome. We read up on the science, the management, the promise, took seriously the chance that Celera would change the world, and bought a stock that has the potential to grow exponentially in the next ten years. Ain't no hocus-pocus to any of this.

Your Investigation

The earnings page of any good financial daily makes for good, raw data. We prefer *Investor's Business Daily (IBD)* because we believe that the present incarnation of *IBD* is the investor's best friend among financial newspapers. Not only does that newspaper contain more useful numbers than any other on a daily basis, it presents them in a way that simplifies the process of locating good stocks.

The earnings page, for example, first divides all the companies that reported earnings the day before into two groups, the "Ups" and the "Downs." Because we're looking only at top-quality growth companies, we completely ignore the downs, those companies whose most recent earnings came in lower than the corresponding numbers from the year before. In general, about a third of all earnings reports are downs, which means that *IBD* enables us to scan the earnings page in two-thirds the time it would take using the *Wall Street Journal*.

As you comb through the "Ups" from top to bottom, scour the list of companies sporting positive earnings growth above 25 percent. Of course, this isn't all you're going to find out about these operations, but this is a fine place to start. (Keep in mind, this isn't the *only* way to find stocks—we've just given you several good ideas above that we would prioritize above this one. However, if you're intellectually curious and more into this stuff than most, this scan of the *IBD* earnings page is a good habit to get into.) Soon we'll fill you in on the eight principles that will help you sort out the likely winners from the likely losers, but let's take our baby steps first. When we find a company report that qualifies, we clip it out with scissors, glue the clipping to a sheet, and type the stock into our database. (In time this process should all be done electronically, but we haven't yet found an efficient way to do this, so for now we think of this effort as "charmingly analog.")

Keep this up for three months—that is, one quarter—and you'll have encountered an earnings statement from virtually every U.S. public company. You should end up with a list of one hundred to 150 top companies, most of them unrecognizable names, that include some of the greatest newcomers to our stock markets.

Wow! That may sound like a lot to do. It certainly is about a daily commitment and one that will require occasional hours spent on weekends in order to get it all in a spreadsheet. If you have the time to do this, we think your investment returns will justify the time spent. At the very least, you will wind up thoroughly educated.

If you do have some time, just not *quite* enough, you have two alternatives. One is to play a hit-and-miss strategy, combing the earnings page when you can but not worrying about those days when you can't. Not everyone needs a hundred-stock database. If you spend, say, one hour one day a week, you'll still have twenty-plus companies to add to your list, and twenty potential new investment ideas in three months will suffice for most people. A second option, which you can combine with the first, is to take a group approach to this work. This is where the power of the online world comes in. Merge your list or spreadsheet of stocks with those of others. Let's say you commit to clipping earnings reports from interesting companies on Mondays. Find someone who'll do it Tuesdays, then you both find someone to do it Wednesdays, and so on. Combine your lists every weekend into one spreadsheet and e-mail it to everyone, and you have a good gig going. Cooperating never seems to occur to our species often enough.

In fact, at Fool.com we have a large number of people focused on this approach to locating stocks, which takes place in our Foolish Eight section (we'll detail the eight things we look for—the meaning of this "Eight"—later on). There you can find others' lists of qualifying companies, as well as our own recently updated list. These are all time-savers for those who don't have the time to do all the work.

High Quality

Now that we've laid down what we think are the clearest roads to finding potential investments—your industry, your interests, your insight, your investigation—we're obliged to emphasize that finding the best products around doesn't mean you've found the best companies in which to invest. Beware the one-trick-pony business, aiming to thrust, say, a terrific new brake system for tractor trailers out to market while showing no other products in the pipeline. Brake It Down Inc. (ticker: UNE) goes public to raise cash; it generates awesome sales and earnings on its Gimme-a-Brake throttle for a full year; it saves a wagonload of cash by not spending anything on research for future product lines. Then money-laden management heads for the hills, leaving shareholders on a downward roll with bandless brakes.

An awful lot of the fireworks that greet initial public offerings fizzle quickly after liftoff. Know thy company, dear Fool. True, you can't hold yourself responsible for learning everything possible about a business. That's management's full-time job—to think strategically, plan prudently, pursue growth aggressively. But your analysis will improve your returns.

In making your first growth stock investment, your responsibility is to perform enough research so that you believe (or don't) that a given company will match up well against its competitors, outdo market-average growth, and remain focused on long-term prosperity. Warren Buffett has said, "You can't do good business with bad people." Investing is no different. After all, when you buy a small piece of ownership in an operation, you do business with the executives of that company. It's your charge to make some determinations about the quality of that team.

So look to high-quality companies succeeding in industries that you understand from your own experience, whether that experience comes from your job, your home life, or your vacation.

Steering the Tottering Boat

With the outboard mounted firmly on the boat, you're set to cruise the open water in search of profitable fish, but don't forget whose hand is on the wheel. Yours. No one in the financial world has your and your family's long-term best interests closer to their heart than you.

Once you recognize that you are solely responsible for the investment decisions you make, you'll start making better decisions. Much of the zeitgeist seems to flow around excuse building, which has our courts overwhelmed with nuisance suits and our universities blustering with complaint. Be contrary in this respect; if you plan to venture out from index funds, take it all head-on. Building a Foolish portfolio with steady blue-chips, monster growth stocks, and a smattering of precariously priced shorts can prove awfully profitable.

But do always remember that if your dory does start taking in water, you have the strongest, handsomest, and most dependable dock on the lake in index funds.

·10·

Getting Information
on Companies

· · · · ·

We're drowning in information and starving for
knowledge.
—*Rutherford D. Rogers*

After you've honed in on the companies you're interested in learning about, it's time to start digging. No right-thinking Fool (and what other kind is there, really?) would dream of buying a stock based merely on cocktail party chatter, a broker's recommendation, or even a discussion board overflowing with exuberance. Even if the stock is one you discovered on your own, you shouldn't just run out and buy shares. First get your hands on the company's financial information and get to know the situation thoroughly.

One of the best places to start is at the company itself. Give 'em a call and ask for the *investor relations department* and request an *investor information packet*. A full packet contains the following, all of which you would want and should ask for:

1. The *annual report* (most recent)
2. The *10-K* (most recent)
3. The *10-Q* (most recent)
4. *Press releases* (all recent ones)
5. *Analysts' reports* (any available up-to-date ones)

Are you wondering what all this is going to cost you? Nothing more than a holiday bottle of wine for your postal carrier, who'll be delivering all the packets you order. These packets are free! They may not include analysts' reports, since these are often reserved for clients only. In that case, you may have to go to multex.com and actually pay for the reports, if you want them.

While you're waiting for that packet to arrive, stop by the company's Web site. It's usually pretty easy to guess at the URL—what do you think, for example, you'll find at www.nike.com? Bingo. (If you can't guess the Web address, slide on over to www.companiesonline.com for listings.) Just click over to their investor relations or their About Us section and see what the company says it does. It will often give an overview of its business, its history, recent activities, and plans for the future. Recent press releases will tell you what products are in the pipeline or what services they'll be offering soon. You can also find press releases at www.prnewswire.com and www.businesswire.com. If the company's Web site has an investor relations section worth its salt, you may not even have to order the materials listed above via the mail. Perhaps they'll all be right there at your fingertips.

SEC Filings

Once you've checked out operations, take a look at some recent public filings. Every three months, U.S. companies are required to file a report on their business with the Securities and Exchange Commission (SEC). They travel under the name "10-Q" for the first three quarters. In the final quarter of the year, businesses file their "10-K," a much longer, comprehensive report. SEC documents are arguably the best place to obtain comprehensive, raw information about a company. The 10-K and 10-Qs supply a complete description of operations, competitors, management's compensation, business risks—all manner of useful information. You can often find them on the company's Web site, or at Fool.com (in our Quotes and Data section, under a company's Financials), or straight from the SEC at www.freeedgar.com. We'll talk more about how to read SEC filings a little later on.

Fool.com

It used to be that investors had to pay out a couple of hundred bucks a year for a daily financial newspaper, then another few hundred in financial magazines and newsletters, to get commentary on businesses, interviews with CEOs, analysts' ratings of stocks, and the like. The digital world is changing all of that, distributing information across America with greater efficiency and less expense.

Consider that Fool.com offers all of the following:

- Dynamic news throughout the day, starting with our Breakfast News at 9 A.M. Eastern every market day and finishing up with a recap after market close
- Fifteen-minute-delayed quotes
- Several model portfolios (including the Rule Breaker and Rule Maker portfolios, managed by your authors), published in full view for investors to analyze, track, compete with, or just follow
- Industry analysts ready and waiting to answer questions on individual stocks and their sectors
- Research reports penned by Fools on many of the world's top companies
- An entire Fool's School offering up-to-date and relevant assistance on managing your 401(k) plan, retirement investing, portfolio management, tax strategies, and investment theory
- A massive collection of other Web resources
- Lots of Fun and Folly games and contests bringing some levity to the serious world of investing
- Individual discussion boards for ongoing chat about almost every stock on the major exchanges (you may find employees of the company you're interested in here, maybe even a CEO or two!)

Among our former volunteer staff whom we mentioned earlier (some of whom are full-time employees today) numbered several doctors, a railroad industry insider, a marketing executive with a Japanese technology multinational, a lawyer or two, a paper-and-forest-products industry analyst, a consultant, a microbrewer, a software developer . . . the list goes on and on. These were all people we met online, and we signed them up to build The Motley Fool's original Industry Area section. In so doing, we leveraged the power of the medium to give our audience the opportunity to ask investment questions on a daily basis of industry professionals whose expertise they would otherwise never have come across. That's what we mean when we say that you're missing out if you're not online—today more than ever.

All of this costs no more than the price of an Internet connection (which is free, if you want it to be!), well below the cost of traditional financial newspapers. In fact, many of them, including *Forbes,* the *New York Times,* and *Fortune,* can be found online for free as well! Even those that charge, like the *Economist, Barron's,* and the *Wall Street Journal,* come at much lower prices than the print editions.

Great businesses are built on providing products and services that are more convenient, more comprehensive, of higher quality, and less precious than the competition. More information and better analysis at a lower cost: It's a model that ought to be most familiar to those in the financial services industry, right? Businessmen should know the business world better than any, no? That certainly hasn't proved true in the cobbling together and distribution of financial information, which runs at such a premium that many individuals have heretofore been unable to access it.

You should take advantage of the greater sophistication that the digital world offers on the cheap. Financial newspapers, magazines, and TV programs pick and choose what they think to be the most important of news stories; they present what they believe to be the proper angle in their editorials. They offer opinions without having the capacity or the accountability to hear back from their often more sophisticated audience, and they do all this at rather great expense. Being Foolish means being wired.

PART IV

COMPANIES
AND QUALITY

•11•

Why Buy Blue-Chips?
· · · · ·

Everything is worth what its purchaser will pay for it.
—*Publilius Syrus*

We talked in Chapter 9 about how you can find good ideas for investments within your own industry and through your own interests, insight, and investigation. Maybe you work for a satellite company that is doing what you think is groundbreaking communications work. That may make for a solid investment. You shop at Home Depot (NYSE: HD) every week to get the next perfect tool that's going to prompt you to finish that basement you've been working on for the last five years. Everyone else seems to love Home Depot too, so that's an intriguing possibility. Every afternoon for lunch you down a tin of Saltee Sardinez from Joe's Fishery, Inc. (ticker: SARDEENZ). If America ever catches on to that snack treat, you could have a real winner!

It might be useful to classify these investments, in order to get a sense of the level of risk you're taking in your investment. Any company of any size can rise or fall precipitously in a given year or month or week, but you can be pretty sure going in that Home Depot won't go bankrupt anytime soon. Joe's Fishery is small and relatively new, so it could go belly-up, but its products seem to be catching on. Your satellite company, on the other hand, has a much more uncertain future, since its system isn't even in place yet. It may never make a dime.

Let's look at the first type first, the Home Depots of the world. These are the large-cap companies, the established leaders, the so-called blue-chips of the investment world.

A quick word about what we mean by large-cap. Large capitalization is one of the four categories of market capitalization. Market cap is the market price of the entire company, calculated by multiplying share price times the number of shares outstanding. The four typical categories of market cap are large-cap, mid-cap, small-cap, and micro-cap. Everyone has his own definition of these categories, but the numbers below present a dependable enough guide, circa the year 2000:

Large-cap	over $5 billion
Mid-cap	$1 billion to $5 billion
Small-cap	$250 million to $1 billion
Micro-cap	below $250 million

The Dow

Some of the largest corporations on the planet have their homes in the Dow Jones Industrial Average (DJIA). The Dow is the most familiar of market indices, the one that the network news commits a good four seconds to every night of the week. "The Dow was up 58.75 points to 11032.50," Tom Brokaw recites, leading into another pet-food commercial. So little has been taught to U.S. citizens about investing and the stock market that most viewers probably better understand, and care more about, the pet food.

What is the Dow? It's one of Wall Street's measuring sticks, an index comprising the shares of thirty public U.S. companies in industries ranging from agricultural equipment to automobile manufacturing to oil exploration to fountain beverages. The unique factor that binds the thirty companies together is their hugeness. Each company has more than $10 billion in sales over the past year, which land it in the top fifth percentile of publicly traded U.S. companies. The market caps of the Dow Jones Industrials range from $12 billion in the case of International Paper (NYSE: IP) to $500 billion for General Electric (NYSE: GE). Most of them have a slew of wholly owned subsidiaries sporting brands that you might not associate with the parent company. Did you know, for instance, that Procter & Gamble (NYSE: PG) owns, manufactures, and markets Tide detergent, Cover Girl cosmetics, and Pringles? How about that it not only makes Crest toothpaste and Duncan Hines brownie mix but also produces soap operas, including *As the World Turns* and *Guiding Light*? Or that Philip Morris (NYSE: MO) owns

Kraft? Billion-dollar companies are by necessity diversified into a variety of businesses and involved in a multitude of investments that often aren't readily apparent to consumers or investors.

The Dow Jones Industrial index houses businesses that provide the foundation for corporate activity in the United States and around the globe. Below we list the thirty current companies for your perusal.

Alcoa	Honeywell
American Express	IBM
AT&T	Intel
Boeing	International Paper
Caterpillar	Johnson & Johnson
Citigroup	J. P. Morgan
Coca-Cola	McDonald's
Disney	Merck
DuPont	Microsoft
Eastman Kodak	Philip Morris
ExxonMobil	Procter & Gamble
General Electric	SBC Communications
General Motors	3M
Hewlett-Packard	United Technologies
Home Depot	Wal-Mart

S&P 500

We talked a little bit about the S&P 500 in the discussion of index funds. It's important to remember, though, that the popular index does not act as a proxy for the American market as a whole. The Wilshire 5000, as the largest comprehensive index of U.S. firms, performs that function better (though not completely). The S&P 500 is widely regarded as the standard for measuring *large-cap* U.S. stock market performance. It is used by 97 percent of U.S. money managers and pension plan sponsors.

Like the Dow, it is designed to encompass a representative sample of leading companies in leading industries. It's not, therefore, an index of the top five hundred companies in terms of market cap, sales, or any other set metric, but a broad reflection of industrial activity. It includes companies like General Electric (yes, Dow stocks are all also in the S&P 500), Best Buy (NYSE: BBY), First Data Corp. (NYSE: FDC), Hershey's (NYSE: HSY), and Potlatch Corp. (NYSE: PCH). Warren Buffett's Berkshire Hathaway (NYSE: BRK.A), on the other hand, despite having a market cap in excess of $80 billion, is not included in the index, since it is considered a holding company and not an industrial concern.

Unlike the Dow, which is weighted by share price, the S&P 500 is weighted by capitalization. That means that a large company in the index will exert a greater influence on the index's returns than a smaller one. Say that General Electric had a market cap of $500 billion and that the index as a whole had a capitalization of $10 trillion. GE would make up 5 percent of the index. AutoZone (NYSE: AZO) has a market cap of $5 billion, so that it represents only 0.05 percent of the index. Any price movement in GE will have a more profound effect on the index than a change in AutoZone.

The NOW 50

So important do we find the concept of indexing that we designed our own index, The Motley Fool NOW 50, or just NOW 50 for short. The NOW 50 began at 2000, tracking on the first day of trading in the year 2000, and was designed to address some realities in the marketplace that the Dow and the S&P 500 did not.

The NOW 50 contains, oddly enough, fifty large-cap, globally relevant companies, ranging from Biogen, at $8.8 billion (as of this writing), up to the aforementioned General Electric, at $560 billion. Unlike the Dow or the S&P 500, NOW 50 companies are not required to be American in order to be included; the NOW 50 is the only one of the three that includes international companies. So, while Sony may fill your entertainment center and Nokia may provide your cellular phone, HSBC your banking, and DaimlerChrysler your mode of transportation, you will not find any of these companies in either the Dow or the S&P. Given the increasing irrelevance of national borders in the commercial world, we find this quite deficient.

The NOW 50 most resembles the Dow in composition. It is a smaller grouping of companies than the broader S&P 500. But whereas a large number of companies in the S&P would elicit blank stares from consumers and even investors, every one of the NOW 50 companies is recognizable to large segments of the population, either in and of itself or through the services it offers. These companies include some of the most recognizable trademarks. Get off a plane in Brunei and you are still bombarded with advertisements for Coca-Cola, Pepsi, Microsoft, and Dell. Location hardly matters for these brands. They are ubiquitous. Not only that, they're everywhere. (Their presence is so strong we even redundantly write redundantly about them.)

The NOW 50 is, like the S&P 500, market-cap weighted, but it is modified to overweight the smallest companies and underweight the largest. So although GE is fifty times the size of Biogen in market cap, its weight in the index is only fourteen times larger. This is a crucial distinction, because any index is worthwhile only if it represents something larger: the performance of a universe of stocks, or of an economy, or even of an industry. In this case, the NOW 50 is measuring the performance of the most relevant sectors of the global economy, as represented by the best practitioners in their fields.

So, what are these industries? You know them already: telecommunications, consumer brands, health care, biotechnology, food and beverage, the Internet, banking, insurance. They are both the fastest growing and the largest sectors of the modern economy.

And the companies, if there are any here that you do *not* recognize, well, you should get to know them.

A Few Examples

Berkshire Hathaway (NYSE: BRK.A), Warren Buffett's operating company and investment vehicle, is one of the most admired and misunderstood public companies. Berkshire is primarily an insurance company, providing insurance under its own name and also through its GEICO and General Reinsurance subsidiaries. Generally thought of as a fund due to its holdings in other public companies, Berkshire annually tallies operating revenues above $20 billion in its insurance, flight safety, jewelry, newspaper, apparel, household appliance, and myriad other divisions. Berkshire Hathaway's holdings in public companies range from Coca-Cola to the *Washington Post*. Warren Buffett sets the standard for corporate disclosure and shareholder-friendly management.

Amgen (Nasdaq: AMGN) emerged as biotechnology's first megawinner, with some of the earliest and most commercially successful biotech products. If biotechnology is to be the catalyst for change in the twenty-first century, Amgen is a favorite to lead the charge. Amgen's current products, blood cell boosting agents Neupogen (for the red) and Epogen (for the white), are the industry's first bona fide blockbusters. The company's next product to be released, Infergen, could be another big gainer if it demonstrates substantial efficacy at fighting hepatitis. Amgen is more thoroughly reviewed in *The Motley Fool's Rule Breakers, Rule Makers,* our third and final book in this trilogy.

United Parcel Service (NYSE: UPS), or "Big Brown," is the only company in the world that is a demonstrated vendor to every company in the Fortune 1000. UPS is sometimes looked upon as being a proxy for market performance in and of itself, so pervasive is its service. It's easy to see why. If UPS sees a decrease in shipping volume, it is a pretty good sign that the overall level of spending and commerce is dropping. The company delivers more than 12 million packages *per day* around the globe.

ARM Holdings (Nasdaq: ARMHY), based in the United Kingdom, is in some ways the most obscure of the NOW 50 companies, but if you use any technology beyond a can and string for communications, then you are intimately familiar with its products. ARM is a large owner of intellectual property in the semiconductor industry. If you have an Intel-based computer, you're indirectly or directly using ARM. Ditto for Nokia phones and Sony digital cameras.

We think you get the idea. These are companies that are proven winners in their fields and, further, are highly likely to continue to be so. Here is a complete list of the NOW 50 companies as constituted for the year 2000:

ARM Holdings	AT&T
Amazon.com	America Online
American Express	American International Group
Amgen	Applied Materials
Automatic Data Processing	Berkshire Hathaway
Biogen	Cable & Wireless
Charles Schwab	Cisco Systems
Citigroup	Coca-Cola
Costco Wholesale	DaimlerChrysler
Dell Computer	DuPont
EMC	Enron
ExxonMobil	Gap
General Electric	HSBC Holdings
Home Depot	Hughes Electronics
IBM	Intel
Johnson & Johnson	Lucent Technologies
McDonald's	Medtronic
Merck	Microsoft
News Corp.	Nokia
Oracle	Pepsico
Pfizer	Procter & Gamble
Schlumberger	Sony
Sun Microsystems	Texas Instruments
Time Warner	United Parcel Service
Wal-Mart	Yahoo!

Some of these companies are in fact "high risk." Amazon.com, for example, has to this point never made an operating profit. But the likelihood of NOW 50–caliber companies collapsing, as compared to smaller, less established companies in the same industries, is fairly low. Not all of the NOW 50 companies may be within every investor's comfort level for risk, but this index is an excellent place to start paring down from the thousands of publicly traded companies.

Why Invest in Large-Cap Companies?

Why? To outperform. There's no reason to invest in anything unless you believe that by doing so you can outdo the uneventful 11 percent in compounded growth you'll get via an index fund. It's very dangerous to ride speculative stocks, bonds, futures, commodities, gold coins; to trade options; to hop in on any cool-sounding, indecipherable wireless-cable deals. We don't think you'll outperform the market with them, and we've dedicated a section of our book (Appendix E) to the matter. The unfortunate thing, of course, is that these are just the sorts of unstudied dice rolls that thousands of greenhorn investors casually toss each year. All it takes for some is a few moments of weakness on the line with a jelly-voiced broker. This isn't investing, of course, it's gambling—an excellent long-term approach to losing money.

Investing in large-cap companies in the Dow, the S&P 500, and the NOW 50 offers considerably less intermediate- and long-term risk. Does anybody think we won't see Coca-Cola, McDonald's, IBM, AT&T, General Electric, and the like in the year 2010? Investors in this group of stocks are a bit like children in a playpen—there aren't a lot of sharp objects, and it ought to be a lot of fun.

The second great reason to invest in large-cap companies is that you end up working from a small sample of potential investments. Perhaps the greatest mistake individual investors make is trying to follow too many stocks. Our three major U.S. exchanges—the American Stock Exchange, the Nasdaq, and the New York Stock Exchange—list over nine thousand stocks. It's tempting to spread open the financial pages on the weekend, peek in on thousands of stock quotes, and muse, "I will conquer you all!" But it ain't gonna happen. Investors who try to manage too much research typically run unprofitable or underperforming portfolios. It may help you sleep better at night to start by staying on top of only a few stable stocks, from five hundred of the strongest, most profitable, and most immense companies in the world.

That's not to say that they are completely safe. Many companies have risen to S&P 500 or even Dow 30 heights, only to fall back down the heap. The Dow has dropped the likes of Bethlehem Steel (NYSE: BS), Sears (NYSE: S), and Goodyear Tires (NYSE: GT) because of their shrinking performance. Woolworth, which has since changed its name to Venator (NYSE: Z), not only fell out of the Dow in 1997 but has since even been removed from the S&P 500. You need to watch even the blue-chips.

·12·

Why Small-Cap Growth Stocks?

• • • • •

Think naught a trifle, though it small appear;
Small sands the mountain, moments make
the year, and trifles life.
—Edward Young

Small-capitalization growth stocks (small-caps) make a handsome foil to the world's blue-chips. It's not hard to figure out why. Since 1925, small-caps have as a group well exceeded the overall returns of larger stocks. A study by Ibbotson Associates, the esteemed Chicago research firm that tracks the performance of stocks and mutual funds, shows that from 1925 to 1996, small-cap stocks posted average annual returns of 12.6 percent, versus a large-cap return of 10.6 percent over the corresponding period. That may look like only 2 percentage points, but when you compound that return, the difference, as you now know, is huge. How huge? A $1,000 investment earning 12.6 percent annually is worth $4.5 million seventy-one years later; a $1,000 investment bringing in 10.6 percent over that time ends up worth just $1.37 million. So when you examine it historically, it's clear that investing in anything else means a lower, slower flight to fame and fortune.

Despite this, many people resist investing in small-caps because of the inherent risk associated with them. You can make a lot of money in these stocks, and you can lose a lot, too. That's because little stocks often react to dramatic news like gnats in the wind (whether the wind is blowing for or against them). But is that reason enough to avoid some of the best bets on the market? Nay. If these people didn't so

Wisely avoid these stocks, they'd understand and appreciate the value (pun intended) of strong small-cap representation in their portfolios.

That said, small-cap stocks are not the right choices for people who can't afford the short-term risks. Do not risk investing in small-cap stocks if you'll need the money to make your mortgage payments! It's the very same story if you're a retiree who cannot tolerate losing capital you need to live on. *Never* invest money you can't afford to lose in small-cap stocks.

But as we wrote earlier, consciously taking on smart risk remains the best way to succeed in investing. We embrace risk because the opposite is timidity, which is what most of the world is good at. Always remember, dear reader, that it wasn't the Wise who discovered the New World. Join us as we emulate Columbus and head for deep water.

Now, before stirring small-caps into your investment cauldron, you must first thoroughly understand the ingredients and their effects. Handled properly, small-cap investing is tremendous fun and exceptionally lucrative.

Why? Well, big stocks generally fluctuate less than small stocks, in much the same way that airplanes are less affected by wind than are hot-air balloons. This reminds us of a useful point for investors: Size correlates directly with inertia. As you've already seen, we suggest that you may want your first-tier investment to be blue-chip stocks. We intentionally pile up this large-cap ballast in order to steady our balloon without compromising its ground speed. On the other hand, you'll meet some people whose balloons have no sandbags at all, wild-eyed people with hot-air portfolios full of penny stocks top to bottom. Look fast, 'cause if the wind shifts, you won't see them anymore. With such out-of-balance portfolios, they won't be able to right themselves if (no, when) the market goes the wrong direction. Then again, you may have friends who make the opposite mistake, heaping their vessel with far too many sandbags. Their balloons never get off the ground. As is always the case in life, one must constantly work toward a happy medium, erring on the side of neither dearth nor plenty.

Why You Shouldn't Buy Small-Caps

In Foolish style, let's first spend some time examining why you *shouldn't* buy small-caps.

For one thing, you definitely shouldn't buy small-caps if you don't know what you're doing. You'd be surprised how many newcomers plunge right into the market just because they happened to get a hot tip when they had a little money on hand, without having the faintest idea of what they're doing. The market, in this context, should be treated like deep-sea diving. Would you debark a diving bell at five hundred feet without ever having read an instruction manual? We hope not. Fortunately, you now have your Foolish instruction manual for investing, and you've figured out that no matter how hot a tip is, there's homework to do before you make the buy. (Guess what: There's even *more* work to do *after* you buy a small-cap stock.)

You should stay out of small-cap stocks if you don't have the time or are unwilling to follow them. Small-cap growth investors must scrutinize their investments on a more regular basis than equity investors of any other stripe, just as you have to spend more time keeping an eye on a crawling baby than on your typically immobile two-week-old infant.

Another reason to avoid small-caps is if you instinctively shy away from risk. While we celebrate taking risk—the *right* risk—we don't look down on those who eschew it. Everyone is different, and the good news is that a motley variety of market-beating stock-picking approaches exists. So if you're not risk tolerant by nature, don't try to be something you aren't. Avoid small-caps.

We've already mentioned yet another reason not to buy these things: if you need the money elsewhere. If you're putting your lunch money (or its equivalent) down on the market, you're hoping to hit the lotto jackpot. Again, the most frequent mistake new investors make is to invest as if they were playing the lottery—buy enough long shots and one of them has to hit! We've met plenty practitioners of this philosophy. (See Appendix E.) Both the lottery and this investment style are, as the Italians say, a "tax on imbeciles." Well, we say, "No new taxes!" Don't waste your money on lotto. You'll lose. Lotso.

All right, that's quite enough on why you shouldn't buy small-caps. If you've worked your way through the above and decided that you're still interested, then carry on.

Why Even the Family Goldfish Should Hold Some Small-Caps: Getting In First

Having learned what "small-cap" means and in which situations it should be avoided, let us delve more deeply into the advantages of small-stock investing and why even Irving, your family goldfish, should probably own a few of these shares.

The primary reason for buying small-cap growth stocks—aside from their superior historical performance—is that mutual funds and institutions often cannot buy them . . . yet. Or even if they can, mutual funds and institutions cannot build up any meaningful holding. "Meaningful" here is defined as "in a sufficient quantity to make any noticeable difference to the fund's overall performance."

The reasons partly involve the natural dimensions of the situation and partly involve SEC regulations. The natural dimensions are obvious: At last count, the average mutual fund had about $700 million in holdings. So, let's set up our own fund for discussion's sake. We'll call it Joe Fund, and it's going to be absolutely average; it has $700 million in holdings and wants to make lots of money. If Joe Fund's manager (Joe) wanted to hold ten stocks, he would divide that money into ten parts of $70 million each. Now, the total value (as measured by market capitalization) of many excellent small-caps is right about $500 million. Further, the management team often owns 15 to 40 percent of the company, so that a large portion of shares is simply not available on the open market. Thus, you can see that any serious attempt by Joe Fund to establish a meaningful stake in these companies would more often than not involve virtual buyouts of the targeted companies! At the very least, if mutual funds were seriously to attempt to buy 20 to 30 percent of a stock they loved, they'd push up the price so quickly that the latter half of their buying would be at prices far beyond the attractive initial entry point. Not a formula for good investment returns . . . especially when it comes time to *sell* a big stake. The price could be driven down just as far and as fast as it was driven up.

So, what would *you* do if you were Joe managing the fund and wanted to invest in small-caps? You'd end up having to spread out your holdings into, say, fifty separate stocks in order to avoid the dangers of buying too much of a company. Do you have fifty good investment ideas? We expect not, because you're human, after all. Well, so are money managers. We know of very few money management teams— let alone individuals—who can effectively keep up with fifty or more investments. And every additional investment makes it that much more likely that an investment portfolio will do no more than duplicate the market's performance.

Add to all of this some SEC regulations and a fund's own chosen limitations as published in its prospectus, and you generally wind up with a portfolio that cannot put more than 5 percent of its assets into any given stock or buy more than 5 percent of any given company. That means that Joe Fund can't put more than $25 million into our small-cap company. It will have to find 28 such companies in which to invest in order to use up its $700 million in assets. If Joe went shopping for $300 million companies, he'd have to find forty-six, taking a $15 million stake in each. Joe Fund probably isn't going to waste its time with tiny stocks that won't have any effect on its bottom line.

To reiterate: The first reason that you want to buy these stocks is that mutual funds cannot . . . yet. The idea is that the small investor *can* buy these stocks, getting in early on some of the great emerging growth stories of American business. Microsoft, Intel, and Wal-Mart all began simply as initial public offerings on the Nasdaq. Mutual funds couldn't really buy them back then, when they were small-caps. Over the course of time, as these companies became mid-cap and then large-cap companies, mutual funds and institutions have moved in, in a multibillion-dollar way. The ideal for the individual investor in this situation is to have been the person able to *sell* the shares to the institutions when the big guys finally became convinced that one or another of these stocks was worth owning. (Although, in the case of these three companies, the best plan of attack would have been never to sell at all. But that's a separate story—see Chapter 19.)

Now it must be said that some of the best-performing mutual funds historically are small-cap growth funds. These include, among others, T. Rowe Price New Horizons, RS Emerging Growth, and Janus Venture Fund, all of which have compiled some of the best market-beating records over the past decade (past performance being, of course, no guarantee of future returns). But what happens then? More investors hear of these funds and invest *their* money in them, too. The fund's assets swell, forcing managers either to invest that money into new stocks they don't like as much or to put more and more money into their favorite existing ones, at significantly higher prices in most cases. And if a small-cap growth fund's assets *still* continue to grow via appreciation, it often has to close itself to new investors altogether (as the T. Rowe Price fund has) or risk walking away from investing in small-caps anymore!

By investing directly in the stocks yourself, you gain the ability to profit hugely off stocks that mutual funds couldn't buy for their customers in sufficient amounts. You get in before the big guys get in, and once they decide to get in, the big dollars they throw at your stock help push it up for you. The best buy of all is the purchase of a small-cap just before the institutions "discover" it. By concentrating a portion of your portfolio in excellent small companies in dynamic growth situations, you give yourself a great shot at beating Harry, your mutual-fund-owning neighbor who plays the tuba, by a wide margin.

Why Even the Family Goldfish Should Hold Small-Caps: Other Reasons

You already have a couple of good reasons for buying and holding small-cap stocks: They have been the best-performing category historically, and you can beat the institutions into these stocks and then *use* the institutions to prop them up further. The good news doesn't stop there, though.

Here's something to recognize and applaud: Small numbers multiply much more rapidly than big ones. When earnings double, a stock's price may very well double. The question is, which company is more likely to double in size in the next two years (all other things remaining equal)—a company with $10 million sales, or one with $10 billion in sales? Right, the smaller one. It's a lot easier to triple and double again in size quickly when you're starting from a base below $100 million . . . a lot more difficult anywhere above that.

Earnings grow fastest among small companies. And what often accompanies earnings growth is share price growth. It's an argument made down through the decades, perhaps most convincingly by Peter Lynch in his wonderful book *One Up on Wall Street*. It didn't hurt that Lynch put his money where his mouth was. He's made a whole career off expounding his love of growth stocks and generating superior returns by investing in them.

This concept has found such acceptance since Lynch wrote his book that you'll often find a lot of future growth priced into a stock. Companies that would have remained small-caps in earlier markets are now finding themselves bid up into mid- and large-cap ranges, based much more on future rather than present earnings. That has made our job harder, since we have to pay very close attention to business quality and potential instead of spying power in their financial statements. It also depletes the returns and augments the risk that investors in low- or no-earnings companies take, since they are already priced for success. If they don't deliver, the pain shareholders feel will be excruciating.

That hasn't, however, stopped us from looking for quality among the start-ups. We believe that it is still possible to score big gains, even in this environment.

And another reason to like small companies is that they are typically closely held by management. That means that the people running the company have a significant financial stake in the success not *just* of the company but of the stock itself. In fact, in many cases, the performance of the stock has a much *greater* influence on the wealth of the management team than does their annual salaries. This is a good thing, quite the opposite of Big Company America, where Forbes 500 operations pay their senior officers huge salaries without in most cases involving them meaningfully in the ownership of the company. (Some get some huge bonuses in stock options, which rewards them well when the stock does well over the short term—supposedly in response to their management. But this is not for the *long term,* which Fools care most about. And further, many of these managers sell out most or all of their stock options as soon as they're able to be "exercised"—activated.)

Fools favor companies that are at least 10 percent owned by insiders, and the place you're going to find these companies is mainly among Nasdaq small-caps. What this means is that if you invest in one or another hot dog stand, the guy running it probably cares even more than you do about whether or not the dogs are selling. He's probably running your business as if it were the make-or-break opportunity of his financial life. Hey, it probably is, since if he's like the typical small-company management, most of his wealth is tied up in his company's stock.

Because small-cap stocks have such a proven record of achievement and because they'll always represent an exciting way to invest one's money, these stocks have garnered increasing amounts of attention from individual investors as well as the media at large. (Whether it's the recent ubiquity of Nasdaq television commercials or the emergence over the last decade of *Investor's Business Daily,* the names and profiles of good small companies are easier to come by than ever.) But while everyone's hearing about them these days, very few really know how to locate the best ones, how to value them, and which ones to buy and hold. Before we talk about the qualities we look for in a company, let's learn how to read their financial statements.

PART V

THINGS TO
LOOK FOR

·13·

Selecting the
Best Growth Stocks

· · · · ·

I have called this principle, by which each slight variation,
if useful, is preserved, by the term Natural Selection.
—Charles Darwin

Convinced of our need to fight the good fight and buy up some of
these growth stocks, our first task is to discover how to select the
best ones. We're not going to decide which ones to *buy* yet, necessarily,
only how to develop a list of quality stocks to watch. Let's start by introducing Messages Inc.

Messages Inc. (ticker: MESS)

> NOTE: Throughout this section we'll be looking at Messages Inc., an
> upstart company bringing some ingenious new ideas to a fairly dull
> mature business. This fictional company, based in Reno, Nevada, ex-
> hibits dynamic growth of the very sort Fools favor, though the situa-
> tion grows a bit more complicated (and educational) as we delve
> deeper. Messages won't be coming public anytime soon, probably,
> so we're going to fast-forward several years for the following chap-
> ters.

So, a friend turns you on to this new investment idea—a company
you've never heard a thing about. That's quite surprising, given the
story you now have before you. Messages Inc. It's the newest thing . . .
recently mentioned on the nightly news, you're told. Hmm . . . Well, at

least your friend has been kind enough to provide you the company's investor information packet. Let's read the company description.

Messages Inc.™ manufactures, markets, and distributes written communications included with traditional novelty items. The company's primary business involves tiny scrolls inserted into fortune cookies, except that **Messages** has radically redefined the meaning, function, and popularity of these items. In 1998 the company pioneered the use of flavored scrolls with the introduction of its new TastiScroll® technology, a line of paper breath fresheners. In late 1999 the company introduced new concepts for the messages themselves, creating the popular InfoCookie®. InfoCookies, whose predecessors focused entirely on conveying "fortunes" of little redeeming value, now feature stock tips, lucky lottery numbers, winning picks for NFL games, and revenue-generating suggestions for entrepreneurs. The InfoCookie won the Best of Show prize at the 2000 Consumer ProductFest, and helped **Messages** reach 25 on the year 2001 list of the Forbes 200 Hottest Small Companies.

The company forecasts dynamic growth into the twenty-first century on the wings of its two-tiered expansion strategy: (1) vertical growth, involving further development of message concepts for the InfoCookie (Braille messages, audio messages, custom birth and death announcements, etc.), and (2) horizontal growth, involving the deployment of messages over a wider range of consumer gift items (airline snack packs, compact discs, piñatas, etc.). **Messages**'s InfoCookie brand name poses, in the company's estimation, significant barriers to competition.

Messages™ is a registered trademark and markets its primary product line under the service marks "More Than Just a Cookie" and "We're Talking to You."

With interest, you peruse further the company's news announcements and press materials. You notice that much of Messages Inc.'s publicity revolves around stories of people whose lives were radically changed by messages they'd read: those who made money on the stock tips, lottery winners, and entrepreneurs turned on to their winning product ideas by suggestions contained on the company's edible scrolls. Amazing. You wonder right away whether Messages has run into legal problems from people who may have acted on some of these money-making tips, failed, and blamed the cookie. But in a precedent-setting 1998 case, Judge Marcia Ito ruled the company "not responsible for losses incurred as a result of its products," adding that "these are basically just a novelty item, fortune cookies whose messages adults shouldn't take seriously." While the company itself might disagree with the reasoning, it obviously agreed with the ruling. Legal problems appear to be a nonissue for an investor.

Business is booming. The start-up company's sales have already reached $50 million over the past twelve months and are mounting at an impressive rate. A few analysts have trotted out impressive earnings estimates for the next few years. Is that at all surprising? Nope. The production cost of these tiny TastiScrolls must be negligible, while the faddish enthusiasm that the market has taken to the product has enabled this company to charge rates far above its production expenses. The company's common stock has done exceedingly well, and many are now speculating that Messages might make an attractive acquisition for a bakery products conglomerate, like Sara Lee.

Messages Inc. grabs your attention even further when, a few days later, a *New York Times* op-ed piece skewers the company's newest business plan to make a large portion of the "Inspected by No. X" messages in new garments *edible*. The article contends that by conditioning consumers to blithely ingest their "Inspected" slips, the company will induce thousands of people to eat chemically treated paper that is not at all edible. That's because Messages's TastiScrolls are expected to penetrate only 30 percent of the "Inspected" slip market, meaning that *fully 70 percent* of these slips will be quite inedible. Reaction to the piece causes the stock to drop from $15 to $10 in one day, as critics suddenly reach a consensus that the *Times* has put a permanent kibosh on Messages's aggressive "horizontal" expansion plans.

Ah, but the competitive business advantages of the product eventually far outweigh short-term admonitions, and in the coming weeks the company continues to announce sales deals with domestic and multinational corporations. Corporate partners simply cannot deny the entertaining enhancement of including InfoCookies and other imaginatively placed messages in their products. The "brand enhancement" of inserted messages enables a diverse group of manufacturers to differentiate their product from competitors by creating incredible—and edible—goodwill with the customer. It's a winning formula, and the company before you is at present a huge winner.

Now that we've gotten to know a little about this company, it's time to match it up to our growth stock selection criteria. *Is it worth adding this company to the list of stocks I follow?* you ask yourself. Well, you have the research material in front of you. Let's go through an eight-item checklist and see.

Eight Key Items

For the purpose of determining a given stock's suitability for our portfolio, we look at a checklist of eight items (our so-called Foolish Eight). The point of this chapter, as stated above, is to help you generate this list of *potential* picks. The list itself does not comprise our final selections, but it is often from this list that we end up picking our eventual selections. Fortunately, each of the concepts below is so simple—in most cases, nonmathematical—that any novice can learn it without difficulty. And keep in mind, these measures are best used for finding growing small-cap companies. Many of these measures do enjoy use outside of the search for small growth companies, but our list is tailored to small-caps.

To that end, not all of what follows is qualitative judgments; the first four points are mainly quantitative restrictions put in place to narrow the field, to keep our watch list from getting too big or unwieldy. We have no desire to follow 748 different stocks, and we don't expect you do either. It's kind of like looking only for astronauts who are young, in top shape, don't have asthma, and don't suffer from any notable manias, phobias, or dependencies. Now, we *could* try to go to the moon with a team of fat old drunks, but our country—not to mention our investment portfolio—increases its odds of success through more demanding criteria.

Keep it simple.

1. The Company's Sales: $500 Million or Less

If we can agree that all stocks *can* be reasonably valued, then it follows that the least followed and least familiar ones have the greatest potential for not yet having been fully evaluated. It is among America's small companies that you're most likely to find an uncut gem—one that, as we've said before, institutions won't be able to buy yet. That is why we use limits on a *company's sales* to weed out the ones we want to follow from those we don't. Leave behind all the monster corporations for now, General Motors and Coca-Cola and all the rest, and set your sights on the lesser-knowns.

Please don't limit your investment prospects to companies with which you are immediately familiar. That you are familiar with them already suggests, in most cases, that a lot of other people are, too, including a lot of institutions. While this doesn't mean that any company you already know won't sport a great stock, it does mean that we think you should instead focus on developing a small-cap growth list of lesser-known, upcoming companies—the ones that so often put up the greatest investment returns of all.

Keep in mind companies that did *$500 million or less* in sales in the past year. It's companies that have $500 million or less in sales that are mostly likely to double and triple in size over the next few years. And the nice thing about limiting yourself to $500 million in sales is that you can quickly eyeball an earnings report in your newspaper and see that a given company does or does not fall within these bounds. The Web site Market Guide also provides a screen that can hone in on this group.

Since Messages racked up sales of only $50 million over the past twelve months, it's certainly small enough for us. We move on.

2. Daily Dollar Volume: From $1 Million to $25 Million

In Part IV we discussed market capitalization, but capitalization is not the most useful measure for investors intent on classifying and generalizing about the *size of stocks*. In fact, once we've located a likely small-cap stock, we almost never use the capitalization figure. Much more important to us is the company's *daily dollar volume,* and so that's our second Foolish requirement. The optimum range is from $1 million up to $25 million.

Whereas capitalization measures the total amount of value of a company's equity (remember the formula: *share price times number of shares*), our daily dollar volume figure tracks the total amount of money that trades in a given stock on an average day. This figure enables one to measure and follow a stock's *liquidity,* which we consider far more meaningful than market cap. Particularly in the case of small- and micro-cap investing, the liquidity of stocks can greatly affect how they trade.

Like market capitalization, figuring the daily dollar volume is simple multiplication. To get the figure, just multiply a stock's share price by its *average daily trading volume*. You may already know a good source for average daily volume. Most online quotes will include the number. Another place to find this information is probably, once again, *Investor's Business Daily,* which each day prints for every stock both the number of shares that traded in it and the percentage change from the norm that that figure represents. Dipping open your *IBD,* you locate the following in the paper:

Stock	Vol. (100s)	Vol. % Change
Messages	3430	−65

From these figures, you'll need to deduce the average daily volume. Often, online quotes will list the average daily volume for you, but it's a piece of cake to calculate it yourself. The number 3430 is that day's volume, expressed in hundreds. In other words, 343,000 shares exchanged hands. The "−65" lets you know what percentage change that figure was from the average of the last fifty trading days. In this case, Messages's volume of 343,000 shares was actually 65 percent below recent norms. To calculate the normal figure, therefore, you simply take 343,000 and divide it by 1 minus .65—that is, by .35. (You use 1 minus .65 because 1 represents 100 percent, or average daily volume, and in this case you were .65 below that, at just .35—or 35 percent—of daily volume.) Let's do the math: 343,000 divided by .35 equals 980,000 on the nose. In other words, we have just figured out that the average daily volume for Messages is 980,000 shares.

Now all that's left to do is to calculate the daily dollar volume in this stock. Let's take a more complete look at the listing:

Stock	Vol. (100s)	Vol. % Change	Closing Price
Messages	3430	−65	12.63

We've already calculated the average daily volume: 980,000 shares. Multiplying by the closing price of $12.63, we come away with an average daily dollar volume of $12,372,500. That means that a typical six-and-a-half-hour trading day sees more than $12 million of Messages stock change hands. Yowser.

Now, while the previous explanation took the better part of a page to explain, the actual time that it'll take you to do these calculations is minimal. Of course, if you are capable of setting up a spreadsheet to do this, even less time is required; you just type in (or import) the numbers and let your computer do the calculations.

A daily dollar volume of $12 million may sound like a fair amount, but it's peanuts compared to most stocks you've heard of. Apple Computer, for example, trades over $225 million a day. Microsoft, at last check, traded ten times more than that. But $12 million is a very significant number to Fools, because it comes under our $25 million daily dollar volume maximum.

With few exceptions, we add only those stocks that trade $25 million a day or less to our checklist. Messages, at $12 million, fulfills this criterion. Our reasoning, again, is to follow only those stocks that remain relatively undiscovered by institutions. We are intentionally seeking less *liquid* situations, situations in which institutions would have difficulty liquidating (cashing out). Institutions intentionally *avoid* these situations until stocks grow big enough to trade enough . . . it is at that point that institutions buy and stocks really begin to fly.

By limiting the amount of daily dollar volume to $25 million or less, you're using the advantage available to you as a small private investor. You're scoring touchdowns against the big guys on *your* turf, turf too awkward for them to touch yet. That's not supposed to be the case. The popular press always seems to be emphasizing how *difficult* it is for the little guy to swim in institution-infested waters. But we're telling you that you can swim circles round the institutions, especially if you gain energy from feeding on the plankton.

Before we close this point, you may be wondering whether we're therefore recommending that you seek out penny stock situations featuring securities that trade $100,000 to $500,000 a day, or many days not at all. Never. Don't get too *illiquid*. Stick to higher-quality companies that trade over $1 million a day and have Nasdaq listings.

3. Minimum Share Price of $7

The third Foolish requirement is also in place mainly to limit the field. It's simply a stock's share price. *We want stocks trading above $7.* Anything lower than that drifts into the land of instability. While it's true that low-priced stocks move more than their higher-priced brethren, it's also true that businesses don't see their stocks drift this low without good reason. Stocks with prices below $7 also become much more difficult to trade, and we generally don't waste our time with illiquid junk.

4. Net Profit Margin: At Least 7 Percent

The fourth Foolish requirement is also designed to limit the field. But whereas a company's sales and dollar volume and share price relate merely to size, a high *net profit margin* relates mostly to quality.

Let's learn just exactly what the net profit margin is by referring to Messages's financial statements. If you're right now looking at an income statement for the first time, you'll soon see how little you had to fear all those years.

Statement of Income (numbers in 000)	Messages Inc.
Revenue	50,000
Cost of sales	21,000
Gross profit	29,000

Operating expenses:	
Selling, general & admin.	12,000
Research & development	6,000
Total operating costs	18,000
Income from operations	**11,000**
Interest income	**50**
Income before taxes	**11,050**
Income taxes	3,650
Net income	**7,400**

All numbers in bold represent sales and profits; nonbold represents subtractions, or costs.

The income statement is an extremely simple and useful table. It simply shows a business's sales on the top line and its profits on the bottom. (Note that all numbers in the table are expressed in thousands, as the "numbers in 000" indicates. Numbers are sometimes listed in millions and even billions, so always check the multiple.) Between a company's top-line sales and its bottom-line profits are its costs of doing business, appearing on the income statement as deductions from the top line. In Messages's case, we see that it did $50 million in *Revenue* for the year last year, almost all of it via TastiScroll proliferating like kudzu across Georgia. From this figure, we must deduct $21 million for the factory costs of manufacturing these products, also known as *Cost of sales*. The number we're left with is *Gross profit*, or $29 million. Some financial analysts like to use a measure of profitability called the "gross margin." This is simply gross profit—$29 million—taken as a percentage of (divided by) overall sales: $50 million. Messages's gross margin (29 divided by 50) is thus 58 percent.

The next deduction we'll take is in the so-called *Operating expenses,* comprising *Selling, general, and administrative* costs (SG&A) and *Research & development* costs (R&D). SG&A typically includes salaries, advertising and marketing expenses, office expenses, insurance, rent, and other miscellaneous fun stuff, like executive weekend trips to Kennebunkport or Taos. Messages racked up $12 million there. Research and development expenses represent the amount that a company pays to develop new products; in Messages's case, our psychologists are studying human behavior to determine which products will serve as the best vehicles for new messages by the year 2005. The psychologists' conclusions, mainly involving attempts at sticking messages wherever they'll best fit into mass transit, cost a total of $6 million last year in development expenses. Adding SG&A and R&D together, we reach our operating cost of $18 million.

Income from operations isn't too difficult to calculate next: $29 million in gross profits minus $18 million of total operating costs. Hmm. Looks like $11 million. (Can you believe accountants get paid so much to do this stuff?)

Most profitable small companies have little debt and not much cash, so that the line item that follows, *Interest income* (or, it could be expense), is usually small enough that it's relatively insignificant. Yep, that's pretty much the case with Messages.

Now it's time for *Income taxes* . . . dreaded beast. Most corporations these days pay out about one-third of their profits to income taxes. The corporation that we're subjecting to such extreme scrutiny isn't very different in this case. Messages paid almost exactly one-third last year, or about $3.7 million. What is left over, as you already know, is the bottom line, profits, a.k.a. *Net income,* since it's income after having netted out everything else.

Congratulations! You just learned in about a page what takes a third of a term in a typical accounting course.

Back to the matter at hand, we're actually in search of *net profit margin.* Above, we read about gross profit margin being simply gross profit taken as a percentage of overall sales. Net profit margin is simply *net income* (Messages's is $7.4 million) taken as a percentage of sales.

Thus, Messages's net profit margin is $7.4 divided by $50 . . . 14.8 percent. *Our Foolish requirement is that the companies we follow should show a minimum net profit margin of 7 percent.*

What does 14.8 percent—or our minimum of 7 percent—mean? And why do we bother making this our fourth Foolish requirement? Fools prefer this figure high because a high net profit margin indicates a company that is either soundly beating its competition or (Fool's choice) has no competition at all. In our capitalistic world, a high net profit margin is an achievement, a mark of excellence. That's because anybody who can manage to make 14.8 cents off every dollar of sales (as Messages is doing) must be doing something right. High margins automatically invite copycats, competitors who will be happy trying to run you out of business by selling the same product for profits of 10 or 12 cents off every dollar of sales. Again, it's called capitalism, darling of the consumer, bane of the complacent business. Now, a company that actually *maintains* a high net profit margin over the years gives clear numerical proof of its superiority.

A bit more context helps here. The typical net profit margin will vary from industry to industry, while in most cases remaining below 7 percent. Bargain-basement retailers and supermarkets typically sport margins of less than 3 percent, many closer to 1 percent. Why would that be? It's not hard to imagine. Retailers like Kmart have built billion-dollar businesses out of offering consumers the lowest price. In a cut-throat competitive world, it stands to reason these guys ain't taking too much to the bank. (You'll notice, for instance, that Kmart does "blue-light specials," as opposed to "red-carpet specials." Or red-carpet anything. At their present rate, we're not even sure these guys are still going to be in business by the time we eventually launch the third edition of this book.)

Pop quiz: What margins are typical of airline companies?

If you answered "negative," you win the little white furry thing on the third shelf up. Airlines, almost as a rule, don't turn profits.

Technology companies are typically where you'll find the best profitability, the highest margins. That's because when a successful company carves out its own niche with a revolutionary product, it can get away with charging higher prices (taking in more profits) because no one else is making, say, cold-fusion automobile engines.

Reminds us of the situation in the pharmaceuticals industry, where new products have been creating lucrative niches for years. In fact, it was the impressively high net profit margins of drug manufacturers like Merck and Bristol-Myers Squibb that drew the attention of the Clinton administration in the first place, bringing about that administration's efforts to regulate the health care industry (and creating, by the by, a wonderful place to jump into Merck stock, which the Fool Portfolio did at $30.25 in the summer of 1994, ripping off a 60 percent gain in less than a year). Anyway, as Kipling may have written, "Ours not to reason why, ours but to make jokes about all the people who think that the government should run our health care system."

High margins aren't necessarily only for high-technology and drug companies, though. We've found some great small companies in a wide variety of industries over the years, everything from fashion accessories (Fossil—Nasdaq: FOSL) to hair- and tattoo-removal (Candela Corp.—Nasdaq: CLZR—which you're gonna want to own when today's teens hit thirty-five!).

Messages at this point has met all four of our Foolish criteria, being both small enough and profitable enough. Time to push on.

5. Relative Strength: 90 or Higher

Foolish requirement number five introduces one of our favorites: *relative strength*. Relative strength rates the performance against one another of every stock listed on our major markets. The rating system gives a numerical grade—just like the ones Mr. Spicer used to scrawl in bright red ink on your algebra quizzes—to the performance of a stock over the past twelve months. (The range is actually 1 to 99.) Thus, relative strength is a momentum indicator. A relative strength of 95, for example, indicates a wonderful stock, one that has outperformed 95 percent of all other American stocks over the past year.

Though the concept dates back a long time, we first read about relative strength in William O'Neil's book, the bluntly titled *How to Make Money in Stocks*. (O'Neil also happens to be the publisher of *Investor's Business Daily*, in which relative strength is printed for every stock, every weekday. Thank you, sir!) Mr. O'Neil favors purchasing stocks with high relative strengths, an approach that we have found very successful. O'Neil writes—somewhat Foolishly, we might add—"If . . . you buy equities that haven't yet moved or are down the most in price, because you feel safer with them and think you're getting a real bargain, you're probably buying . . . sleepy losers. . . . Why buy an equity whose relative performance is inferior and straggling drearily behind a larger number of other, better-acting securities in the market? Yet most investors do, and many do it without ever looking at a relative strength line or number."

Here we see the two fundamental mentalities one can take to purchasing securities on the stock market: that of the Pendulum and that of the Horse Race. The Pendulum claims that what goes one way will, in time, go the other: Buy stocks that are down and out, because they can swing only so far one way before you make money by going the other. On the other hand, the Horse Race mentality suggests that you should bet on the pony that's in first place coming down the stretch, because who else is going to win? The Foolish mentality on growth stocks runs much more toward the latter approach.

It really all comes down to physics, actually. Way back in the late seventeenth century, Sir Isaac Newton penned the first law of motion: "Every body remains in a state of rest or in a state of uniform motion (constant speed in a straight line) unless it is compelled by impressed forces to change that state." This is the fundamental principle of relative strength, as well: Until "impressed forces" show up "to change that state" of a stock, your likelihood of turning a profit—maybe a quick, *big* profit (the best profit of all)—is very good. In other words, if it's already rising, chances are it will keep rising. Mere coincidence, by the way, that Newton was appointed master of the mint in 1699?

Tomorrow's strong companies and stock market heroes typically flock like geese in the high ranges of relative strength. This contrary notion confounds the Wise, who, when they see a stock with a fifty-two-week high of $22 hitting new lows at $10, purchase the stock because it looks "cheap." The high-flying nature of turbocharged relative strength stocks, on the other hand, offends their staid sensibilities. They may even get blue in the face telling you, "The P/E is too high!" or, "It's already had its run!" High-flying stocks, in fact, are the frequent targets of Wall Street journalists, who can always be depended upon to try to pick off the latest high flier in their *Barron's* or "Heard on the Street" columns.

Preferring to bet on the winning horse, we limit our field to stocks that have a relative strength of 90 or more, taking Mr. O'Neil up on his idea. This underlines one of our basic beliefs as regards the free-market capitalism this country has practiced better than any other: While the door to competition will always remain open and every business is vulnerable at all times, over the long term the winners generally keep on winning. (We find it as true of human capital as it is of financial capital, by the way.) When you select companies whose recent past performance is A-grade, you are selecting from a group of companies that (1) are doing something right and (2) have the market taking notice. This does not mean a company will be a great investment; this only indicates the likelihood of it being a better investment than if its performance were poor. Such is the philosophy behind including relative strength in our investigations. It shouldn't be looked at in isolation, but rather as part of the Foolish Eight total package.

Messages, at $12.63, happens to have a relative strength of 92, which not entirely coincidentally happens to meet our fifth Foolish requirement. Although the company's stock still sits a few points off its recent high after the *Times* piece, it's nevertheless up from a low of $3.50 toward the end of last year and has been a stellar market performer. Just the sort we like to welcome into Fool Stables.

6. Earnings and Sales Growth: 25 Percent or Greater

Our sixth Foolish requirement calls for a company we're following to demonstrate *sales and earnings growth of at least 25 percent when compared to the same period the year before.* We could lower this limitation to 15 percent or 20 percent, but then all we're doing is diluting the amount of growth that we consider worthy; we're not going to do that. We could also raise the limitation to 30 percent or 40 percent, but our experience suggests that 25 percent makes a better cutoff because it doesn't restrict the field too much.

Corporate financial statements are prepared and published four times a year, at three-month intervals (quarters). You should be following your stocks *at least* this often so that you're on top of your company's developing story. Additionally, the reports compiled by financial analysts typically make quarterly projections of sales and earnings (with guidance from the company itself), numbers that you should have fairly well committed to memory for the upcoming quarter.

Why is this important? Well, you've just checked in with your broker and heard that Forever Lightbulbs, your favorite stock, has lost $5 in morning trading. "Down five?" you cry into the telephone receiver. "Any news?" Your broker informs you that Forever reported its earnings that morning, showing sales and income leaped 100 percent in its most recent quarter, when compared to the like quarter the year before. Does this news anger you? That pretty much depends on how well informed an investor you are. In many situations, 100 percent growth looks wonderful. But here, the four analysts following Forever had predicted 150 percent growth year to year. These quarterly numbers are therefore somewhat of a disappointing shock to the Street, but still perfectly explainable. Your job now is to plug in the new numbers and reevaluate the stock.

It is this act of reevaluating on a quarterly basis that should inspire you to keep a handle on the date when each of your companies expects to publish its next earnings report. If your broker can't furnish the date for you, you may obtain it from the company's Web site or by dialing your company directly and asking the representative in Investor Relations. (A mini primer at the end of this chapter explains how to do so Foolishly.)

For those who don't know how to calculate growth rates, most Web sites offer past percentages and future projections. It's enough to note in passing that Messages's sales and earnings are up more than 80 percent in its most recent published annual report. No significant competition, here, yet . . . the innovative company was first to market with its product and carved out a brand name, InfoCookie, that consumer awareness studies ranked even with Kentucky Fried Chicken. Messages easily passes our sixth test.

7. Insider Holdings: 10 Percent or More

As we mentioned last chapter, a respectable amount of *insider holdings* is an attractive attribute in a stock, one that we actively seek out. *Fools typically prefer to see at least 10 percent of a small-cap growth company owned by management, if not a good deal more.*

We've already gone over this point, so there's not much to add here other than that you should almost never be dissuaded by news of insiders selling their shares. Many insiders have most of their wealth tied up in their own company's stock. Just like you, they have loved ones to put through space camp, lots and lots of Ben & Jerry's ice cream to buy, and a fraudulent oil field or two to unknowingly invest in (and later take a tax loss on). In other words, they too have costs that their salaries cannot always cover. Selling their stock is their way of getting rich, and in many cases they've worked hard as hell to earn it.

So, next time someone points out to you that one of your stock's insiders is bailing left and right, ignore this person. Insider sales occur about ten times more often than insider buys, and are only in the very rarest situations cause for concern (for example, if multiple insiders sell out all or most of their positions in one pop, at about the same time).

What is Messages's management's stake in its own stock? Of the 10 million shares outstanding, fully 3.5 million sit in the coffers of Norman Vincent Steele, the founder and CEO of one of America's most talked about companies. Indeed, 35 percent is a high mark, well above that of most company managements. If Steele continues to think positively about holding his shares, and if over the next decade Messages can grow in line with some analysts' humongous expectations, our man may just become the Bill Gates of the next generation.

8. Cash Flow from Operations: A Positive Number

We've saved the figure that's hardest to explain to the very end. Number eight is *cash flow from operations*. Cash flow is a measure of the movement of money through a business. It is reported in the statement of cash flow that usually appears at the end of a company's financial statements. We want this number to be positive.

What does positive operational cash flow mean? It means that in the course of running its business, the company has managed to *generate* cash rather than consume it (which would be indicated by a negative number). You want your companies to crank out free cash from operations, making the necessary funds available for internal expansion, acquisitions, dividend payments, or whatever. A company that has negative cash flow has to borrow money in order to maintain and grow its business. For a small company, that's a discouraging indication that the company will have to either take on debt (borrow money for the short or long term) or issue more shares of stock (diluting the all-important earnings per share; see Chapter 18).

You might ask, "Doesn't *every* profitable business generate positive cash flow?" The answer is no. Messages is unfortunately one such example. Following the strong fiscal 2000 report that we've been looking at in this chapter, the company will go on to turn in a disappointing 2001, detailed next chapter. So, despite its obvious profitability, Messages goes *cash-flow negative,* which is perhaps the only thing we don't like about MESS stock right now. Let's preview the situation (the brunt of the analysis of the company's finances for 2001 does appear next chapter).

In 2001 Messages reports sales of $97 million in a further explosion of market penetration based on both brand-name expansion domesti-cally *and* an unexpected swelling of international sales, as the "mes-sages" concept suddenly seizes the imagination of the Far East. Unfortunately, foreign customers are notoriously slow in paying, taking several months. Further, in order to grow its sales so fast and generate publicity, Messages has extended extremely favorable payment terms to these foreign customers, allowing them to finance their purchases of Messages products at a low low low 0.5 percent annual interest charge, no money down. In other words, as it turns out, Messages has practi-cally been giving the product away overseas. All of this has substan-tially bulked up the company's accounts receivable.

When you look hard at it (we'll talk about how to do this in the fol-lowing chapter), you discover that Messages's customers are taking an average of more than four months to pay for their TastiScrolls. Mean-while, Norman Vincent Steele has to pay salaries, advertising and mar-keting costs, Mr. Landlord, and his sugar suppliers, within *one month* of services rendered. The predicament hurts Messages's finances pretty badly, though it simply represents a natural outgrowth of the com-pany's business plan. Anyway, MESS now occupies the uncomfortable position of having to pay its costs three months before getting paid by its customers. Despite the impressive profitability we discovered in the income statement earlier this chapter, Messages is cash-flow negative; the act of growing its business consumes cash, rather than creates it. Unless the company can turn this situation around by making stricter payment demands of its customers, more business will only mean more short-term cash consumed, and an even greater need either to borrow money or to sell more shares in order to generate the cash on hand necessary to meet a three-month cash shortfall.

A company with *positive* cash flow, on the other hand, signals a savvy management team and a strong business, the very sort of situation we like to buy and hold. (We'll read a lot more about cash-flow statements in the next chapter.)

Well, our darling stock met seven of our eight criteria, so we're left to ponder whether or not we should continue to pursue Messages. You don't think we'd write a whole chapter about the company behind this epoch-changing piece of technology and drop it flat just before the chapter on "Making Sense of Income Statements," do you? No way, Manet.

Let's thank our friend for turning us on to this one and for sharing his packet of financial info with us. It's time for us to procure our own set of statements. And maybe get a sample of the product, check out the quality of its breath mint . . . maybe try one or two of those TastiScroll stock tips.

Your Call to the Company Requesting Info

So, you have the phone number: 1-800-MESSAGE. Cute. Okay, time to call the company. But how do you reach the people you need to reach? And once you do, what should you say?

Well, first, let's list what you'll need to ask for—a full information packet, which we outlined on page 85.

Good news: *All* of this information will be furnished to you free of charge, no strings attached. Isn't America great?

Let's dial the number.

MESSAGES HQ: Hello, Messages Incorporated! How may I direct your call?

YOU: Hi, there! *[Never hurts to be friendly]* Um, Investor Relations, please?

[At this point, the receptionist will say either this:]

RECEPTIONIST: Do you just want financial information sent out to you, or would you like to speak with someone?

[In which case you exchange:]

YOU: Oh, I'd just like financial information.

RECEPTIONIST: Fine, I'll be happy to take your name and address, or you could leave it on Lucky Mintoro's voice mail. She's the director of Investor Relations.

[OR, the receptionist will say this:]

RECEPTIONIST: One moment, please! I'm transferring you to our Investor Relations Department.

[Either way, you name the five pieces of literature you seek.]
[Then, if you do end up talking directly with Lucky Mintoro . . .]

YOU: Oh, and would you please include my name and address on your investor mailing list? I'd like to receive regular updates on the company.

LUCKY MINTORO: I'd be more than happy to do that. Yes.

YOU *[If you're really gung ho and have the technology]*: Do you e-mail or fax out your press releases hot off the wire? Because in that case, I'd love to be on your list, as well.

LUCKY MINTORO: Sure.

  [OR:]

LUCKY MINTORO: No.

YOU *[just to be obnoxious]*: Really? *[Stunned.]* Wow. I can't believe that. *[Totally let down.]* Oh well . . . *[If enough of us do this, we Fools will one day have every company in America e-mailing or faxing its press releases. Bear the torch. Keep the faith.]*

[And now it's time to draw the call to a close.]

YOU: Thanks for your time, and continued best of luck to Messages. I won a bake sale raffle last week using the lucky number from my latest InfoCookie! Anyway, I think it'd be really cool and first-rate if you would consider dropping by Fool.com and answering investor questions. They have an active discussion on your company, and we're not looking for any "forward-looking statements," or whatever. Just some occasional factual help, as you see fit. You'd be making a great statement with your presence, that your company cares about its private investors. Plus—

Okay, we're getting carried away. (Fortunately, we have had in the past and present, and will in future have, company officials occasionally answering questions or clarifying information directly on our Web site's discussion board. So, darn right, let these people know they're wanted!)

Anyway, the call ends. Easy, isn't it? You've learned the eight things to look for when selecting a top small-cap growth stock. And now, when the stuff arrives a week later, it's time to learn all you can about Messages.

•14•

Making Sense
of Income Statements

• • • • •

*What you have become is the price you paid to get what
you used to want.*
—*Mignon McLaughlin*

All right, after a few days you've got Messages Inc.'s information
packet. Now you have its full financial information in front of
you. You've never really looked at one of these packets, so what do you
look for?

The first thing you see upon opening the manila envelope is the col-
orful dossier containing the company's annual report, press releases,
SEC documents, et cetera . . . and what else? A cinnamon-flavored message, of course! (It says, "Buy MESS below $20," showing you that Lucky
Mintoro has a very good sense of humor.) Looking it over, you see that
the folder has been artistically rendered with color photographs, expensive graphics, and the Messages logo plastered right smack in the
center. Welcome to one of the first lessons learned about a company's
financial information packet: It's as much a marketing device as anything else. As you read through the text portions of the annual report
and press releases, you'll want to keep this observation foremost in
mind. By sending you the darn financial info in the first place, the company is hoping to sell you on its stock.

Many different (and conflicting) inferences may be drawn from the
presentation of a company's packet. Should an annual report look expensive, or not? Every color photograph, every additional page of fine

paper—these things cost money. When the company could be spending the money on its operation, do you really want an outfit in which *you're* invested to ring up a big expense on the annual report (a charge included on the selling, general, and administrative line item of the income statement, by the way, to review from last chapter)?

Then again, if you peel open a company's investor information packet and see grainy black-and-white pictures of drab people in a corporate headquarters sloppily appointed, do you want to invest your money there? Some financial commentators have said that's *exactly* the situation you want to invest in, but we're not so sure. If a company is that poor at selling itself in materials targeted at investors, how successful do you think its marketing campaigns will be? Can people who so fail to communicate their story in a compelling way to individual investors ever succeed in communicating that same story to the institutions who have the greatest power at moving the stock?

We'll un-Wisely leave this question alone, preferring instead merely to gaze bemusedly over the material, paying due attention to the cosmetic touches before digging in.

This chapter is about digging in, digging deep into a company's financial statements and departing with a firm understanding of how financial statements can help you make investment decisions for and against the companies whose reports you come across. But we're bringing more than just our pickaxe to Chapter 14; we also have crashed this party with our handheld weeder. That's because although it's all very well to break a sweat digging profitably through the numbers, you'll save yourself even more time if you know how to weed out the meaningless stuff and spend all your time examining what counts. Thus, please read this chapter free of delusion; we do not presume to cover financial statements exhaustively in all their intricacies, with all their manifold footnotes and exceptions. If you're that much into this stuff, read some of the investment books that attempt to do this, then *write your own* with a conscious effort to crack a joke or two. You'll need your readers to be giggling along as they read about amortization, revenue recognition, nonstatutory stock option plans, and warranty reserves.

(Seriously, though, we do cover accounting information, education, and issues at Fool.com, so whether you're looking for beginner info or something more technical and complex, we either already have it or will look into adding it, at your behest.)

Below is what a perfect Fool should spend time investigating and pulling out of the standard available financial information.

The Income Statement

We've already seen the income statement once before, but in somewhat abbreviated form. Let's now look at the actual version as it appears in the company's annual report.

Statement of Income (numbers in 000)	Messages Inc.		
	2000	**1999**	**1998**
Revenue	**50,000**	**27,000**	**8,000**
Cost of sales	21,000	12,400	3,400
Gross profit	**29,000**	**14,600**	**4,600**
Operating expenses:			
Selling, general & admin.	12,000	5,250	2,200
Research & development	6,000	3,750	2,000
Total operating costs	18,000	9,000	4,200
Income from operations	**11,000**	**5,600**	**400**
Interest income	**50**	**50**	**50**
Income before taxes	**11,050**	**5,650**	**450**
Income taxes	3,650	1,875	0
Net income	**7,400**	**3,775**	**450**
Earnings per share	**$0.74**	**$0.38**	**$0.04**
Shares outstanding (000)	**10,000**	**10,000**	**10,000**

All numbers in bold represent sales and profits; nonbold represents subtractions, or costs.

The picture that emerges is of one of the nation's best-looking up-and-comers, the sort that should keep making next year's "200 Hottest Small Companies" lists. Sales and earnings growth is outstanding, profit margins improve with the passage of time, management is allotting a healthy amount to development of new products. Messages seems to epitomize what every small-cap growth company fan could possibly seek out.

And that's why it is so disturbing, to the savvier Messages shareholders, when the company posts the numbers below, for fiscal 2001:

Statement of Income (numbers in 000)	Messages Inc.	
	2001	**2000**
Revenue	**97,000**	**50,000**
Cost of sales	46,500	21,000
Gross profit	**50,500**	**29,000**

Operating expenses:		
Selling, general & admin.	27,500	12,000
Research & development	4,500	6,000
Total operation costs	32,000	18,000
Income from operations	**18,500**	**11,000**
Interest income	**100**	**50**
Income before taxes	**18,600**	**11,050**
Income taxes	6,000	3,650
Net income	**12,600**	**7,400**
Earnings per share	**$1.05**	**$0.74**
Shares outstanding (000)	**12,000**	**10,000**

All numbers in bold represent sales and profits; nonbold represents subtractions, or costs.

On the face of it, we still see tremendous growth. *Revenue* exceeded analysts' expectations, coming in up 94 percent to $97 million, while *Net income* rose some 70 percent. But look deeper and you may change your mind about this report. Certainly the market didn't like it, dropping MESS stock from $18 (to which it had risen) to $14 in one day. Let's examine this income statement for a few more Foolish indicators that we seek in every statement of operations. It's another checklist. Take note!

1. Make sure margins remain at consistent levels if they're not actually rising.

A company's profitability directly affects its stock price, mainly through the vehicle of earnings per share (EPS). If a company's margins (a.k.a. level of profitability) decline, that decline translates directly to the bottom line, or *Earnings per share*. That decline will in turn dramatically affect the performance of a stock.

Messages's net profit margin in the year 2000 was an impressive 14.8 percent ($7.4 million divided by $50 million). But in 2001 the company followed up with only a 13 percent net margin (you already know how to do this: $12.6 million divided by $97 million). Still very high, but lower than the year before. A bad sign. Stocks often trade off of forward expectations, and forward expectations are deeply rooted in trends. Because the trend here is falling, even a Fool couldn't express much surprise in MESS stock's 22 percent decline the day that these numbers were released.

We prefer margins to remain at the same levels or (even better) rise slightly and consistently over time. This is the sign of good management and a healthy and competitive enterprise. This is the boxer who, light on his toes, can still shake and bake around the ring in round eleven.

It remains always to examine the cause of rising or falling margins; you should attempt to reach an understanding of the reasons behind any significant change in a company's financial statements, just as you would in your own bank account. In Messages's case, we find the primary problem relates to its *Cost of sales,* which ate right into the company's gross margins. It appears that in the effort to ramp up production of new messages for innovative new inserts—particularly the construction of its scratch-'n'-eat mentholated series—the company couldn't achieve factory efficiency. Perhaps the company should never have introduced this new product at all. Or maybe the margin decline is a onetime event.

2. Make sure research and development (R&D) expenditures aren't getting shortchanged.

Perhaps the foremost financial trick that companies use to match or exceed their earnings estimates is to reduce their *Research and development* (R&D) expenditures. What they are effectively doing is what the federal government has been getting accused of doing for years: jeopardizing the future by enhancing (or just preserving) the present. In an effort to save face today, companies that reduce R&D are imperiling themselves down the road.

Why would a company do this? Because unfortunately most companies feel tremendous pressure to meet or exceed the earnings estimates put forward by the analysts tracking them. In this day and age, if a company fails to meet estimates (as was the case with Messages) it can expect its stock to star in that day's "Market Losers" news segments. And it can sometimes take a long, long time for institutional confidence—and strong stock price performance—to reappear.

Having furnished the context that explains why companies feel the heat to hit estimates, we can now look down the income statement and see which of the costs deducted from sales is most under the company's control *and* least likely to exert any effect in the "now now now, earnings earnings earnings" atmosphere: research and development. R&D, as we mentioned last chapter, is simply the bucks you supply to a few mad scientists hidden away somewhere in the bowels of your corporate headquarters. Who's going to notice if you happen to shortchange these guys for a quarter or a year?

A Fool, that's who. Because we watch very carefully the amounts our companies are spending on R&D, particularly high-tech and medical companies, which rely so much on developing the superior technology that will put everyone else out of business. Look back at MESS's financial statement. Horrors! Messages just so happens to have spent *less* on research and development in 2001 (just $4.5 million) than it did in the year 2000 ($6 million). That's quite a bad sign, and it suggests that management may consciously have underfunded its development efforts in order to prop up its earnings per share. It is possible, of course, that a company's R&D needs can change, permanently reducing the amount spent. Quite unlikely for a small, high-growth situation, but possible. Anyway, your job will be to find out.

The traditional and best way to look at R&D is as a percentage of revenues for that year; doing so, we see that R&D accounted for 12 percent of revenues in 2000, and just 4.6 percent of revenues in 2001. This is a dramatic reduction; at your first convenience, you should be back on the phone to Investor Relations, chewing them out and asking why. They may have managed to keep earnings per share up over $1 for the year, but how well will earnings fare in another year or two? The company has claimed plans to release its Virtual-Reality InfoCookie Experience modules in the first half of 2003—you still think it's going to make that schedule?

If Messages is not willing to maintain a consistent annual percentage for R&D costs, it'll only be that much more likely to get swept under the rug when Microsoft comes out with a better Virtual-Reality Info-Cookie Experience module.

Watch this figure carefully, dear reader.

3. Make sure the company is paying full income taxes.

Always look at your company's corporate tax rate. You can deduce this simply by taking the amount paid in *Income taxes* as a percentage of income before taxes. Refreshing our memory in Messages's case, we see:

Messages	2001	2000
Income before taxes	**18,600**	**11,050**
Income taxes	6,000	3,650

So in 2000, the company paid 33 percent ($3,650 divided by $11,050), while MESS paid a slightly lower rate (32 percent) in 2001. This is fine, about what one would expect. Don't get hung up here on fine distinctions regarding a percentage point or two—that's for margins, where percentage points really count. No, in the case of taxes, you should never worry about slight changes between apparently high tax rates; who the heck can ever figure out tax returns anyway? The rules change slightly every year to keep accountants in business. Don't let this bog you down.

The reason we do make a point of talking about income taxes here is that some companies record much lower income tax rates due to *tax-loss carryforwards*. Our government gives money-losing enterprises credits against future taxes when (and if) they eventually turn a profit. Messages Inc., back in the prehistoric days of 1996 and 1997, lost a spot of money as a start-up. If you turn back a few pages, you'll see that the company's 1998 income statement shows it paying no income tax at all. The carryforward credits are the reason. (If a company lost lots and lots of money early on, in many cases the now-profitable company won't use up all its credits in one year. These are then carried forward even further, to be used over the coming years at management's discretion.)

In closing up this section, we simply caution you to make sure you're not using artificially high net income and earnings-per-share figures if the company was using an artificially low tax rate (in most cases, below 20 percent).

4. Keep an eye on growth in shares.

Companies issue more common shares when they need to create cash; with an investment bank serving as liaison, the public purchases the new shares, filling the corporate coffers. Reasons to issue new stock abound. Some companies are cash-flow negative, as we learned last chapter, and therefore need the bucks to fund expansion. Others might issue new shares or convertible warrants to pay off a new acquisition. Whatever the reason, whenever new stock is issued, the existing stock generally becomes devalued by the market. From a current shareholder's point of view, it's kind of like finally fulfilling your lifelong dream of purchasing the *Mona Lisa* and then finding out that there also happen to be three others in a dusty old backroom of the Louvre. Bummer.

As mentioned earlier, when we settle into the process of actually valuing stocks, earnings per share is an important figure for investors to watch. To review, *Earnings per share* is simply the profits of the company (*Net income*) divided by the total number of shares of common stock (*Shares outstanding*). So obviously, when a company issues more shares, the earnings per share will decline (all other things remaining equal). Because many stocks trade mainly off a multiple of earnings per share, this is not a good thing.

In 2001 Messages issued 2 million new shares for no good reason we know of at present. (We may learn more later.) What that meant is that despite sales and profits gains of greater than 70 percent, earnings per share rose only 42 percent. We've already discussed what that did to the stock.

Suffice it to point out now that you should scrutinize total shares outstanding. If you see significant increases or hear of a new company share offering, always ask yourself *why*. Did your company need the money, or did it just want to cash in off a high share price following a great run in its stock? And if your company did need the money, did it need it for *good* reasons (like to launch a new subsidiary, or for development of a new product), or *bad* reasons (like to stay in business)? Oh, and by the way, no cause for complaint if total shares outstanding increase in bits and pieces from quarter to quarter, since extra shares are often rewarded to management and employees as incentivized compensation. But if you see a large unexplained jump in the company's share total, or a consistent pattern over three to five years of significantly more and more and more shares, your guys are diluting the growth of their earnings per share. You can find better investments elsewhere.

The P/E Ratio: The Market's Price Tag

Now that you've got a handle on the income statement, here is a quick word on one of the most common methods people use to evaluate stocks: the *price-to-earnings ratio* (P/E ratio). P/E equals the price of a stock divided by its company's earnings per share over the past twelve months.

Let's take two examples.

- *Yuckie Yogurt Corp.* (ticker: YUCK), the retailer of exotically flavored frozen yogurt, has earnings per share of 50 cents and a stock price of $5. *Its P/E ratio is 10* ($5 divided by $0.50 equals 10).
- *Doors Incorporated "C"* (ticker: REMAC), the software conglomerate whose operating software, Doors, has suddenly cracked a competing brand's seemingly unshakable hold on the PC market, has earnings per share of 50 cents and now trades at $30. *Its P/E ratio is 60* ($30 divided by $0.50 equals 60).

The P/E for a given stock varies based on changes in price (which happen every day) and changes in earnings (which happen once a quarter). Think of it as the price tag that the market has put on the shares. The market is saying, in effect, "If you want to buy stock in Doors, you're going to have to pay sixty times the company's earnings."

Buying stocks like Doors Incorporated that trade at thirty-five times earnings or higher (as do many of the best growth stocks) is akin to shopping at Tiffany—high prices for desired goods. Purchasers of stocks at ten times earnings or less have opted to shed their discretionary income on the equity equivalent of a blue-light special.

The less you pay up to buy a stock, the lower your risk. Would you prefer to buy our ingenious developer of the Windows ripoff at forty times earnings rather than its current sixty times earnings? We think so. You should, anyway, just as you'd rather pay $1 instead of $4 for the exact same half gallon of jalapeño-flavored Yuckie Yogurt! Likewise, the more you pay up for a company's stock, the more risk you're accepting. The company had better produce the gigantic earnings growth for which you're paying such a premium, or you're in *big* trouble.

Looking closely at the examples, notice the extreme disparity. Both companies, after all, have trailing twelve-month earnings of 50 cents per share, but YUCK is trading at $5 per share and there's REMAC at $30. This seems just too good a deal to pass up—one in a lifetime—so you stake half of last year's salary on Yuckie Yogurt. For the same amount of earnings, you have had to pay only $5 per share . . . quite impressive in comparison to the Fools who are paying six times that for Doors. Darned clever of you; you've outsmarted the market. Yuckie's share price, you convince your in-laws, should probably race to $30 sometime soon . . . a cool 500 percent profit. You're seeing big things: a week in Paris, then a leisurely yacht cruise along the Côte d'Azur. Not that you wouldn't stand for 200 percent and a *weekend* in Paris—lose the yacht—just the same. No need to be greedy.

What a desperate and woeful state you'll be in when, a year later, Doors Incorporated has run to $52 a share, even as YUCK's management has dismantled and sold its seventy-third Yuckie Hut year-to-date, inducing a decline in the stock price to $1.25 per share. Well, you can still take your in-laws to Hardee's . . . if they'll treat.

The lesson: The P/E need not (and often does not) correspond between stocks; some stocks may be considered underpriced at fifty times earnings, whereas others may be grossly overpriced when their P/E rises to 12. This is because the market's price tag is based on past history, present circumstance, and future projections, all of which vary from company to company. Think of the P/E as representing the present circumstance (stock price) divided by past history (trailing twelve-month earnings per share). Finally, the future projections (or growth rate) made by analysts have a great effect on how high a stock's P/E gets. The term "analysts," as you know, refers to those fearless Wall Street professionals who research companies and their stocks with an eye toward predicting their future performance, numbers, valuation, and current attractiveness as an investment. Don't bet the house on analysts' estimates of future growth, since they are usually guided by the company itself. They are wont to change. Still, it will take a lot of experience and understanding of the company to come up with more accurate future earnings estimates.

So now you see why you didn't have to pay up much to buy Yuckie Yogurt. The market remained unconvinced that the company's Froz-Gurt Cubes would ever sell.

Fool Ratio

Many investors make the mistake of viewing the P/E ratio alone, in a vacuum, as if the number 17 or 5 or 43 could serve as an effective valuation tool on its own. You'll occasionally hear such an investor say something like, "Will you look at that P/E of 60! The stock is *outrageously* overvalued!" To our Foolish ear, that's kind of like saying, "Look at the thermometer; the temperature is 60! Outrageous!" But unless we know what season it is and what are the average outdoor temperatures during that season, we have nothing to relate the comments to . . . they are non sequiturs.

First Foolish lesson on P/Es: They need to be placed in a context that gives them meaning. And here's where a very general rule of thumb comes in handy: "In a fully and fairly valued situation, a growth stock's price-to-earnings ratio should equal the percentage of the growth rate of its company's earnings per share."

The growth rate is the subjective piece of the pie. The P/E ratio is hard fact, reported everywhere. Thus, what'll eventually force you to use your noggin in this scenario is the analysis of a company's growth. When we talk about growth rate, we're talking primarily about the future earnings-per-share (EPS) growth rate. Growth in sales is of no use if it is being canceled out by swelling costs. We want EPS to outpace everything else on the income statement.

Let's say Doors Incorporated has just reported EPS of 60 cents this year. How much will EPS be next year? The most relevant numbers—earnings estimates—are the ones that haven't been reported yet. A whole industry has sprung up to estimate those numbers and to provide them to investors.

You can find analysts' estimates in the Quotes & Data area at Fool.com and on many other financial sites on the Web. In the case of Doors, a quick check on the Fool reveals that analysts expect the company to earn 90 cents EPS in the upcoming year. The one-year growth rate, a straight percentage gain calculation, is 50 percent. So what does this really mean? In this case, the company is currently earning 60 cents per share and we expect EPS to grow by 50 percent over the coming year, to 90 cents per share.

If you want to look more than one year into the future (and what Fool doesn't want to look as far forward as possible?) simply use analysts' growth estimates for two, three, or five years into the future, if available.

All right. We know the P/E now, and we can calculate growth rates. Here comes the fun, putting the two together.

A fundamental Wall Street axiom is that a stock's P/E should equal the company growth rate. Convenient, huh? Thus, if a company is growing at 20 percent, the P/E should be 20 for a fair, full value. The technical underpinnings of the theory have something to do with anticipated cash flows looking years ahead, but the actual principle itself has melted away over the years. It's now become a generally accepted investment principle. It's actually kind of like the NFL's quarterback rating; nobody really knows the formula but everyone takes it for granted.

This is the basis for the Fool Ratio. You calculate it by taking a stock's current P/E ratio as a percentage of its growth rate. (For this reason some analysts call it the price-to-earnings-to-growth ratio, or PEG.) It's that easy.

Let's apply the Fool Ratio to Doors Incorporated. We know that the P/E is 60 and that analysts expect the company to grow at a rate of 50 percent next year. Simply divide 60 by 50 to find that the PEG for Doors is 1.2.

Simple, isn't it? Well, it's not so easy when you are looking ahead two or three years, or an odd number of quarters. For those situations, we have created a little program on the Fool.com site known as the PEG Calculator (a.k.a. PEGulator) that takes all the work (we mean *fun*) out of finding the PEG. All you need is the current price, the current twelve-month trailing earnings, the estimated earnings, and the number of fiscal quarters between the last actual earnings and the date of the earnings estimate. You plug the numbers into the PEGulator and out pops the PEG.

What to do with that number? We said that the Fool Ratio takes as its basis that the P/E and growth rate would be equal when a stock is fully and fairly valued. That means that a PEG of 1 would indicate full valuation. Anything less than 1 would point out that the expected growth rate has sped ahead of the P/E, which means that the stock is selling for less than its growth rate would normally demand. A Fool Ratio more than 1 indicates a stock that is more expensive than you would expect, based on its growth rate.

We used to interpret Fool Ratio results as a clear indicator of absolute over- or undervaluation. We would make buys based on low PEGs and sell or short high PEGs. We've found, however, that Mr. Market often has a good reason for his valuation. If the Street doesn't have confidence in Doors's ability to reach its 50 percent growth targets, it will price it accordingly, leading to a low PEG. If the market starts to believe that Doors will blow the doors off its 50 percent annual growth estimate, it will bid the stock up, giving it a high Fool Ratio. That means that, counterintuitively, a high Fool Ratio often points out a company that the market has great faith in. And the market is very often right to believe in the best companies.

Also, a "normal" (or mean) level for a company's PEG ratio will, in our experience, change based on the present-day environment for interest rates. When rates are low or going lower, money piles into the stock market, fleeing from interest-bearing vehicles like CDs and money markets since the rate of return on those is less attractive. This pushes up stock market valuations. In the late 1990s we saw good companies with Fool Ratios over 2, and their stocks still did well over the following twelve to twenty-four months. Conversely, during eras with high interest rates, expect the normal PEG ratios to trade well below 1. Thus, even this Fool Ratio cannot be viewed out of context.

The key point to take away, and the reason we teach this ratio, is that for companies with profits (the ratio does not, of course, exist for companies where there is no "E") you can get a pretty good gauge on how their stocks are being priced according to their growth rates. This is a critical bit of context that the Wise too often lack. Again, go back to the line that kicked off this section: "It has a P/E of 60! How overvalued!" Well, if the sustainable growth rate for the enterprise over the next three to five years is 60 percent or higher, we don't think so.

Use the Fool Ratio carefully. It ultimately provides only an impression of a stock's valuation. It's then up to you to determine *why* the market has that impression.

·15·

Balance Sheets and Cash Flow Statements

· · · · ·

A Fool sees not the same tree that a Wise Man sees.
—*William Blake*

The Balance Sheet

We've given a basic picture of the income statement at this point. Time to move on to the second financial statement that we watch: the balance sheet. Unlike the income statement, which reads like a top-down yearlong story of a business's progress, the balance sheet gives the reader a single snapshot of the company's books on the *last day* of the reporting period. The statement comprises two sections, *assets* and *liabilities* (the latter is grouped with shareholders' equity). The balance sheet is so called because these two sections *balance* each other out in terms of value. Assets are balanced by liabilities, and when you run out of liabilities all else is considered shareholders' equity, which is the basic net worth of the company. That's a pretty understandable concept, no? If you subtract liabilities from assets, you have the amount that belongs to the owners. (Welcome to the wonderful world of financial accounting, where these guys make up their own definitions and their own rules and the rest of us just sit back and pay them to do our taxes.) (All right, that's probably enough cheap shots at accountants for one book. We'll stop now.) Both the assets and the liabilities sections are further divided between *current* and *noncurrent* items, where the currentness of the item in question refers to how quickly it could be recouped should the business be liquidated. Current items are those that are to be paid or collected within one year.

We're about to take up the balance sheet Foolishly, fixing on the items that matter to us. So again, we won't be laying out every term. You're paying us to take you to the stars' homes, not explain the history behind the street names that link them together.

Balance Sheet (numbers in 000)	Messages Inc.	
	2001	**2000**
Current Assets:		
Cash and cash equivalents	24,000	20,000
Accounts receivable	34,000	14,000
Inventory	20,000	10,000
Prepaid expenses	1,500	1,000
	79,500	45,000
Property & Equipment:		
Subtotal	12,000	6,000
Less accumulated depreciation	1,200	800
	10,800	5,200
	90,300	50,200
Liabilities:		
Current Liabilities:		
Accounts payable	6,500	3,200
Accrued expenses	18,000	10,000
	24,500	13,200
Long-Term Debt:	0	0
Stockholders' Equity:		
Common stock; $.01 par value	2,400	2,000
Additional paid-in capital	26,300	10,500
Retained earnings	37,100	24,500
	65,800	37,000
Total Liabilities and Stockholders' Equity	90,300	50,200

1. Cash: very, very likable.

The very first line of the balance sheet is always named *Cash and cash equivalents,* or some similar phrase. This is the amount of money a company has sitting in the bank. The cash equivalents part of the definition simply refers to the cash, unnecessary for running a business, that is currently earning a speck of short-term interest. (If a second line below it is labeled anything like *Short-term investments,* that line should be *combined* with the cash line; both serve similar functions and should always be grouped together, for our purposes.)

Our only real rule with company cash is that we like to see lots of it.

Companies build up cash for several reasons. The first one is the best of all: Good operations generate cash. To review, operational cash flow is simply the dough that is piling up in the course of the company running its business. We call businesses that take in more than they put out "cash generators," green machines cranking out seven- and eight-figure additions to this most-favored-status line of the balance sheet. Watching a cash generator do its thing can bring tears to a good capitalist's eyes, an emotional response to finance that can only be augmented by actually being *invested* in such situations. One of the great lines from Peter Lynch's book *Beating the Street* (1993) captures the feeling perfectly: "It's no accident that there's a snapshot of Fannie Mae [his favorite company] headquarters alongside the family photographs on the memento shelf in my office. It warms my heart to think of the place. The stock has been so great they ought to retire the symbol."

But there are other ways to come by cash as well. A common one is a share offering. We have mentioned companies that issue more shares of common stock in order to raise cash. When those offerings occur, the resultant cash comes right to this asset line.

Some analysts like to express the amount of cash a company has in per-share amounts. All you'd do is just divide the cash and cash equivalents figure by the total number of shares outstanding. For example, Messages has built up an impressive $24 million in cash by the last day of 2001. With 12 million shares out, Messages sports cash alone worth $2 per share. This means that no matter how many earthquakes shake the company's Reno, Nevada, headquarters, ain't no way this stock is dropping below $2. (Stock prices *can* conceivably fall below a company's cash per share, but this extremely rare occurrence generally would happen only if the business's cash flow was so extremely negative that the cash on its balance sheet showed little likelihood of being there much longer.)

But cash means more than just a dependable rock-bottom stock price. It also represents the power to pay off debts, if a company has them. Or it could represent the potential to acquire complementary businesses, or buy out a competitor. The best growth companies on the planet create future growth with their own cash.

Develop a bias toward stocks backed by cash-generating businesses that have a wad of bills sitting in the bank gathering interest (and ready to be deployed whenever a good opportunity presents itself!).

2. Avoid too much debt.

The inverse to cash is *Long-Term Debt*. Like people taking out thirty-year mortgages, many companies also borrow to fund future opportunities. Companies routinely take on debt to fund acquisitions, new product developments, franchising expansion, and so forth. Consider a few examples. Disney assumed more than $10 billion in debt to buy out Capital Cities/ABC. Trump Hotels and Casinos has borrowed more than $2 billion to buy up casino properties in Atlantic City. Tricon Global took on more than $3 billion in debt to finance the expansion of its KFC, Pizza Hut, and Taco Bell restaurant chains.

Debt is just one of the financing tools available to companies across the planet. It's not always completely horrible to expand rapidly through the use of debt, but it's a dangerous game. We vastly prefer businesses that don't take on much debt, if any. We like them to be so profitable from operations and growing so rapidly that they don't need the risk of significant interest expenses; they don't need additional capital to thrive. These will make for some of your very best investments, through good *and* bad economic periods.

Oh, *Long-Term Debt* (if it exists) is an item found midway down the liability side of the balance sheet, just after *Current Liabilities*.

3. Make sure growth in accounts receivable and inventory approximates sales growth.

Accounts receivable and *Inventory* both constitute assets, insofar as both represent money that the company would receive if it were liquidated. Accounts receivable measures the amount of money that a business is owed by its customers, not all of whom pay 100 percent cash up front for every product. Inventories are an asset because they represent finished or near-finished products that the company simply has not yet sold.

Both of these items are indeed considered assets because they have monetary value to the company, but from an investor's point of view they're more like liabilities. Gaze through a Foolish lens and you can well see that both accounts receivable and inventories represent momentary failures on a company's part to convert its business into cash. Accounts receivable are what your loan sharks have failed to collect so far, and inventories are what your unctuous salesmen have not yet managed to foist off on your unsuspecting customers.

Both these assets will always exist as inevitable components of running a business (unless you're a lightweight software company). What you as an investor need to track is how the *growth* in accounts receivable and inventory tracks against overall sales growth. You'd ideally like to see this growth rate decline in comparison to the sales growth rate. However, that's the ideal; a more realistic expectation is for the growth rates of accounts receivable, inventories, and sales to move roughly in sync. If that's the case, you have nothing to worry about.

When, on the other hand, accounts receivable and inventories for a company you hold are rising at a significantly higher rate than sales, or demonstrate a huge one-quarter jump, you need to consider very seriously whether you want to remain in that investment. Accounts receivable in particular are worthy of your scrutiny and respect as a financial indicator. We've seen many otherwise healthy small-cap stocks literally fall apart (lose 80 percent or more, quickly) because they failed over time to collect what they were supposedly owed, creating a *huge* cash flow drain. (We say "supposedly owed" because in some situations it may have been questionable whether a company really had made the sales it claimed in the first place.)

Classic case in point at Fool HQ was Styles on Video, the manufacturer and marketer of "hair imaging systems." The Styles on Video product, essentially a computer hooked up to a video camera, enabled customers to see what they would look like with a selection of different hairstyles. The simulation was achieved with the video image by superimposing these other coifs in a seamless manner right over the top of the customer's existing hair. This was a story that—so sue us—we bought.

We first acquired the stock in our personal accounts via an April 1993 spin-off from another company whose shares we owned. Styles on Video then proceeded to rise from our cost of $5 to over $15 by January 1994. As it was quite near its full valuation at that point, we actually cashed the stock at a very nice profit. We weren't about to hang a photo of the SOV corporate headquarters next to those of our loved ones, but we were seriously thinking of submitting to the humiliation of a Styles on Video photo session and printing up the results in Ye Olde Printed Foole.

That winter, we were invited to join a prestigious investment club in Washington, D.C., one that featured exclusively older men (mostly friends of our father). We proudly accepted, the youngest new members in years. What young rakes we were, and what pressure we felt to make a good stock pick or two.

We began our very first meeting with three words in our mouths, "Styles on Video."

We explained how much we'd regretted selling in the first place, now that we'd seen the latest earnings estimates from Thomas James, the regional brokerage firm that had SOV down for $1.35 per share for 1994 and $2.40 per share for 1995. We told the whole humorous story about the "hair imaging" and went on to discuss the company's R&D plans for (no joke) "eyewear imaging" and "weight-loss imaging." Our trusting fellow club members, of a generous spirit, agreed. Our club bought a fair amount of it.

Imagine our quiet disappointment when two months later our mailbox turned up a fresh copy of the company's brand-new annual report for the year ended December 31, 1993. We've cobbled together below the relevant figures from a few different statements, for your reading pleasure. Check out these numbers.

Styles on Video	1993	1992	
Sales	8,553,000	2,680,000	up 219%
Accounts receivable	3,594,000	505,000	up 611%
Net cash flow	(2,570,000)		
Cash and cash equivalents	2,107,000		

What you've just looked at was very bad news. Allow us to explain. First, you see the *Sales* growth: up 219 percent! So far, so good. Now look at the growth in *Accounts receivable:* up 611 percent. Bad. *Real* bad. The growth in receivables was way, way ahead of sales growth. In fact, the year-over-year receivables growth of $3 million–plus far outstripped the company's entire $2 million in net income. Glancing at *Net cash flow* from operations (a figure we went over last chapter), you see a big fat negative $2.6 million; *Cash and cash equivalents* were *less,* reported at $2.1 million.

Take the time to incorporate what you've learned so far and then ask yourself what was going to happen to this company in 1994. Its sales were projected by analysts to leap from $8 million to $23 million. What might you expect that would do to Styles's accounts receivable? Does the term "explodamundo" in any way convey our meaning? And what would that receivables explosion create? A gigantic cash flow problem. And how much cash did the company have in its coffers to solve the problem? Far too little.

Right about that time, a couple of things happened. The first is that despite these disgusting-looking numbers, CNBC financial television correspondent Dan Dorfman gave the stock a big plug, quoting an analyst who was very bullish on the company's "explosive" prospects. The second thing that happened is that we were stricken with acute and irreversible mental paralysis that prevented us from acting on what we knew for the benefit of our investment club. That we might actually announce to the club that we wanted out of this pick just a couple months after we made it was too intolerable a notion. How embarrassing! Plus, the stock had stayed propped up pretty high (in the $15 to $16 range), and staying the course was the way of least resistance.

We should've shorted the bejesus out of it. (We discuss shorting in Chapter 22.)

You can only imagine our chagrin when Styles on Video declined from $15 to $10 to $5 in the course of a few months, and halted trading altogether less than a year later, after some of the company's management resigned to go to work for the firm that audited its statements! (We'd never heard of such a thing, and are now curious whether that auditor is publicly traded so that we might short it instead.) Meanwhile, our Washington Investors Club was left with worthless shares thanks to our first-ever stock pick. Could we have made a more striking first impression? (Fortunately, we can laugh about this, since most of the rest of the members of the club set the example by laughing it off in the first place.)

Styles on Video is our definitive accounts receivable story, though as we mentioned earlier, numerous examples of similar demises exist. Unless they have a lot of cash, small businesses have to maintain a tight control on growth in receivables and inventories; the imperativeness of this simply cannot be overstated. Don't even bother considering investing in any companies that are having problems in this arena. You can find too many better ones that aren't.

Incidentally, beyond just looking at the growth rates in accounts receivable, we also watch to see the percentage of overall sales that receivables make up. This is a useful measurement to track quarter by quarter because you can see what portion of sales is getting paid for right away. In the case of Messages, we see 2001 receivables at $34 million, with 2001's sales being $97 million. That means that receivables are running at 35 percent of sales ($34 divided by $97), or, expressed in calendar terms, receivables take about 4.2 months (35 percent of a year) to pay off. Messages fans, 35 percent is a discouragingly high figure. It gets even worse when put in the context of the previous year, in which sales were $50 million and receivables were $14 million. That's 28 percent, meaning our receivables-to-sales ratio is already high and trending higher. It appears that bakers are welching on their InfoCookie fees. A strong, well-managed business won't permit this to happen.

Finally, please note that the reverse equivalent of accounts receivable and inventories is *Accounts payable* and *Accrued expenses,* which are liabilities that a company *owes* but which (paradoxically, again) a company should do its best to increase. That's because the longer a company can string out its suppliers and creditors, the more use the company will get out of the cash it keeps on hand (for operations or interest). It's called smart cash management. However, in most strong small-cap growth companies, accounts receivable and inventories will still far exceed accounts payable and accrued expenses, making these latter balance sheet items less meaningful.

4. Do whatever ratios catch your fancy.

Some people go overboard analyzing the various ratios calculable from the data in a balance sheet. We don't find many of these terribly meaningful, but we'll share with you a couple of things you can learn.

The most common ratio associated with balance sheets is probably the *current ratio*. The current ratio provides an investor with a basic test of short-term liquidity, since it simply takes the *Current Assets* (cash, receivables, inventories, et cetera) and divides them by the *Current Liabilities* (accounts payable, accrued expenses, et cetera). Ideally, this figure will fall somewhere above 2-to-1 for the typical American industrial company, tending toward higher ratios for small caps. What the current ratio tells you is how nimbly a company may be able to act to take advantage of an unforeseen circumstance.

In reality, of course, even a high ratio may not help in times of trouble. Taken on its own, the current ratio doesn't actually tell you much about a company's liquidity, because it depends on the company's ability to convert its current assets into cash. That's not always possible. If, for example, TastiScrolls were found to cause mild increases in the libidos of laboratory rats, one might think that Messages would be far better prepared to deal with this potential crisis with a current ratio of 5 than with a ratio of 1. In the wake of the FDA investigation, however, Messages is going to have to write off all of its current inventory. What's more, some of its customers might decide that they aren't going to pay the money they owe Messages, since they can't sell their TastiScrolls either. Messages's inventory and accounts receivable balances won't add up to a pile of glucose in this situation.

For what it's worth, let's calculate Messages's current ratio for 2001 and 2000:

	2001	**2000**
Current Assets	79,500	45,000
Divided by Current Liabilities	24,500	13,200
Equals Current Ratio	3.2	3.4

Messages's current ratio for 2001 was 3.2, which is certainly acceptable. Note that this is *down* from the previous year's mark of 3.4.

You can apply the current ratio to any annual report you look at, though we've never let it make or break an investment decision for us. We like to see the ratio remain even or trend slightly higher, but you won't find us getting emotional on the subject. Still, a survey of the current ratio can be a useful way to discover potential new investment ideas among financially healthy mid-caps. Just look at the company's snapshot in the Quotes & Data section of Fool.com.

A second ratio, very similar to the current ratio, is the *quick ratio*. The quick ratio is more "cashcentric" (to coin an abominable-looking term); it is simply the *Current Assets* minus *Inventory* divided by the *Current Liabilities.* It gives you an even better read on how prepared a company might be to encounter unforeseen difficulties or opportunities, or just to meet current short-term debt obligations, so you want to see as high a number as possible.

	2001	2000
Current Assets	79,500	45,000
Minus Inventory	20,000	10,000
Divided by Current Liabilities	24,500	13,200
Equals Quick Ratio	2.4	2.7

Messages's quick ratio declined from a powerful 2.7 in 2000 down to a still-impressive 2.4 in 2001. Still, this drop may portend ill.

Another fairly common ratio is the *debt-to-equity ratio.* As you know, companies issue bonds or shares of stock in order to raise money. One of the fundamental differences between debt (bank borrowings or bonds) and equity (stock) is that debt has to be repaid. From a stockholder's point of view, therefore, the less debt the better, unless the company can make well more money from that debt than it will have to pay out in interest. If a company maintains little debt, it retains the ability to go out to the capital markets and float a bond or convertible in order to raise cash, should the need arise.

To calculate the simple version of this ratio, you simply need to locate a company's long-term debt and its equity. *Long-Term Debt* sits in the liability portion (noncurrent) of the balance sheet. Equity may be culled from the *Stockholders' Equity* section of the balance sheet, below liabilities. Take the values for *Common stock* and capital surplus (also known as *Additional paid-in capital*) and add them together. Then you just divide the debt figure by the equity figure. You want this figure to be as low as possible, with zero being the preference, in most cases. Messages, because it has no debt, has a 0 debt-to-equity ratio.

A final ratio we'll mention is perhaps the most important, but again not one upon which we found any investment decisions. It's called the *return on equity ratio,* one additional measure of corporate profitability. For this one, you divide the *Net Income* by the *Total Stockholders' Equity* from the balance sheet (the bottom line). By so doing, you are measuring the amount of profit a business generates relative to the amount of money shareholders have put into it. A respectable figure is 15 percent; a strong figure runs over 20 percent. As with most of these ratios, you want to see a high number that remains high over time either by standing pat or increasing slightly. For outstandingly profitable emerging-growth companies, this number may start out ridiculously high (50 percent or even greater, in some cases) and trend down as the company grows. This should not be counted against a stock.

	2001	2000
Net Income	12,600	7,400
Divided by Shareholders' Equity	65,800	37,000
Equals Return on Equity	19.1%	20.0%

Messages produced net income of $7.4 million in 2000, and a check of the balance sheet reveals total shareholders' equity at $37 million that year. Thus, the return on equity was 20 percent. The next year, as you might expect by now, was a tad worse: Return on equity for 2001 came in at 19.1 percent.

◆ ◆ ◆

Having drawn to an end of our Foolish discussion of the balance sheet, you've now plotted enough points on your map that you can safely navigate the crucial parts of the terrain while still leaving yourself room to explore the out-of-the-way places, should you so desire. (We'll mention a few others we like in Part VI.) We close our discussion of making sense of the financial info by turning to the cash-flow statement.

The Statement of Cash Flows

By now you've already heard a fair amount about cash flow; we've stressed the importance of positive operational cash flow again and again. In Chapter 13 we learned that positive cash flow is one of our Foolish Eight criteria for selecting growth stocks. And in this chapter we have told the sorry tale of Styles on Video, the company that was sunk by its own negative cash flow. We ascribe profound importance to a business's ability to spin off—not consume—cash. Your own portfolio should be replete with, if not totally dominated by, *cash generators.*

Novices sometimes have difficulty conceiving of the cash flow statement. If it's measuring income and expenses, how is it any different from the income statement? The answer is that the cash flow statement simply provides you a different way of looking at income and expenses. The statement of cash flows is most akin, in fact, to your monthly bank statement. If you view your own personal or family bank statement as a business, you'll notice that the various income and expense items that show up there are all accounted for *when paid.* On the other hand, the corporate income statement—*unlike* your bank statement—contains items (like sales, for instance) that have been recorded but not yet paid for. This is perfectly legitimate accounting but not the most useful way to focus on the guts of a business. The guts of a business reveal exactly when and what money is going out and when and what money is coming in. That's exactly what a cash flow statement shows and why we watch this report so carefully.

Now the cash flow statement is actually three statements in one, because accountants organize all inflows and outflows in three categories:

1. Operating activities (the most important one), or the company's businesses
2. Investing activities, generally expenditures on hard assets such as property and equipment
3. Financing activities, typically inflows like common-share offerings and outflows like repayment of debt

The cash-flow adjustments coming out of these three separate categories are cumulative, and the bottom-line result of this statement is usually called "increase (or decrease) in cash and cash equivalents." As you may recall, that's the very same top line item in the asset side of the balance sheet. Here we have yet another example of how the income statement, balance sheet, and statement of cash flows hang together; the reason that financiers often link these things into a single spreadsheet is that when you change one figure on one statement, you'll often affect at least one other figure on one of the other statements. As investors, we like to see the cash and cash equivalents line increase with the passage of time; it's to the statement of cash flows that you go to understand why (or why not) a company's cash is increasing.

We typically don't spend much time looking at anything but the first section on operating cash flow. With that in mind, let's end this chapter with a look at the operational portion of Messages's cash flow statement:

Statement of Cash Flow (numbers in 000)	Messages Inc.	
	2001	**2000**
Cash flows from operating activities:		
Net income	12,600	7,400
Adjustments to reconcile net income to net cash provided by operating activities:		
Depreciation	1,200	800
Effects of change in operating assets and liabilities:		
Accounts receivable	(20,000)	(5,000)
Inventory	(10,000)	(4,000)
Accounts payable	3,300	2,000
Accrued expenses	8,000	4,000
Net cash provided by operating activities	**(4,900)**	**5,200**

Determine the driving reasons behind a company's cash flow (or lack thereof).

In many cases, the top section of the statement of cash flow makes for the single most enlightening reading in a business's financial reports. You should always scrutinize this section with the intention of coming away with a pretty clear picture of just exactly how a company is managing or botching its finances.

The top line of *Cash flows from operating activities,* and generally the biggest cash flow source, is *Net income.* Just below that appears an addition in the form of *Depreciation,* a technical term that you really don't have to know for our purposes. (But for readers who want a taste, here goes. Depreciation is basically the allocation of the cost of fixed assets [plant and equipment] over their useful life.)

Adding together net income and depreciation gives you a figure that some analysts refer to as "gross cash flow." In Messages's case, this would equal $13.8 million for 2001. But we're just mentioning this by the by . . . we don't use this definition. We prefer instead to make the normal adjustments of balance-sheet items to reach the operational cash flow.

We've already learned about the balance sheet, having featured several items on it (like accounts receivable). The bottom (*Effects of change . . .*) section of *cash flows from operating activities* simply presents the changes of these items from the previous year to the current one, making each an adjustment to cash flow. So, for example, if you go back and review Messages's balance sheet, you'll see that the company reported accounts receivable at $34 million and $14 million for 2001 and 2000, respectively. The difference between these figures is obviously $20 million. That very figure, $20 million, appears as the 2001 change in *Accounts receivable* on the cash flow statement. The number is reported in parentheses, meaning it is accounted for as a deduction from cash flow. This makes sense, given that the company is now owed by its customers $20 million more than last year, a cash drag.

One can thus go on to fill out the rest of the bottom section by making similar adjustments for all other significant operating assets and liabilities. Of course, this isn't necessary, since the company's accountant has already done it for you. The resulting sum is then deducted from net income and depreciation to obtain the operational cash flow.

For the first time, we can now see how clearly Messages screwed up its 2001 cash situation. After showing a positive flow of $5.2 million in 2000, the company went cash flow negative to the tune of $4.9 million in 2001. This partly explains floating another 2 million MESS shares in 2001; foreseeing the business going cash flow negative, perhaps management wanted more working capital on hand to start the new millennium.

Our review of the cash flow statement helps us see the main reason behind Messages's problems: a gigantic leap in accounts receivable from $5 million to $20 million, indicating the company is having trouble collecting money owed by its customers. As an investor, you would want to focus on this primary issue going forward.

The cash flow statement gives you the opportunity to see what's going on in a company's bank account. Take advantage of this by poring over the statement and formulating a notion of what's working financially and what isn't.

Read the management discussion of "liquidity and capital resources"!

Required by law to appear in annual reports and 10-Ks, this write-up makes for the best few paragraphs of substantive reading you'll get anywhere in a company's information packet. We're mentioning it in this section because the "liquidity and capital resources" text relates directly to the business's cash flow, to which you'll often read several overt references. Here you have the opportunity to hear straight from management how it will manage its cash and finances in the next year. You'll learn the size of any credit lines that your company has established at banks, and how far (if any) it has drawn off those lines. You'll sometimes get estimates of a company's capital expenditures over the next year, and explanations of how the company will fund those expenditures (*from operating cash flows* is the best explanation). In short, this section provides you a nice read on a company's immediate financial future, in no-fluff talk.

◆　◆　◆

Okay, that's it . . . a list of items we look for in financial statements. Oh, sure, other things will occasionally catch your eye—and should—but what those particular things are will emerge out of your own experience and expertise. For now, by learning how to digest and understand the most important parts of financial statements, you're prepared to invest Foolishly.

PART VI

RULE MAKERS, RULE BREAKERS, AND MORE

Quality Versus Valuation

. . . . .

*What we obtain too cheap, we esteem too lightly; it is
dearness only that gives everything its value.*
—*Thomas Paine*

In outlining some methods for identifying investment possibilities
and some basic metrics that you may want to use to assess them,
we've covered two types of companies—big stocks and small-caps.
Our truly favorite methods, for which we have designed real-money
portfolios at Fool.com, are fleshed out much more completely in our
1999 book, *The Motley Fool's Rule Breakers, Rule Makers*. In this part
of the book, we'd like briefly to summarize those strategies and a few
others we have developed for evaluating stocks worthy of more investigation.

The basic premise of both Rule Maker (Tom invests this way) and
Rule Breaker investing (David invests this way) is that you are looking
for the greatest companies in the world today. They are either the Rule
Makers (legal monopolies that dominate their industries for years and
provide huge profit streams) or Rule Breakers (upstart companies that
you identify early on as entities that can potentially slay Goliath and
create huge shareholder value in faster amounts of time). We therefore
look at the world of business this way: Every great business begins as a
Rule Breaker and hopes to transition in time to eventually dominating
its industry (often an industry the company helped to create), ascend-
ing to the throne as Rule Maker.

With both approaches, we focus first and foremost on the *quality* of the businesses that lie behind the stocks we buy. We don't get hung up on the *valuation*. The twentieth century showed that if the true underlying quality of a company goes up, eventually the valuation of that company rises to meet it. The Rule Maker and Rule Breaker approaches are based on that notion.

We therefore largely ignore the weekly fluctuation of stock prices and, instead, concentrate on the merits and shortcomings of the actual business. If you can find the best-managed, most profitable companies with increasing potential . . . tomorrow morning's share price shouldn't concern you. Have breakfast with your husband. Or give your grandmother a call. Or read your morning paper. Or surprise your kids and wake *them* up for a change, and play with them before school. But don't sweat the daily wiggles of your company's stock charted on a graph digitized on the Internet or spinning past you on a television screen.

Our aim is to find companies that we want to own, with whom we want to be partners, perhaps for the remainder of our lives. When we find them, we half lash ourselves to the mast and hang on for the ride. Some of our investments will perform poorly; others, moderately well; and some we expect will dominate. That mix should turn $20,000 literally into millions of dollars in a handful of decades.

No doubt you've run across those investors mentioned earlier who think that no stock should trade above a certain price-to-earnings ratio—say, 30 times earnings. Other investors believe that unless you discount forward all predictable cash flows through a business, you have no chance of accurately estimating the present or future values of that business. Still others see valuation as a hand wave or a swizzle stick appearing on a stock chart.

So many opinions, so little time.

But if you are going to invest in stocks, shouldn't you want to work very hard to determine the fair value of a company like Williams-Sonoma? Or a business like Tootsie Roll? Or a stock like TCBY Yogurt?

Our unusual answer to that one is, "Well, only if it helps you sleep at night."

We say this because our quite contrary take is that any intense process designed around arriving at a present-day fair price for a given stock greatly underrates the long-term merits of the business that underlies it. Because of the myriad reasons for the financial industry to be concentrated on what's happening today, the context of historical performance gets left behind. One share of Coca-Cola purchased at its IPO in 1919 for $40 was worth $6.7 million eighty years later (with dividends reinvested).

If we grant that finding companies like Coca-Cola is a challenge, will you grant that if you can find them, worrying about their P/E ratio today, or their projected cash flows over the next five years, or the images on their stock graph, is worrying about something that more often than not will end up being inconsequential? Given the performance of just Coca-Cola (and there are other examples), at what point over the last eight decades would it have been smart to stress out about the stock's immediate fair price? We submit to you then, dear Fool, that valuation isn't half so important as quality and the durability of the business model.

In fact, we'll go so far as to say that the quality of the company is at least a degree of magnitude more important than the immediate value of its stock price. We've dubbed this principle *QuaVa*. (It sounds a bit like "guava," as in the guava juice we will sip together in the British Virgin Islands a couple of decades down the line as our investments play out and bear the juicy fruit.) "QuaVa" stands for our belief that QUAlity comes before VAluation. This isn't to say that we'll shield our eyes from the stock price. Nor is it to say that we don't attend to the intermediate-term performance of a stock. Nope, we'll confess to doing both. We will say, however, that in our investment portfolio, we'll be concentrating our work on *the strength of the businesses that we own* and searching for clues about their viability over the next ten years.

Certainly, this runs contrary to much of what we see on financial television and read in the papers. We expect to be in the minority with this one. And by largely ignoring the stock price and concentrating instead on the business and its performance in its industry, we'll make some *timing* mistakes as investors. We'll buy a stock at 40 times earnings that six months later could be had for 25 times earnings after a strong quarterly earnings performance but a broad-market decline of 20 percent. Darn! Other times we'll get lucky, buying a stock for 25 times earnings that quickly zooms to 40 times earnings on a handful of new partnership agreements.

We do think, though, that in ten years and twenty, the single best way to grow your savings is to become a part owner of the very best businesses you can, with management committed to enduring growth for their shareholders. If you choose right, that growth will compound (multiply manifold) in your portfolio for a long, long time. This has been the case for outfits like Hershey, Microsoft, IBM, General Electric, Sears, Wal-Mart, and Disney. The twentieth century in America has provided enormous long-term opportunity for public corporations and their shareholders. We expect the same in the twenty-first century. And for that reason, we're going out in search of long-term quality, not inexpensive pricing in the short term.

The old saw of "Buy low, sell high" has too many people concentrated on the *when* of investing. Most of us should not be focused on the *when* but on the *what*. This too runs against conventional wisdom. For the highest-quality businesses are the best performers over time, but also happen to appear "overvalued" by traditional valuation measures, all the way up. Microsoft has never looked "undervalued," and yet there was no better stock to have held through from the mid-eighties.

Speaking of Microsoft . . .

·17·

Rule Makers

* * * * *

*He was never so highly esteemed as when every one saw
that he was the sole master of his forces.*
—*Niccolò Machiavelli*

Rule Maker investing makes a good starting point for new investors, since it is focused on big companies—*huge* companies—
that rule their industries. Viewed from the Rule Maker's perspective, all
small companies are constantly in danger of blowing up and dropping
to zero. As established behemoths, Rule Makers are in little danger of
going belly-up anytime soon. In fact, they have by definition realized
spectacular gains in the past through excellent business performance.
In this chapter we'll offer you a list of attributes that Rule Makers share.

Please note that these guidelines are loosely drawn. They're not hard-
and-fast rules. Very few companies will satisfy everyone, and the few
that do may be unsuitable for other reasons. For instance, a great-looking
clothing company may have been run by an executive team that was
just thrown in jail for illegal accounting—we're not about to invest
there. Or contrarily, a health care company may satisfy only half of our
criteria now, but for other reasons we believe that the business is
headed into increased profitability and a great future. Another example: Though we, as investors, love to see a company with a treasure
chest of savings and no long-term debt, there are plenty of companies
"heading that way." Companies that, after taking on some debt a few
years back (when, say, they acquired a profitable competitor) have re-
lentlessly been paying down those loans ever since. The direction of a

business is as important as—often more important than—its present location.

The Rule Maker criteria rest on the premise that understanding a company's business—both its location and its direction—is essential to successful investing. The following eleven guidelines aim to help you synthesize the essential elements of a company's business model. In addition, the criteria serve as prerequisites for a company's earning the esteemed title of Rule Maker. Indeed, these criteria set a very high bar. Only the best of the best are able to clear it. Again, rarely will a company ace all of the criteria, but the best Rule Makers fulfill most of them.

Finally, Rule Maker analysis is both qualitative and quantitative in nature. The first five criteria focus on qualitative aspects of a company's business. The second six are numerical metrics based on the company's financials. Together, the eleven guidelines serve as the basic measures of excellence for evaluating Rule Makers.

So, without further ado, here are the Rule Maker essentials:

1. Dominant brand
2. Repeat-purchase business
3. Convenience
4. Expanding possibilities
5. Your familiarity and interest
6. Sales growth of at least 10 percent year over year
7. Gross margins of at least 50 percent
8. Net profit margins of at least 10 percent
9. Cash no less than 1.5 times total debt
10. Foolish Flow Ratio below 1.25
11. Cash King Margin of at least 10 percent

You'll notice some of the RM criteria are very similar to benchmarks we outlined in our previous book and even some of the tools used to hunt for growth stocks in the last chapter.

1. Dominant Brand

True Rule Makers are looking to establish a direct connection with billions of consumer minds, day in and day out. They'd like to draw a clear distinction between their product and the generic, competing brand. For example, when you ask for a hanky during allergy season, there's a good chance you'll call for a Kleenex. And when you head out to buy a pair of jeans next month, you might tell a friend, "I'm going to buy some Levi's."

When a product achieves that instant recognition, that consumer habit, it is Foolishly said to have *mind share.* It has burrowed a small home into your cerebellum. And when this happens en masse—when you, your neighbors, your colleagues, and your enemies all say, "Haaa-choooo! Ugh. Eeew! Do you have a Kleenex, Joe?"—you have an increasingly defensible business. Having one product with mind share, or better yet, several, is the first sign of a Rule Maker business.

2. Repeat-Purchase Business

We love these businesses because every time a sale is made, the customer is reminded once again of the value of the company's product. The more often this free advertising occurs, the better. A product that is used often but purchased infrequently, such as software or an automobile, benefits from frequent (and hopefully positive) customer contact. However, future income is more predictable when the product or service is actually repurchased often.

Not surprisingly, the more people who know and appreciate the product, the better chance the company's stock will reward shareholders—because in business, it's much harder to reverse the purchasing behavior of millions (or billions) of consumers than it is to reverse the purchasing behavior of a few large, wealthy buyers. If, for instance, one of the five corporate buyers of your $10 million video technology takes its business elsewhere . . . you just lost 20 percent of your business! Ouch. Much better is a mass market base that doesn't shift and that doesn't have an ability to shake the foundation of your business in an instant.

Please note that this should not be interpreted to mean that software or technology companies can't be Rule Makers. On the contrary, Microsoft and Intel, for example, are Rule Makers. Their high gross and profit margins make it easy to overlook any disadvantage that comes from the relatively infrequent purchase of their products, especially since most buyers of their products use them almost daily.

3. Convenience

To establish Rule Maker authority, a business must position its products as the most accessible and convenient in its industry. History shows that in virtually every consumer sector, there are few ways to underrate the value of being the leader in convenience for customers. Whether it's buying midlevel shelf space in a supermarket, placing the gas station fifty yards closer to the exit ramp, delivering books right to the doorstep, selling coffee on the corner, or preloading software on a computer, convenience for the customer is crucial to a company's long-term success.

To be sure, rating a company's convenience is a subjective endeavor and relies on your ability to make a judgment call, comparing a company to its lead competitors. Try to determine if a given company provides the most accessible products or services in its industry. The gold star goes only to companies with best-of-class convenience.

4. Expanding Possibilities

Even more important than the past is the future. We're looking for companies with a direction that's even sweeter than its present location. Sure, historical performance leads us to some great companies, but it doesn't correlate perfectly with future results. Instead, we need to think seriously about a company's future prospects. Is the world going to be buying Pokémon in 2010? Does Coca-Cola's brand name have staying power? Are video rental stores going out of business?

Now, the most common mistake an investor can make (financial reporters are particularly prone to this) is to be pessimistic about everything. Gloom-and-doomers can find potential calamity in the cards for any business. You can imagine them taking the following positions:

- With Coca-Cola, caffeine will be their eventual undoing.
- Microsoft? When the Justice Department breaks up that monopoly, it'll fall apart.
- The Gap . . . they're in a fad business. They can't possibly have staying power.

We're not saying that making these determinations is easy or that you shouldn't be skeptical. You'll want to probe your own habits, your own thoughts, read through the company's statements, and ask questions on our discussion boards to decide if the business you're studying has staying power. And because this one isn't quantifiable, you'll want to return to it again and again. When in doubt, try asking yourself the following questions:

- Do my friends know about and use the company's products?
- Is worldwide expansion believable for their stuff?

5. Your Familiarity and Interest

On the face of it, the last of our qualitative criteria for finding Rule Makers seems absurd. How does your interest and familiarity with a corporation improve its chances of excelling? It doesn't, really. This requirement, rather than being applied to public companies, is applied to you, the investor. Without an understanding of what your businesses really do, you open yourself up to subpar returns. The likelihood that you'll understand whether the bumps and bruises along the way are minor nicks or life-threatening injuries for your company is very high if you can understand and follow its progress.

Thus, this criterion of the Rule Maker is that you find it easy to follow the operational direction of the business. It proposes that you'll dramatically improve your chances of scoring above-average investment returns if you weed out the unfamiliar and concentrate on companies whose products, marketing approach, management, and reputation with customers you'll enjoy following. Whether it's dedicated to the business of NASCAR racing, selling sandwiches, or manufacturing personal computers, a company will more likely serve you well if you know it well.

For the next six criteria, we'll turn to the quantitative side of business analysis. Ahh, the numbers . . . something to hold on to . . . something to tap into your calculator or spreadsheet! Or perhaps numbers make you shudder . . . don't worry, though. Remember: FIFTH-GRADE MATH! And we explain the math step by step in our book *The Motley Fool's Rule Breakers, Rule Makers* and online at Fool.com in our Investment Strategies, Rule Maker area.

6. Sales Growth of at Least 10 Percent Year over Year

Sales growth is the most fundamental indication of an expanding business. We're looking for companies that are growing sales (a.k.a. revenue) by at least 10 percent per year. This metric is easy to calculate. Using a company's income statement (available online, or by calling the company), simply divide the current year's sales by the previous year's sales and subtract one.

7. Gross Margins of at Least 50 Percent

Strong sales growth is dandy, but only if each dollar of sales is profitable. Rule Makers will rarely make a long-term investment in companies that aren't profitable. Riskier investments in smaller, unprofitable companies can make sense. But since Rule Makers focus on mature, consumer-brand behemoths, we want to see substantial profits already in place. So, continuing with the income statement, let's look at gross margins.

Gross margins show what money is left from revenue after the cost of the goods sold is subtracted. We want to see gross margins poking up above the very lofty perch of 50 percent. In other words, we'd like the company's cost of making its product or providing its service to be no more than half the price of what it sells at.

To calculate gross margins (again, from the income statement in company reports), divide gross profits by sales. We're looking for that number to be above 50 percent.

8. Net Profit Margins of at Least 10 Percent

It's nice to know that a company can sell its products for double the cost of producing them, but that'd be of little positive consequence if the promotion and overhead expenses associated with that product ended up wiping out the profits. We want the company to still earn good money, even if they pay out $1 million for that advertisement on the Super Bowl. And we don't want the government's 35 percent tax bite to whittle the bottom line into nothingness.

Therefore, our next objective is that net profit margins be at least 7 percent. The calculation is net income (after all expenses, including taxes, marketing and administrative expenses, and so forth) divided by sales. So, simply divide the company's net earnings by its total sales to figure the net profit margin.

9. Cash No Less Than 1.5 Times Total Debt

We say it of your personal finances, and we'll say it of Rule Maker companies. We'd prefer the financial statements to show little or no debt. Who wants to own a business that announces phenomenal earnings today only because they borrowed heavily from tomorrow? If we want to invest in a company that's going to thrive for ten years or more, we don't want short-term profits at the expense of long-term survival and success. Nay, dear Fool . . . we'd prefer to find companies that grow their business *out of profits from operations* and, thus, don't have substantial interest payments to make to the Man in the years ahead.

Because most companies will and must borrow money at some point, we don't want to cross off our list all businesses with some debt on their balance sheet. Therefore, we require that a company's cash be at least 1.5 times greater than their total debt (including both long-term and short-term debt). A moderate amount of debt doesn't particularly worry us. But if and when bad things do occur, when something goes bump in the night, it's essential that the company have ample and immediate cash resources to deal with the problem. We want them to get their business back on track quickly, earning moola for shareholders. And make no mistake about it, over the course of a decade or two, or three, bad things will happen to every company, even the greatest ones. Do you remember New Coke? How about Microsoft's MSN Online, Version 1? And what about McDonald's infamous McDLT? Or who remembers their McLean sandwich?

Things can and will go wrong. We want companies with the cash to buy themselves out of trouble when it comes knocking on the door. We want businesses with cash that amounts to 150 percent of (or 1.5 times) their total debt.

10. Foolish Flow Ratio Below 1.25

Next up, we want to see efficient use of that cash. In the day-to-day management of a company's operation, money is going to rush through the front door from sales, and it's going to fly out the window and the back door from expenses. Businesses survive on cash. That's their oxygen. Without dollars coming in, they can't pay for employees, for equipment, for insurance, for holiday parties, for new technology, for anything. So, how a business manages the dollars that flow through its daily operations is of critical importance.

We want our companies to bring money in quickly, but to pay it out slowly. More cash coming in today, less cash going out today.

But, you ask, "How can we possibly measure that?" Well, with a little something we call the Foolish Flow Ratio. The Foolish Flow enables you to cut through accounting shenanigans and artfully constructed income statements to get a clear snapshot of how a company is managing its cash.

The simple calculation is:

$$\frac{\text{current assets } \textit{minus} \text{ cash}}{\text{current liabilities } \textit{minus} \text{ short-term debt}}$$

Cash means cash and equivalents, marketable securities, and short-term investments (as found on the company balance sheet). *Short-term debt* means notes payable and the current portion of long-term debt (also from the company's balance sheet).

Guidelines for the numbers? We accept Flow Ratios that run lower than 1.25, ideally below 1. If they get below 1, that means the business is able to delay more payments than it's carrying in costs of inventory and unpaid bills. In this group below 1, you'll find companies like Microsoft, Yahoo!, and Intel—companies in such strong position that they have leverage over their partners, including those that supply them with raw materials or services and those that help them distribute stuff to the end consumer.

The Flow Ratio is one key measure of quality for Rule Makers. Again, we want companies that have a Flow Ratio less than 1.25, and ideally less than 1.

11. Cash King Margin of at Least 10 Percent

The Cash King Margin follows in the footsteps of the Flow Ratio by revealing important truths about the cash dynamics of a business without unnecessary complexity. The Cash King Margin is the equivalent of the standard net profit margin, except that it measures profits by using the cash flow statement instead of the income statement. What's the difference, you say? Everything in the world.

You'll recall that the income statement measures earnings, whereas the cash flow statement measures cash. We prefer the latter. Here's why: Accountants have been known to massage the income statement in order to produce "earnings." The income statement includes a lot of stuff that can get between sales and net income, and a lot of those items don't have much to do with a company's cash profitability. In contrast, the cash flow statement reveals the unmitigated truth of what's going on inside the business. While standard net margins are important, what hits the bank account at the end of the day—*cash,* as measured by the cash flow statement—is a lot more real from an economic standpoint. The Cash King Margin lets us shove all that income statement stuff aside and see what really happens to the money that the company is bringing in via sales.

Here's how the Cash King Margin is calculated:

$$\frac{\text{operating cash flow } \textit{minus} \text{ capital expenditures}}{\text{sales}}$$

To calculate the Cash King Margin, you need only two line items taken directly from a company's cash flow statement: operating cash flow and capital expenditures. With only a little practice, your eyes will soon clue in directly on these two important numbers, and all the other numbers will fade to the background.

Supersize the Company!

Finally, it will probably come as no surprise that Rule Makers tend to be enormous in size. This is not so much a criterion as a mere statement of fact. We tend not to look for Rule Maker companies with anything less than $1 billion in annual sales. And we look for companies with a total value, or market capitalization, of at least $5 billion. Most Rule Makers have sales figures and market caps substantially larger than $1 billion and $5 billion, respectively. But those are good baseline numbers.

Let's just repeat the eleven criteria for those still taking notes (very diligent of you):

1. Dominant brand
2. Repeat-purchase business
3. Convenience
4. Expanding possibilities
5. Your familiarity and interest
6. Sales growth of at least 10 percent year over year
7. Gross margins of at least 50 percent
8. Net profit margins of at least 10 percent
9. Cash no less than 1.5 times total debt
10. Foolish Flow Ratio below 1.25
11. Cash King Margin of at least 10 percent

By the way, we have two free Rule Maker spreadsheets at rule-maker.Fool.com that will help you evaluate companies using these criteria.

Rule Breakers

* * * * *

That which does not kill us makes us stronger.
—*Friedrich Nietzsche*

On August 4, 1994, an obscure, real-money public stock portfolio opened up shop and announced its intention to purchase shares of America Online. With no one in particular taking notice, we bought America Online at a now split-adjusted price of 46 cents a share. Less than six years later, the stock traded at $60: Our $1,848 then had appreciated to $241,080—a gain of 12,900 percent.

We bought Amazon.com in the summer of 1997 at a split-adjusted $3.19 a share. That was several months after its strong initial public offering (IPO), and *Money* magazine had in fact recently published an article about how overvalued the stock was. Market pundits too numerous to name fervently agreed. Three years later, Amazon.com stood at $38, so that our $8,408 had turned into $100,158—a gain of 1,091 percent.

These companies were classic Rule Breakers. They both possessed the six attributes shared by all revolutionary capitalistic enterprises that will lead to the greatest returns the stock market has to offer. AOL and Amazon.com are only some of the more recent companies continuing a storied tradition of Rule Breakers that have created astounding amounts of shareholder value throughout history: Coca-Cola, Wal-Mart, Microsoft, Cisco, and Starbucks. The best stocks of the past century began as flat-out Rule Breakers.

But oh, by the way . . .

On December 23, 1994, we bought Sonic Solutions at $14.25 per share. It was the last trading day before Christmas, the ticker symbol was SNIC, and one of our Fool community members pointed out to us that SNIC read like "St. Nick." Less than a year later, we sold St. Nick for $6.38, losing a full 56.5 percent. Merry Christmas in our face!

You think that's bad? Maybe you were a customer of Fool.com when we purchased ATC Communications for the Rule Breaker Portfolio? It was the autumn of '96, the stock was riding high with its telecom services peers, and we got the shares for $22.88. Six months later, having missed the earnings estimates put out by Wall Street analysts, ATC had dropped to (yikes) $5. Believing the company to be undervalued, we held on. (Fortunately, we did not add to the position—Fools rarely add to losers.) We eventually liquidated what little value was left below $4 a share in October 1997.

First, *any investor who takes any real risk investing in common stocks will have some spectacular losers,* and no true Rule Breaker investor should shy away from this reality. This style of investing is not for the faint of heart.

And second—the good news—*the money that you make on your winners if you are patient should dramatically surpass what is lost on your losers.* Compare the very best investment we've ever made (AOL, gaining $239,693) with the very worst investment we've ever made (ATC Communications, losing $12,000), and the overall result of a $227,693 gain bears eloquent testimony to this critical but simple point.

With its large risks and rewards in mind, let's break down the six attributes we look for in every Rule Breaker investment:

- Top dog and the first mover in an important, emerging industry
- Sustainable advantage gained through business momentum, patent protection, visionary leadership, or inept competitors
- Strong past price appreciation equivalent to a relative-strength performance of 90 or greater
- Good management and smart backing
- The stronger the consumer appeal, the better: to attract, to habituate, to profit, and to protect
- Grossly overvalued, according to at least one significant constituent of the financial media

Top Dog and the First Mover
in an Important, Emerging Industry

We buy only top dogs and first movers. Not the third player among Internet search engines. Not the second-best-tasting soda. And not the fourth tier of the hottest industry *du jour*.

How do you determine who's the top? Here are four ways:

1. *Look at the company's market cap*. The top dog is obviously going to be the company with the biggest market cap in its space. But hey, aren't we looking for smaller companies *before* they've been discovered by everyone and his uncle Tony? So why are we looking for big market caps? Well, it's all relative. Big market caps in young Rule Breaking industries generally aren't so big compared to more mature industries.

2. *Look at the company's sales and earnings*. Starbucks is a Rule Breaker that has significant sales and earnings; not only is it the top dog in coffee, but we can't identify any single company that is effectively playing Reebok to its Nike. Amgen is also a top dog with the biggest sales and earnings in its biotech field. How do you quickly look up sales and earnings for companies you're researching? Go to the Quotes & Data section at Fool.com. Once there, type the ticker symbol of the company you're considering into the Data field, and select the GO button under "Financials." There you'll find trailing twelve-month info about sales and earnings. And if you don't know the company's ticker symbol, look it up—also available on that page. Realize, however, that many young Rule Breakers (and AOL was one of them) will not have positive earnings for several years. This is often the case, and when it is, the size of sales is your guide.

3. *Read industry rags*. Every meaningful technology or business today has a trade publication that covers it. These publications are, in our experience, several times more knowledgeable and informative about their subjects than the comparably scanty coverage their industry will get in personal finance and investing magazines. If you know of some emerging technology that you want to learn a lot more about, particularly to divine just who exactly is the first mover with it, locate the trade magazine. The *EE Times* covers engineering and semiconductors, for instance, and you can read it at http://www.eet.com. If you don't know the trade title, ask around among your fellow Fools. They're pretty much all online now.

4. *Use The Motley Fool discussion boards.* Our discussion boards have individual conversations on every company of any significant degree of public interest. That would include all possible top dogs. When you go to the boards at http://boards.Fool.com just type in the stock's ticker symbol or company name! Or if you're searching for companies to study and don't know where to start, click to visit the most active discussion boards on the site. Buzz in the form of active discussion at the Fool often uncovers Rule Breakers. Discussion boards enable us to work together to figure out lots of stuff about the financial world, not the least of which is finding out who exactly is a top dog out there.

By the way, in important, emerging industries the phrases "top dog" and "first mover" are virtually synonymous. The company that moves first in a big way to dominate an upstart industry does indeed, in the vast majority of cases, wind up the top dog.

Sustainable Advantage Gained Through Business Momentum, Patent Protection, Visionary Leadership, or Inept Competitors

The second attribute we must consider is that of the *sustainable advantage,* of at least two to three years' duration, preferably far longer. You might know the technology, or the people managing the business, or the industry in which the business is springing up. But until you know the *business of the business,* the business itself, you really don't know much at all.

"How do they make money? How do they make more money than that?" And (critically), one step further, "How will the business protect that money?"

Okay, given that it is the business model that will create sustainable advantages, we should anatomize the business model itself. It can be broken down into four attributes, a way of thinking borrowed from the outstanding book *The Profit Zone* by Adrian J. Slywotzsky (recommended to all Foolish readers):

1. *Customer selection:* Who is the customer?
2. *Value capture:* How does the business turn those customers into profits?
3. *Strategic control:* How can the business protect those profits?
4. *Scope:* How much bigger, and in what ways, can the business grow?

As we look at Rule Breakers to espy which have a two-to-three-year *sustainable advantage,* we are focused on that third component of company biz models: *strategic control.* How might a company protect its profit streams from competitors?

Here's an answer for one Rule Breaker, eBay (Nasdaq: EBAY): On an online auction site, a buyer will look for wherever the most sellers are. A seller will want to find the most buyers. They therefore court each other. And thus, the site that maximizes its customer base will have a possibly unbeatable sustainable advantage.

Another: Pharmaceutical or biotech companies can patent drugs. Once discovered, a drug (and its profit stream) can be protected for twenty years.

As you evaluate potential Rule Breakers, you should be insistent on finding those with effective strategic controls. If a possible Rule Breaker does not have effective controls, the only sustainable advantage we can foresee would be huge business growth—sheer, flat-out momentum as you can see your Rule Breaker upstart growing over the next two to three years much faster and bigger than any competitor. That would be a sustainable advantage too, but is about as tenuous as we can let it get.

To understand business, you have to understand business models. Built into any good business model should be one or more clear-cut methods by which a company can protect its profit streams. These are known as *strategic controls* and are virtually synonymous with the third attribute of the Rule Breaker: a two- to three-year sustainable advantage.

Strong Past Price Appreciation Equivalent to a Relative-Strength Performance of 90 or Greater

We discussed this criterion in Chapter 13. A student of business and the public markets will note a tendency that, as we have written previously, derives from physics. In stock market terms, it reads this way: The rich get richer, and the winners keep on winning. It seems to us that the safest bet—we must repeat—the *safest bet* about a well-managed company and an outperforming stock is that both the company and the stock will, all other things remaining equal, *continue* to be well managed and outperform.

High relative strength can be an *excellent* indicator, not just of past pedigree but of future success! A high relative strength (as found in *Investor's Business Daily*) indicates that the company is doing some things really right. Additionally, and as important, it shows that the market is taking notice.

Good Management and Smart Backing

Another attribute of the Rule Breakers is that they have strong, visionary leadership. Great people make a great company. To do this, you need to get personal—in two ways. First, you need to concern yourself, to think a lot, about the *people* who are managing the business, because we ultimately invest in people when we lay our money down.

Thanks to the Internet today, you have an unprecedented ability to check up on the people of your business. For any Rule Breaker prospect, it's a hot enough stock that you'll have any number of media interviews with the movers and shakers in the company. Read them. Actively draw conclusions about the people you're reading about. Check their backgrounds in the company's prospectuses and 10-K. Where'd they go to school? What are their outside interests? Do they serve on boards of other good companies? Also, see how much each owns of the stock you're looking at. That can be telling, too.

We said above that you should get personal in two ways. Here's the second: You'll also get personal by realizing that one investor's list of Rule Breakers will inevitably differ from another's, for a very good reason. They're different people. Thus, get personal about your own list of Rule Breaker prospects. Whatever we Fools may invest in as Rule Breakers should emphatically not be the same as your list . . . unless you share almost all of our traits . . . say, you're our evil third brother who was carried off by vultures at birth. (Do not bother us, Mordred.)

The Stronger the Consumer Appeal, the Better: To Attract, to Habituate, to Profit, and to Protect

The fifth attribute of a Rule Breaker is that it is developing a *strong brand*. What is a brand? The simplest explanation is *a well-known name and logo*. For many Rule Breakers, however, this will be a goal and not yet a reality, so that's why we write "developing." If ten years ago you or we could have known and invested in today's top hundred brands in the world, we would indeed be very rich. That's because long-term stock market value correlates very highly with brand recognition. The two biggest brands in the world, Coca-Cola and Microsoft, happen to be one of the top-performing stocks of the twentieth century and *the* top-performing stock of the past fifteen years, respectively.

Interestingly enough, both America Online and Amazon.com appear on a list of top brands today, even though both have been public companies for less than a decade. These two have, not surprisingly, scored gigantic wins for their investors.

As you look over your own list of Rule Breaker prospects, ask yourself which have the chance one day to be a household name. Because *those* are the ones most likely to provide dependable, market-crushing returns. All other things remaining equal, the businesses known by tens of millions of people will be more stable and more powerful than those known by hundreds of thousands will. This is largely the same point drawn by Rule Makers about broad-based repeat-purchase businesses providing their own stability.

Since it is the rare Rule Breaker that can make any serious early run up the global best-known-brand lists, we are left with trying to figure out what our prospect's brand might *one day* be. We think "a simple, memorable, extremely positively portrayed name backed by a company that is focused on making that name ubiquitous and making that name good" is a pretty good summary of what we look for. If that's not enough for you, consider an alternate opinion. Harry Beckwith, in his wonderful book *Selling the Invisible,* says that a brand is a promise that a company makes to its customers, and fulfills every day. That sense of focus on the customer and consistent dependability is another way to evaluate your company's brand.

"The stronger the consumer brand, the better," is the way we phrase this attribute in our book *The Motley Fool's Rule Breakers, Rule Makers*. We're getting across that brand really matters, as we know how well it correlates with long-term returns. At the same time, we use intentionally loosey-goosey language because one must evaluate brand for different businesses in different ways. It matters more for an Internet destination than it does for a biotech company, for example. But in the end, whether you're Coke selling to consumers or Cisco selling to businesses, you want your company's name known the world over.

Grossly Overvalued, According to at Least One Significant Constituent of the Financial Media

Are you ready for our final Rule Breaker attribute? It is that a Rule Breaker must have been called *overvalued* at some point within the past few months by a significant constituent of the financial media.

Not undervalued. You want it to be *overvalued*. At least, you want everyone thinking that way. Here's why. If everyone already loves your Rule Breaker, everyone already owns it. Who's going to come along and buy it up? If, on the other hand, you've found the top dog and first mover of an important, emerging industry with a sustainable advantage, excellent past price appreciation, the best people you know driving the business toward it possibly becoming a household name, *and* numerous market commentators all telling everyone it's overvalued, we submit the odds are on the *company's* and its *investors'* side. Further, the commentators have scared large numbers of people out of the stock, which is exactly why our sixth attribute works. Because as the company executes, assuming it does so successfully, those many skeptics whose money was *out* of the stock, it will, one by one, convert to believers whose money moves *into* the stock. This can help create huge gains for patient investors in successful Rule Breakers.

A while back we had Kevin Kalkhoven, the former CEO of JDS Uniphase (Nasdaq: JDSU), on The Motley Fool Radio Show. His company (Uniphase, at the time) came public in the early nineties. Its IPO road show was sparsely attended because the Merrill Lynches of the world were all hyped up, as he tells it, on the coming IPO of Boston Chicken. Fiber optics and the Internet at light speed wasn't sufficiently interesting or believable, if the fleet of limos flocking to Boston Chicken's presentations was any sign. And sure enough, Uniphase came public at just a $30 million valuation. Seven years later, JDS Uniphase is (as of this writing) worth $100 billion (a 330-bagger). Boston Chicken is bankrupt.

Don't forget, though, that this is about commentators, not chicken or fiber optics. You now know the dynamic by which stocks make huge price gains. And you see why Wise commentators letting everyone know a new industry's crown jewel is "grossly overvalued" is the final attribute. It is the final buy signal that we look for!

Let's run through the Rule Breaker checklist once again:

- Top dog and the first mover in an important, emerging industry
- Sustainable advantage gained through business momentum, patent protection, visionary leadership, or inept competitors
- Strong past price appreciation equivalent to a relative-strength performance of 90 or greater
- Good management and smart backing
- The stronger the consumer appeal, the better: to attract, to habituate, to profit, and to protect
- Grossly overvalued, according to at least one significant constituent of the financial media

Some Things to Keep in Mind

In the short term, the investing community can hammer any individual stock, Maker and Breaker alike. Expect the stock price of even the company you most believe in to get cut in half at some point. Oftentimes, the sell-off will be unwarranted; Mr. Market is just playing games with your short-term emotions.

For this reason, we suggest that you largely ignore the short-term wanderings of stock prices and focus on the much harder and yet more rewarding task of trying to accurately project a company's future based on its present financial standing, its managerial strengths, and the scope of its opportunities in the years ahead. Some of these businesses will prove gigantic winners over the next century, just as Hershey's, Johnson & Johnson, and Coca-Cola have rung up bewilderingly great returns for their shareholders over the past eight decades. Others will just match the overall market's average returns. Still others will disappoint. Compaq Computer (NYSE: CPQ) surrendered its enormous lead in the personal computer industry to Dell in the late 1990s. IBM stock (NYSE: IBM) passed almost twenty-five years between 1970 and 1995 without making a dime for shareholders. On par, though, if you select a bunch of great companies and hold them for a very long time, your portfolio should beat the market's average return.

In your search, dear Fool, you must ask yourself: Are this company's products likely to fulfill needs in the future even better than they did in the past and they do today? Does management have the vision and operational skill to continue its outstanding performance? And how much opportunity for growth around this planet (and hey, maybe other worlds someday) is there for this company? These are extremely difficult questions to answer. But to the best of your ability, you'll want to answer 'em. You may get a few wrong . . . but remember, one great company compounding market-beating growth for you over the next four decades will pay down your losses a hundred times over—and then some.

·19·

When to Sell

· · · · ·

[Exit, pursued by a bear.]
—*William Shakespeare*

I have no problem knowing when to buy a stock, but if I just knew when to sell, I'd be a great investor!"

That line expresses the single frustration felt by more investors than any other. If we all just knew when to sell. Heck, if we *all* knew *when* to sell, when to buy wouldn't matter! Ay, there's the rub. Because every time you sell, you're effectively predicting the future. You're effectively saying, "This stock will no longer do well (or well enough)." Foolishly, most of us don't invest under the presumption that we can predict the market; what the heck are we doing presuming to predict an individual stock?

Well, renowned investor and author Philip Fisher affords us some beginning insight when we read his take on the subject: "If the job has been correctly done when a common stock is purchased," Fisher wrote, "the time to sell it is—almost never."

This single sentence pretty much sums up our thoughts on selling. Our method of investing is focused on buying stock in the obviously great large-cap companies (Rule Makers and others), dynamic Rule Breaker companies, and small-cap growth prospects. And perhaps a smattering of other sorts of investments, as well. (See "Chapter 20: Mechanical Investing and the Foolish Four.") *But* (you knew a "but" was coming, didn't you?) we have a little confession to make—despite our best intentions, we're not perfect. Although we diligently research each stock, we purchase, we're bound to make mistakes. Over time, lots of 'em! And when we do, we will often eventually decide to sell the offending stock that we mistook for a good investment.

Deciding when to sell a holding is one of the most difficult aspects of investing. Our selling philosophy can be summed up as simply as (and let's put it in bold): **Sell when you find a better place for your money**. That pretty much covers it, but we want to explain our thinking in a bit more depth. The list of reasons we offer below is far from comprehensive, but instead focuses on what we believe to be the most important issues.

Consider at the start that the market doesn't know what you paid for your stock. It has no idea of your cost basis, in order for you to get back to even (if you're down). It doesn't know, likewise, that you just doubled your money.

No special voodoo sauce will cause your losers to return to even or, alternatively, cause your winners to come falling back to earth, to the price you paid. Don't fall into the "just get back to even" trap; neither allow yourself to start humming, "What goes up must come down."

We're going to explore five valid reasons for selling, broken down between two categories: company fundamentals and portfolio management. We'll finish up with a few closing thoughts on a great way to avoid selling altogether—charitable donations.

Before jumping into the first three valid reasons for selling, let's briefly touch on one reason that you'll notice is conspicuously missing from our list—valuation. Consistent with what we've written before (although many people misunderstand our thinking here, or oversimplify it), we don't really worry all that much about whether a stock is overpriced. In the case of the crème de la crème that qualify as Makers and Breakers, valuation is not a good reason to sell. If you're not convinced, you might want to go back and review "Chapter 16, Quality Versus Valuation," which expounds our belief that business quality is an order of magnitude more important than valuation. Because of their high and sustainable profitability, Rule Makers typically have—and indeed deserve—a premium valuation. Rule Breakers, on the other hand, aren't always profitable companies at the time of our purchase. Some people believe any unprofitable company trading at any stock price is "overvalued." For these reasons, in neither case do we get carried away with timing the market and selling because our stock is "overvalued."

With that disclaimer out of the way, let's jump into this enjoyable topic of selling.

Reasons to Sell Based on
Company Fundamentals

Our initial hope when we buy any stock is that we won't have to sell it for decades, if possible—not until we personally need or want the money for something else. We therefore in spirit agree with Warren Buffett and Philip Fisher that the ideal holding period is forever. Nevertheless, we consider the following three conditions as sufficient, sometimes quite necessary, reasons to sell.

1. Untrustworthy Management
We will not tolerate deceit from management. Less-than-honest management can rear its ugly head in many forms, including a criminal history, bad accounting, and hype-and-bail executives.

Centennial Technologies (OTC: CENLD) demonstrates the danger of a key executive with a spotty legal history. In 1996, the company was a real high flier. Then it came to light that the head of the company had committed several illegal acts, including (as we recall) selling empty boxes of product. This criminal activity, once removed from the company's results, caused actual results to look a good deal worse than had been reported. The end result was that the company's stock price fell through the floor and the stock was delisted from the Nasdaq. This example is a bit extreme; most companies trading on our public markets would and have never engaged in anything like this activity. Even so, this story teaches a good lesson because, interestingly enough, this problem could have been foreseen. The CEO had a history of legal troubles that came to light before anyone learned of the real problems at Centennial. By booting this stock upon learning of the CEO's history, shareholders could have avoided some major losses.

Bad accounting is another telltale sign of suspect management. Here's where we get to pick on a company like Oxford Health Plans (Nasdaq: OXHP). On October 27, 1997, Oxford first announced difficulties and accounting irregularities. It sounded to our Motley Fool news team at the time as if these guys had no real idea about the performance of their business. The events in subsequent weeks only further unraveled any trust one might have still had in the company's management. For over a year, Oxford had been saying that everything was okay—even as other HMO businesses were announcing restructuring plans. Not Oxford. Oxford continued to paint its picture with broad, bright strokes. Then, *ka-blammo!* Check out that stock graph sometime.

Another warning sign of bad accounting is if you learn that the company's accountants are resigning because of some type of disagreement with management. This could occur during the course of a company's annual audit if, for example, a disagreement between the company's management and its CPAs develops over how a specific item should be treated for accounting purposes. Of course, if you should sell here, don't expect to be the proverbially "first one out." As soon as that news hits the wires, you can bet the company's stock will get chopped badly. Like any sell decision, you'll have to do a little bit of wait-and-see and ultimately make the choice yourself. We just want to provide context around the events that are most likely to cause you to consider selling.

Finally, there is the case of hype-and-bail executives who sell their stock ahead of horrible news—yet while leading up to that news, they paint a rosy picture for investors. K-Tel International's (Nasdaq: KTEL) management pulled off just this sort of scheme. In the spring of 1998, the company announced intentions to sell greatest-hits albums and videos over the Internet. Instantly, K-Tel shares boomed on the news and ran from $3 to $40 in a matter of weeks. While the stock was at its highs, company insiders flipped out 2.4 million shares—over 30 percent of the entire company—at prices of $30 to $35 per share. Checked this stock quote lately?

These are just a handful of the deceptive practices that might prompt us to sell a company. Untrustworthy management is incompatible with long-term company ownership. We take honesty so seriously at The Motley Fool that if you even sense an executive is talking out the side of her mouth on some TV interview, you should already be considering the possibility of launching your capital on a "flight to quality."

2. Deteriorating Financials

Even industry-leading Rule Makers are subject to the constant threat of declining demand and encroaching competition. One company's competitive advantage is another company's object of envy. Take Gap Inc. (NYSE: GPS), for instance. Every other casual clothing retailer sees the Gap's stunning success in marketing basic clothing items like khakis and blue jeans, while avoiding trendy fashion fads. If one of these competitors managed in every way possible successfully to emulate Gap's strategy, but at lower prices to consumers, Gap's business would certainly suffer.

Whether the threat is external competition or internal stagnation, for the most part we rely upon the financial statements to show any signs of business weakness, particularly with larger companies. (For smaller companies, more fragile beasts, reasons to sell might be included in a single press release or nightly news item.) Thus, we endorse checking up on the performance of Rule Makers, for instance, on at least an annual basis. A quarterly basis is even better. In conjunction with either the earnings press release or the release of the 10-Q, periodically you should evaluate the company against the basic criteria for which you first bought it (and any others that have popped up since). For example, if this was a growth company you bought into and sales growth just reported was anemic, ask yourself whether it is due to exogenous worldwide economic events or a competitor's better products. If gross and net margins are on the decline, determine whether the cause is a lower-margin product mix or pricing pressure from a competitor.

Also, if the company originally fell short of any of the minimum standards you've set, then you should make sure that it is improving its performance in these areas. If it still hasn't exceeded the minimum thresholds, you should make sure that you still believe its performance in these areas can be rationalized. Ask yourself if your original perceptions of the company, its performance, and its future prospects are on course.

Now, just because a company fails to pass one or even a few of your preset criteria, it doesn't necessarily mean the company should be booted. Criteria are only guidelines, not hard-and-fast rules. Like many a sports team, even the best companies have an occasional "rebuilding year." One good example is Intel (Nasdaq: INTC) in 1998. For a time, sales growth slowed and margins declined, but all the while, the company's 80 percent market share was intact. If a company falls short of some of our standards, we must understand the reasons why. Then we must determine whether it's bearable or not.

As you can see, there's no simple formula for determining whether or not to sell. Only a sober assessment of the company's position relative to its competitors and the economy as a whole will lead to a correct conclusion. If the conclusion of your analysis is that a company's business has—like the octogenarian in the famous TV ad—"fallen and I can't get up," then it's time to move on. This sort of collapse will usually be pretty well represented on the balance sheet, or soon documented on next quarter's income statement. Because we focus so intently on the financial statements, we sometimes do get out of a permanent dog before its howls grow maddeningly loud.

Is this to say that we'll sell any of our stocks that have fallen more than, say, 40 percent in value? *Nyet*. Again, one of the greatest investments of the twentieth century, Coca-Cola (NYSE: KO), fell 67 percent in value in the 1970s. If we believe in the business, we'll hold through that sort of freefall. But if, qualitatively, we think the business model is dead meat and, quantitatively, that death shows up on the balance sheet, we'll look to sell.

3. Mergers, Acquisitions, and Spin-offs

When a company is involved in a major merger or acquisition, it's necessary to reevaluate the combined company. If the new entity doesn't offer the same package of qualitative and quantitative attributes as the stock you'd originally bought, a sell may be in order. The same goes if you own stock in a company that decides to spin off one or more of its business units. When AT&T (NYSE: T) spun off Lucent (NYSE: LU) and NCR (NYSE: NCR) in 1996, you might have decided to keep Lucent and sell NCR just as we did in the Rule Breaker Portfolio. (We later sold Lucent, and as of this midyear-2000 writing, none too soon!)

Reasons to Sell Based on Portfolio Management

Even if all your companies are dominating their markets, warding off competitors, and putting out sparkling financial statements, there are still two more reasons you might conceivably sell one of your companies.

4. A Much Better Place to Invest Your Money

There may be times when you discover a great new investment candidate, a star shot swooping over the left horizon, but don't have any additional money to invest. How distressing! You've found a stock that you just *have* to buy—and you even like the taste of their TastiScrolls—and now you must sell in order to buy!

You take a quick look at your portfolio. You see two stocks: one that has doubled since you bought it and a stock that has been halved. Which do you sell?

You think it's the one that's doubled?

You think it's the one that's halved?

How about the actual correct answer: *Not enough information*?

You see, our answer to that question is simply: whichever holds *less* potential over the next twelve to thirty-six months. Note that we're talking about the future. The future is all that matters! It doesn't matter to us that one stock has already doubled and the other been mercilessly halved. Looking at the two holdings, where you bought them, and what they've done—this is all now a part of history. Fools look through the windshield, not the rearview mirror.

It helps to ask yourself a few questions, of course. In the situation above, ask yourself which of the two holdings has least fulfilled on its contract. Which is doing a worse job of living up to your rationale for purchasing? (It's not *always* the losing one . . . but it usually will be.) Keep in mind as well that if you sell a stock that has doubled, you'll be paying more in taxes. Sell a stock that has been halved and you may actually lighten this year's tax load. These things said, the decision about what to sell still comes down to jettisoning from your portfolio whatever has significantly less potential for *future* growth, all other things remaining equal.

Change gears, but same topic: Rule Breakers begin revolutions. At a certain point, successful revolutionaries must themselves try to rule. This becomes evident in the business world when one or more competitors arises, often mostly just copying the originator. Suddenly, what was once breaking rules now finds itself making rules, or at least trying. Can the onetime Rule Breaker fend off its imitators and ascend to the throne? As you already know, this is the metaphor of business that we use to view the world (in all its other complexities), the story of Rule Breakers and Rule Makers.

We prefer not to sell a Rule Breaker—a company that is still breaking the rules as we have seen them. And our dream is for the Breaker to become a Maker—another situation we generally won't sell out of. The vulnerable time for the Rule Breaker is that time *in between* these two states . . . when a company is what we therefore call a "Tweener." If they should be sold, Breakers will most often be sold during these uncertain times.

When has a company officially Tweened? When one or more competitors have duplicated its offerings (products, services, or both) in such a way that satisfies the average consumer. That is, when the average person cannot find enough specific distinguishing marks between the competitors' offerings to favor the Breaker over its imitator. This is what you're looking for to see if a company has been Tweened. Referring back to our brief summary of business model in the Rule Breakers chapter, the company's "strategic control"—the moat around its fair château—has been compromised. At this point, the Tweener has two directions to go: (1) It will win the game and beat back the competition and make the rules, or (2) It will be replicated, commoditized, and rendered much less relevant, typically with a corresponding lack of future potential for its stock.

So let's say it again: Your view of the future should dictate which stock you choose to sell. That, within the context of any other factors relevant to you as well, such as needing the money for some specific purpose or the implications of the sell for this year's capital gains taxes.

Okay. Let's work through an example that brings this all together. The facts and assumptions are as follows:

- Five years ago, you purchased 100 shares of Virtual Ball Bearings Inc. (ticker: WHY) at $40 per share, plus a $10 commission, for a total investment of $4,010.
- The company has grown at an average rate of 25 percent per year during that time and your stock is now worth $12,207.
- You think that Virtual BB will grow at a rate of only 15 percent per year over the next five years.
- You're excited about your new investment idea, Super Cool Rockets Corp. (ticker: DUDE), which you believe will grow at a 20 percent rate over the next five years, so you want to sell Virtual BB and buy Rockets.
- Super Cool Rockets is priced at $75 per share.
- Your commission to buy and sell stock is $10 per trade.

Let's work through the numbers:

- Your net before-tax proceeds from the sale of Virtual BB will be $12,197 ($12,207 sales price less $10 commission)—a gain of $8,187 ($12,197 less $4,010 cost basis).
- You will pay $1,637 of tax ($8,187 gain taxed at 20 percent) on this gain. This will leave you with $10,550 ($12,197 minus $1,637 minus $10) to invest in Super Cool Rockets stock.
- Since Super Cool Rockets is selling for $75 per share, you buy 140 shares for $10,500. This means that your investment in the manufacturer and marketer of extremely cool-looking missiles is approximately $1,700 less than the value of Virtual Ball Bearings at the time that you sold it.
- If they keep selling the heck out of those virtual bearings from company headquarters in Yonkers, New York, and maintain an annualized share growth rate of 15 percent per year over the next five years, your old investment would have been worth $24,553.
- If Super Cool grows 20 percent per year over the next five years ($75 per share to $186.63), your total investment will be worth $26,127. This is only 6 percent more than the Virtual BB investment would be worth. The value of your Super Cool investment will not become more than the value of your Virtual investment until sometime approximately four years from now.

If all your assumptions hold true, then it would make sense to sell Virtual Ball Bearings to buy Super Cool Rockets. However, if the Rocket Man grows only 18 percent per year, it will be worth $24,021 in five years. In that case, holding on to your shares of WHY would have been the better decision.

Are we being too scientific? Can one actually bank on such assumptions? Well, what this all really means is that you have to make some best- and worst-case assumptions about each stock when considering selling and reinvesting. Since predicting future investment returns will always be guesswork, the best guiding principle we can provide on this point is to make sure you've found a *much* better place to invest your money, if you're considering selling one stock to buy another.

5. Time to Rebalance Your Portfolio

It is not altogether impossible that one stock will substantially outperform all the others in your portfolio. In doing so, that one holding may grow to become a substantial portion of your invested assets. Whether you let your winner continue to run or sell a portion depends largely on your individual tolerance for risk.

On the one hand, your biggest winners are likely the best businesses within your portfolio. By letting winners run, your best businesses organically assume the dominant positions within your portfolio. This is the general approach we take to investing. We tend to let our winners run even when they become a substantial part of our portfolio. This lesson has been borne out of our own experience, and out of watching our dad's investing before us. And as we've pointed out elsewhere, Warren Buffett at various points has had more than one-third of all his billions of assets in a single stock: Coca-Cola. If we've found a great company and think it can grow over the course of at least another decade—perhaps even dominate—then we tend to allow our money to pile up in that stock.

The flip side of this scenario is that whenever a single holding represents a very large percentage (greater than 30 percent) of your portfolio, your portfolio will inevitably be more volatile. So what do you make of volatility? What do *you* make of volatility?

In considering whether to rebalance, keep in mind our previous analysis involving commissions, taxes, and expected returns.

Alternative to Selling: Charitable Donations

Having made it this far, you probably well understand why Philip Fisher and Warren Buffett prefer the joy of buying over the complexities of selling. One of the best ways to avoid selling, avoid the tax man, and make the world a better place is to donate shares as a charitable contribution.

Sharing our wealth in such a way as to add meaningful and sustainable value in the lives of others is not only deeply satisfying and rewarding for all concerned, but also a great way to move dollars out of your own control and into the hands of others, without ever selling or getting taxed. And yet many people don't realize the tax advantages of giving stock.

Say that you want to make a donation to your favorite charity, and figure that you'll sell $5,000 of stock to come up with the money. The stock that you want to sell was bought for $2,000 several years ago, so you'd have to pay $600 in capital gains ($3,000 times 20 percent) on the sale. This would leave you with only $4,400 to donate. The final result—you get a $4,400 tax deduction, the charitable organization gets $4,400, and the IRS gets $600.

If you decide instead to donate the stock directly, you get a tax deduction for the fair market value of the stock, and you don't have to pay any capital gains taxes on the transfer of the stock. If the charitable organization turns around and sells the stock, it doesn't have to pay any taxes on its sale. The final result is that you get a $5,000 tax deduction, the charitable organization gets $5,000 worth of stock, and the IRS gets nothing.

Personally, we like this method a lot better—don't you?

For more information about the logistics and tax advantages of donating stock, visit our Foolanthropy site at The Motley Fool via www.Fool.com/foolanthropy.

Your Own Situation

Obviously, we haven't covered every conceivable selling scenario. You may find yourself needing to sell some holdings just to buy that ski boat or vacation home you always wanted. Or maybe you'll need to cash out of some of your holdings to send Alice to one of those ivy-covered institutions. Countless personal reasons exist why you might sell a stock.

What we have tried to get across is that successful investors generally end up transacting less frequently. The greatest value is created through buying into a great company, being patient and allowing it to show its greatness over time, and then eventually cashing out when you have some better use for the money. Please note that this better use might be another stock or investment, or it might instead be the goal (college fund, retirement) of your investing in the first place. The Motley Fool firmly advocates "buy-to-hold" investing. This means that you put a lot of work in ahead of time to select a great company, with the intention, once you've bought, of holding it right up until the point when you finally want to put the money into play in your own life. But life ain't perfect, and for this reason we never blindly buy and hold. If the company we invested in because of its whizbang gadget never manages to climb out of red ink, we'll sell. You should, too. It didn't work out. Stuff happens.

But when you do find a good or even great company, the longer you hold it, the longer you allow it to crush the market for you . . . *and* the longer Uncle Sam will give you an interest-free loan on your tax obligation. By avoiding the monetary costs of churning your account, you'll be substantially more likely to beat the market. And less time trading and researching new investments means more time for hiking, barbecues, or (noble, noble endeavor) just taking time out to read a great book.

Mechanical Investing
and the Foolish Four

* * * * * *

The scientific method is nothing but the normal working
of the human mind. That is to say, when the mind is
working; that is to say further, when it is engaged in
correcting its mistakes.
—*Thomas Henry Huxley*

We love digging into companies and evaluating their management and considering the implications of various financing deals. We enjoy calculating Foolish Flow Ratios and net margins. Our flavor of stock picking is mostly very analytical. Up to a point. But when it comes down finally to picking *one* company to invest in, gut instinct for us will always play a part. We'll ask ourselves, *Do I really know this business?* And we should all be asking ourselves, *Am I going to have fun at this?*

We've gone over index funds, and Foolish Eight stocks, and how to read financial statements, and we've touched on Rule Breakers and Makers. Out of a large universe of investment approaches of greater and lesser merit, these are the ways we have learned, experimented with, and taught investing. But let's focus on that word "experimented." Because new or other ways to invest will come and go, beyond those you've read here in our guide. And some of the best of these possibilities involve experimentation. Science. Observation of patterns.

It's human nature to look for patterns. Something clicks, and we find ourselves wondering: *Do companies with strong earnings growth outperform the market? Are companies with high debt ratios likely to go down? Do Dow companies with the highest dividend yields perform better than the Dow?* Those are questions that, given access to an historical database with the necessary selection criteria and subsequent stock returns, can be tested.

One prominent emerging investment approach many practice on Fool.com takes such observation and experimentation to the extreme. It's called *mechanical investing,* and its aim is to develop a *completely analytical* method for selecting stocks. Rather than relying on instinct for the final selection, mechanical investing methods rely purely on historical tests, statistics, and algorithms. And rather than selecting an individual stock to invest in, mechanical investors select *strategies,* buying the five or ten stocks that come out at the top of a screen (a screen is a group of stocks that meets or exceeds certain parameters).

Mechanical investing is simply the application of the scientific method to stock selection. The scientific method involves (1) making a hypothesis, (2) observing and gathering data, and then (3) testing the hypothesis against the data and observations in order to (4) confirm or deny the hypothesis. Out of this process comes a Theory (with a capital *T,* there, maestro). Each mechanical investing approach is, in effect, an empirical theory—an idea based on the rigorous testing of historical results. And if you go on to use that theory as your investment approach, you are basing your future hope for profits largely on the soundness of the thing *and* a belief that history will continue to repeat itself and generate similar results.

Mechanical investing is very popular among an enthusiastic group at Fool.com primarily because, with personal computers scanning stock information databases, average individual investors can now test stock selection hypotheses quicker, more exhaustively, and more accurately than ever before. We remember our father's heavy black *Value Line* tome, out of which he taught us to analyze companies. But that was all paper, and needed ongoing paper updates. When Robert Sheard first researched mechanical investing material five years ago for his Motley Fool book *The Unemotional Investor,* he had to use free library copies of the print editions of *Value Line* and *Investor's Business Daily.* (Eventually, we sprang for the subscriptions!) Today, anyone with a computer and a modem can subscribe to *Value Line's Investment Survey for Windows* for under $600 a year and have instant access to all of this data in electronic form, to be sliced and diced, turned over, and tested to one's heart's content.

Here's a typical example of how a mechanical approach comes into existence.

You first imagine a group of screening criteria that you think might lead to stocks beating the market over (say) a twelve-month period. Let's make up the following criteria: companies with at least $100 million sales, companies whose stock beat the market average over the previous year, and companies whose most recently reported quarter represented their single best quarterly earnings per share ever.

Does this sound like a group of companies that might make for good investments? That might beat the market over the succeeding year? Time to find out.

Using a computer and sifting over an accurate and complete database from the past, you start first by going back far enough into the past to gather a sufficient sample size. Let us say, twenty years. You decide, then, to go back to the first Friday of that year twenty years ago and look up the stocks that, on that day, met all three of your screening criteria. Then you check and see how they did over that next year. You take pains to make sure that you are not allowing any knowledge from the future to taint or otherwise influence your selections, and you further ensure that your information source represents the data as it was then, with no "survivorship bias." (An example of survivorship bias would be a historical stock quote service that gives historical quotes only for companies that are still trading today. If you have made the mistake of limiting your test to currently traded companies, you would be eliminating companies that have gone bankrupt or otherwise disappeared. Is this a fair representation of your screen or your mechanical approach?)

Now continue the process for the nineteen consecutive years after that first one, right up to the present day. Once it's completed, you'll be able to judge your results. Often, they will turn out to be junk. Occasionally, the testing of your hypothesis might reveal something interesting, encouraging further thinking and testing. Did you get way too many companies? Are there other good parameters you could add into the mix, next run-through?

And on some rare occasions, your hypothesis might just blow the market away.

"Nothing tends so much to the advancement of knowledge as the application of a new instrument," Sir Humphrey Davis once said. That may be, and within the investing world, those who discover new mechanical investing approaches might well agree. You can think of any new mechanical investing approach, in Sir Humphrey Davis's terms, as an instrument. But how do you tell whether it's a valuable new gadget that truly does advance knowledge or, instead, just a Rube Goldberg machine?

Well, whether we're talking about biology, physics, or analytical investing, you're going to benefit from being part of a community who constantly challenge and criticize one another's ideas. For many mechanical investors, that's where Fool.com steps in. At The Motley Fool, the mechanical investing community plays the role of peer review. A synergy has evolved where ideas are shared, tested, retested, questioned, disparaged, cheered, dismissed, and improved.

Out of this free exchange have emerged a number of strategies with sound rationales that have beaten the market in historical tests and have *continued* to beat the market going forward. So far, as of this writing, we have at most three years of postdiscovery returns on a few of them and shorter periods on many others. The process is continuing, but the initial returns for some of these strategies have been very impressive (in some cases so impressive that we'd look irresponsible if we printed the returns!). Our community has gone beyond developing market-beating strategies, though; they have developed a kind of brain trust that fosters creative thinking while demanding rigorous intellectual honesty. The process has been quite educational, and profitable for many participants.

Data Mining?

Some of this work is occasionally dismissed by some schools of thought or some members of the press as *data mining*. Data mining, in the worst sense of the term, means cherry-picking numbers to arrive at a strategy that, while it looks good in reverse, has very little true substance to it and would be highly unlikely ever to beat the market again. For instance, pretend you ran a screen that showed that companies whose names started with the letter *P* and have green corporate logos beat the market handily when purchased on Thursdays during the summer months, and held for exactly nine months after that. Even the casual reader can tell that this is a silly strategy with no grounding in the sorts of variables that are important and likely to repeat themselves; it's all alphabet, and colors, and flashes of timing. This is data mining done wrong. Sorry to say it, but its substance ranks right down there with astrology.

(By the way, ask your favorite believer in astrology to explain to you why "it works," sometime. Y'know, the "science" behind it. We've received some very creative responses in the past!)

But "data mining" need not be a dirty word, and in reference to a number of mechanical investing approaches we've come across, we think it is very poorly applied if applied in that way. The data miner is simply founding a theory on the existence of historical numbers, and even though in some cases the theory emerges out of the numbers (rather than vice versa), is this, therefore, indicative of bunk thinking or intellectual dishonesty? *Or* just the discovery of a good algorithm? Those familiar with neural network software know that its modus operandi is data mining, which has in fact produced valuable insights across a host of different fields.

In the end you must ask yourself this question: *Does my theory rest on data likely to repeat themselves because of one or more logical, sound, deep, underlying reasons?* If so, we call that good data mining. If not, we call that bad data mining. "Data mining" is a neutral term—a descriptor—not a loaded (and often only half-understood or unconsidered) criticism.

It All Started with Beating the Dow and the Foolish Four

The genesis of the mechanical approach to investing was a strategy called the Foolish Four, which we introduced in the first edition of this book. The Foolish Four was a variation of an earlier strategy from *Beating the Dow* by Michael B. O'Higgins, first published in 1991. Here's how O'Higgins's approach worked.

You start with the thirty stocks that make up the Dow Jones Industrial Average. This acts as a prescreen to ensure that you are selecting from successful, large-cap U.S. stocks. Then you screen those thirty stocks for the ten with the highest dividend yield. (Yield equals dividend per share divided by price per share.) You then buy the five lowest-priced stocks of the high-yield ten and hold them for one year. At that point you recalculate the list, then make any necessary changes. And so forth.

The original Foolish Four (a.k.a. Foolish 4.0) modified the Beating the Dow list by dropping the lowest-priced stock and doubling the investment in the second-lowest-priced stock. Other variations drop the lowest-priced stock only when it is also the highest yielder (Foolish 4.1) or use a mathematical formula that combines low price and high yield into one easily ranked number (Foolish 4.2). Almost any variation on that basic theme will get you a basket of very large U.S. stocks that have been beaten down by the market yet have the potential to stage a relatively quick (one- to three-year) turnaround.

The deeper, logical, underlying reason behind these approaches was this: Higher than average dividend yields are a sign that the market is underpricing the stock relative to its dividend. That's usually the case when a company is out of favor for various reasons, be they lowered earnings, a major lawsuit, a competitive threat, an oil spill, or some other disaster. Wall Street's reaction to such events has often in the past been out of proportion to the likely effects the worrisome event would actually have on the financial health of the company. Nevertheless, short-term investors often dump all over such companies anyway, selling off their stocks and driving the price down.

Thus, Beating the Dow and the Foolish Four variations use the high yield/low price formula to quickly identify companies that may be beaten down yet still have the resources to turn themselves around. (The high dividend is a sign that the company has the financial resources to weather whatever particular difficulty it's in at the time.) So, if you buy such a company when it is down, you are likely to profit, the theory goes, because when these companies turn around, their price grows much faster than usual. Plus you get the higher than average yield.

We loved the Beating the Dow approach (BTD), had used it ourselves profitably for some years, and wrote about it frequently when we first went online and in the first edition of this book. It was simple, it made sense, it had worked for eighteen years *before Beating the Dow* was first published, and it had continued to work for the five years after publication. That's a pretty impressive track record, especially considering that most mutual funds have underperformed the market *and* have less than a ten-year history. We also liked that it selected big-cap companies that, while not immune to loss, were relatively safe and a nice alternative to the kind of high-octane growth stocks that we found most interesting. So we set up a discussion board on our site to discuss BTD, and that's when the magic started. The Foolish Four alternate strategy wasn't something that *we* dreamed up. It was developed by our community, and they went on to develop a number of other variations, all of which beat BTD.

Even though the BTD strategy worked after discovery, it's not doing very well right now, and neither are the Foolish Four versions. Here's a ten-year history of BTD and the three Foolish Four strategies.

	Dow 30*	S&P 500	BTD	F4.0	F4.1	F4.2
1990	−9.14%	−3.17%	−17.34%	−15.06%	−17.61%	−17.61%
1991	30.36%	30.55%	59.14%	89.34%	81.61%	34.81%
1992	11.04%	7.67%	20.19%	29.25%	30.24%	30.24%
1993	17.91%	9.99%	30.49%	37.80%	26.22%	30.26%
1994	3.70%	1.31%	6.10%	−6.88%	4.51%	7.38%
5-yr. CAGR	**9.97%**	**8.69%**	**16.96%**	**21.68%**	**20.79%**	**15.14%**
1995	36.69%	37.43%	30.13%	37.49%	30.42%	47.05%
1996	24.32%	23.07%	26.62%	30.47%	24.34%	26.56%
1997	22.33%	33.36%	17.70%	24.30%	22.31%	19.49%
1998	15.95%	28.70%	12.49%	17.35%	10.75%	15.64%
1999	20.57%	21.04%	−7.60%	−13.37%	−14.54%	21.47%
5-yr. CAGR	**23.79%**	**28.57%**	**15.05%**	**17.78%**	**13.42%**	**25.58%**

*The Dow 30 is the total return for an equal *dollar* amount invested in each of the thirty Dow stocks, including dividends. It will be different from the return of the index, which assumes buying an equal number of *shares*. All of the Foolish Four versions balance their investments by dollar amounts rather than by number of shares.

All returns include dividends and are based on the closing price on the *first* trading day of the year. O'Higgins uses the closing prices on the *last* trading day of each year, so our BTD numbers may not match other published BTD returns, although the averages are about the same. Small differences are probably due to different prices. Larger differences may be due to one or more different stocks being selected. (A small change in relative prices can change the mix of stocks selected from one day to the next.)

The *CAGR* lines tell the tale. The CAGR is the *compound annual growth rate,* the average rate at which an investor's money would have grown had it been invested over the previous five years at the annual rates of return shown. (Note to nonstatisticians: The CAGR is an average *rate,* not the mean average. Mathematically speaking, it's the geometric mean.) While at first glance the second five years appear to be somewhat similar to the first five, that's not the whole story. Remember you have to judge your return *against the market,* represented here by the Dow and the S&P 500. During the early nineties all of these strategies beat the market by wide margins (compound those numbers out and see for yourself). During the second half of the decade they lost to the Dow or, in the case of Foolish 4.2, squeaked by the Dow by less than 2 percent a year (but even that is due only to the good showing in 1995). All the strategies lost to the S&P 500 in this period. We believe in long-term investing and in staying faithful to one's ideologies up to a point. However, we must also not be blind to the possibility of changing markets and a changing world.

Further, the numbers above are only for *one* portfolio each year. The original studies were all based on portfolios that started on either the first or last investing day of the year. Investors starting at other times will have different results, and the average appears to be somewhat lower for portfolios started in months other than January.

All in all we are disappointed. We, the authors, do not practice mechanical investing today, preferring to do our own stock selection. But many people smarter than we are are today extremely involved in mechanical investing, and certainly an extinct Foolish Four (if such be the case) does not logically lead to the idea that all mechanical investing doesn't work. The Foolish Four was indeed a good strategy until the world began to shift away from the dividend (fewer companies in relative terms pay dividends today, and most great growth companies pay none at all). And further, the editors at Dow Jones made some key changes to their industrial average upon which the strategy is based (selecting from the thirty companies) when they booted some sleepy old-timers out and welcomed in bigger growers with scanty dividends (like Wal-Mart). All in all, four stocks were swapped into the Dow in 1997 and four more in 1999 (an unusual number of changes in a very short time period). If you list the Dow stocks according to their dividend yield, seven of those new stocks today (as of this writing) are in the bottom half of the entire list. And *five* of those make up the six lowest-yielding Dow stocks.

If you're using a strategy like the Foolish Four that selects only high-yielding companies, a shift like that shrinks the pool of stocks that you can pick from. It's harder to find good fruit on the shelf when there's less and less of it on the shelf.

Or perhaps the strategy simply became too popular. For a while Beating the Dow spawned a whole industry, where brokerages put together packages of five or ten high-yielding Dow stocks and sold them as *unit investment trusts* (which are something like a mutual fund, but with looser rules). With money from these trusts pouring into the high yielders around the time you'd be buying yourself, and pouring out of others the same time you were planning on selling those at the end of the year—well, sound like a recipe for lowered returns?

Or perhaps investors are today simply dazzled by the prospects of high tech. They are buying "new economy" stocks and ignoring the turnaround potential of downtrodden golden oldies. Maybe that's why the Foolish Four have stumbled. (In which case this sentiment could change in a flash.)

Maybe all of these.

Anyway, to close this section, does the Foolish Four not work? Who's to say for sure? No strategy is perfect, and the approach has had stretches where it didn't beat the market before, notably during the sixties, a decade where go-go technology stocks dominated the market (sound familiar?). Then again, five years of underperformance sure gives one pause. And the dividend-hostile changes to the Dow further undermine our confidence in this particular gadget.

We don't know the answer. No one does right now, with certainty. We'll just have to keep looking. It's part of the learning process in which we are all engaged. If we succeed, we want to know why we succeeded so we can do it again. If we fail, it's even more important to understand why we failed. (Or maybe it's not *more* important, but it sure bugs us until we figure it out.)

Probably the most valuable thing about the Foolish Four is the way that it stimulated interest among many in the idea of using stock screens as the primary criteria for picking stocks "unemotionally." For these investors, selling is no longer a matter of personal choice—they follow the prescription of their strategies and send in buy and sell orders with all the drama and suspense of a called-in pizza order. This idea that one can use set criteria to select stocks and follow a set pattern of investing in those stocks greatly appeals to a certain type of investor. Our typical mechanical investing discussion board participant is highly analytical, mathematically oriented, and logical even to a fault. Is this you?

If so, all this activity takes place in an area on our site called the Foolish Workshop (workshop.Fool.com). There, you'll find board participants have developed hundreds of market-beating strategies, built Web sites where one can see what the historical returns for these strategies would have been over the past fourteen years (some strategies can be tested back to 1969), and constructed other sites that automatically run the numbers to select stocks according to the preset criteria. Most important and enjoyable for us is that they have cooperated in digging up the data needed to back-test various strategies—and some of these are truly Herculean tasks. Of course, when the carrot is big, the rabbits don't mind running . . .

What do *we* do? Mostly your Foolish authors stay out of their way and just watch. We don't personally invest this way because, as we mentioned above, we prefer to pick our own stocks.

By the way, are you curious what some of these approaches are? Well, mechanical investing is an eternal work in progress. A lot of tinkering goes on—hence the "Workshop" title. Strategies are constantly being proposed, tested, combined, rejected and refined. It is useless to tell you about the latest thinking in this community because it will be different by the time you read this. If you're truly interested in these methods, visit us online.

Mechanical Investing: What's Not to Like?

You can start with this word: *taxes*. Most of these strategies perform best when held for less than a year. That means that most of your capital gains will be taxed at short-term rates—in other words, your regular income tax bracket. If you are lucky enough to be in the highest bracket, taxes on these strategies will be twice as high as the long-term capital gains tax rate—close to 40 percent, and that's just the federal bite. Those who draw lower incomes won't be hit as hard but will always pay more than they would if they had held a stock for longer than one year. If you'll please recall our basic buy-to-hold approach, you'll see that we try to pay taxes a lot less frequently than that!

We don't think that tax considerations should be the primary driver of your investing decisions, of course. And for some people who are investing mainly in a retirement account like an IRA, their capital gains are sheltered, not taxed on a yearly basis. But when it comes to choosing for a taxable account between a strategy that creates long-term gains and another that offers short-termers, taxes need to be part of your equation. Because unless those short-term gains are way above the long-term ones, the taxes will wear ya down (to say nothing of all that extra time and attention you spent).

For instance, paying 20 percent on a huge capital gain after twenty-five years may be quite painful, but you are far better off doing it that way than paying a bit each year. The more money you keep in your account, the faster it will compound. We ran a quick simulation comparing two $10,000 accounts that each earned an average annual rate of return of 15 percent. The first account invested strictly in long-term buy-to-hold stocks and managed to avoid trading for thirty years. The second account turned over 100 percent every 366 days and therefore paid 20 percent (the long-term rate) on the amount it grew each year. After thirty years, the high turnover account had grown to $329,393.06 and no further taxes were owed. The buy-and-hold account had grown to $575,754.54, but did of course owe 20 percent on all but the starting balance of $10,000. What, then, remained? Well, after paying the capital gains tax the passive account was still worth $469,803.63, a full *43 percent more* than the high turnover account.

That's the power of compounding. Don't tread on me.

Let's hear it one more time for IRAs! In the context of this chapter, an IRA account—especially the Roth IRA—certainly makes mechanical investing more appealing from a tax standpoint.

What Else?

Glad you asked. We would be remiss if we didn't mention what the Workshop community calls the Maalox Factor. Even—or rather, often—the most successful mechanical strategies can be stomach-churningly volatile. If the market goes down 10 percent, they often fall 20 percent to 30 percent. If the market goes down 20 percent, you probably don't even want to think about where you wound up. On the other hand, if the market is up 30 percent, the strong-growth screens may surge 60 percent. There's ultimately an advantage to volatility—if you can stand the ride.

The problem is that most people don't handle those drops very well. Several psychological studies have shown that the pain of loss greatly exceeds the joy of gain (by a factor of three to one, one recent study suggested). It's one thing to *assure* yourself that you won't wave the white hankie when your strategy comes under fire. It's quite another to sit through a bombardment that drops the value of your portfolio 30 to 40 percent in just six weeks, as happened to many in the spring of 2000. Remember, mechanical investing probably won't work too well if you sell out the very first time your strategy hits the skids. That's another place where the discussion group plays a valuable role. Having the support of others can help many people through their first big blowout. After that, for some it might get easier.

Anyway, if we haven't scared you away from the mechanical investing yet, there's one more thing you need to consider: It's very easy to look at an impressive back test and conclude that you may as well start designing that dream house (or second house, or third house) right now. As important as back-testing is, do remember that it's a rearview mirror, not a windshield! There's a fine chance that some of the screens developed in the Workshop will turn out to be duds—statistical artifacts—even some that look terrific right now. In other words it will turn out that the back test was not in fact *predictive* of the future return of that strategy. That's another way of saying you could lose money over the long term following such a strategy, even if everything in the back test looked good. Or the market could change and even a formerly sound strategy could stop working.

No strategy picks winning companies every time. Mechanical investing simply uses a set of criteria that identifies companies that have a good chance of beating the market. The criteria are suggested by observation and logic, and confirmed—as far as such things can ever be confirmed—by back-testing and real-life performance.

◆ ◆ ◆

Notice in the end that, whether practiced by a brilliant theoretician or a complete novice just following directions, mechanical investing is an act as much of faith as of science.

Science and faith are, by many people, often opposed to each other. But while contrasts exist, their supposed opposition comes much closer to the analogy of opposed digits: thumb and forefinger. Both are flesh, both are connected to the hand, and both are used primarily to manipulate objects. In fact, they work together.

As hell-bent as some are on using analytics and statistics to create empirically based "scientific" answers, mechanical investors are in the end acting on faith, a faith that says, "I believe that what worked in the past will continue to work in the future."

In the end, they are still ultimately investing on the promise of things hoped for, on the sight of things unseen.

PART VII

SOME ADVANCED TOPICS

Using Margin

· · · · ·

Neither a borrower nor a lender be . . .
—*Polonius*, Hamlet, *Act 1, Scene 3*

When you open an account with a broker, you'll be asked on the application whether you want a cash or a margin account. If you choose the cash account, then you can buy only stocks which you intend to pay for at the time you put in your buy order (or in some rare cases, within a few days). Simple.

If you open a margin account, however, you're asking for the brokerage to agree to lend you money from time to time, so that you may use it to invest more money than you have in your account. Neat idea, huh? Pick your stocks well, and you can turn a profit using money that you don't even have. Margin is a secured loan, basically, where the collateral is the existing marginable securities in your account. How much you can borrow is determined by how much is in your account. Currently, you're not allowed to borrow more than 50 percent of the purchase price of the stock you wish to buy. For some highly volatile stocks, certain brokerage firms allow less than that.

For the borrowing privilege, you pay interest to the brokerage, just as with any other loan. In fact, it's a lot easier to open a margin account than to apply for a bank loan! To quote online discount broker Ameritrade, "Having a margin account is like having a pre-approved credit line with your broker." Woo hoo! Party at our house . . . wait, not so fast! There are aspects of margin credit that differ dramatically from pure credit. We'll get to those differences in a bit. Even without addressing the differences, Fools know that credit is a tricky thing, not to be used carelessly.

Just as with a credit card, you're charged interest for the privilege of using the firm's money. While the rates charged for margin are lower than the rates you'll pay to a credit card company, you should still remember that this isn't free money. (Margin rates typically go down as you borrow more, which puts an interesting twist on things, when you think about it.)

There are some restrictions on margin use. Stocks under $5 per share are not marginable. Not that you'd want to invest in a penny stock anyway, right? (Let alone borrow money to buy it! Eeeek!) Initial public offerings (IPOs) are not marginable for a certain period after their debut. Now and then you'll also find that other Nasdaq stocks are not marginable.

The Federal Reserve Board regulates the amount of credit brokerages are allowed to extend to their clients. Currently, the law says you can borrow up to 50 percent of the value of your marginable securities. Another way to look at this is to say that, for stock purchases, you put up 50 percent of the price and your broker puts up 50 percent. In case this is at all confusing, let's introduce some numbers here to help explain it.

Let's say you have $10,000 in your margin-approved brokerage account. This allows you to purchase up to a total of $20,000 of marginable securities. Your ten grand gives you $20,000 worth of buying power.

Suppose there is a marginable stock that costs $20 per share. You could, if you wanted, buy up to 1,000 shares of that stock. At the maximum, you'd put up 50 percent (or, $10,000) of the purchase price for those 1,000 shares, and your broker would put up the other 50 percent.

One thing to remember about margin is that the amount you can borrow is not a fixed number. In this respect, margin differs from the static credit limit given for your credit cards. Margin is tied to the value of the marginable securities in your portfolio. Therefore, your buying power changes daily, along with the changes in your stocks' prices. If your portfolio goes up, the amount you can borrow increases. We'll get to what happens when your portfolio goes down later.

How Margin Works

Margin has a magnifying effect on the gains and the losses in your portfolio. Let's look at the example above again to illustrate this very important point.

Once you've opened your margin account and deposited your money, you're ready to go. Starting with $10,000, you want to buy 1,000 shares of a stock that costs $20. You will therefore borrow $10,000 from your broker at 7.68 percent. Say your order gets filled at exactly $20 a share and (to keep the numbers round) you pay no commissions on that trade. The total invested is $20,000 ($10,000 from you and $10,000 from your broker for 1,000 shares of a $20 stock).

Let's imagine that the stock goes up over the next year to $45 a share. The value of your total investment has gone from $20,000 to $45,000. If you then sold your shares, you'd pay back your broker's margin loan of $10,000 plus $800 interest, leaving you with $34,200. That's $24,200 profit, a *242 percent gain* off of the $10,000 that were your own.

(Now, now . . . pay your taxes, maestro. Okay, you've still netted over $19,000.)

If instead you'd only bought what you could afford, that would have been 500 shares at $20. The stock rises to $45 and, not using any margin from your broker, your investment is now worth $22,500, a 125 percent gain on your original investment, of which you'd have a net profit of $10,000 once you've paid your 20 percent capital gains tax ($2,500).

So in the case where margin was used, after taxes you made $19,000 on original assets of $10,000, as opposed to making $10,000 on that same $10,000.

And it all sounds *just great,* doesn't it? What could be more perfect? *Free money.* Just too easy. *Why doesn't everyone do this?* some may wonder.

Well, that's what your broker would like you to think. Margin loans make high-margin profits for brokerage firms. So from the standpoint of maximizing immediate profit, most brokers would absolutely love it if right now all their clients set down what they were doing, grabbed the phone, and blurted, "Harry, max out my margin and let's exploit all of this buying power! It's like a drug!"

A Fool, however, knows better than to begin the act of planning for his financial future by firmly affixing rosy-colored clip-on lenses to his otherwise spare bifocals. And we trust by now we've clearly enough conveyed that what is good for your broker is generally not, for you. We repeat: Brokers love to see clients use margin, because the interest they charge gives them a guaranteed revenue stream, backed by the holdings in your portfolio. Any advice you may be given to do so is coming from a vested interest—literally—in the matter.

Let's now look at what can happen when Fortune does not smile on your investments. Imagine that your $20 stock falls to $15 over the next year.

In the margin situation, your $20,000 investment has fallen to $15,000. You sell the stock and pay back your broker's $10,000 loan plus the same $800 interest. You're left with $4,200. Or more likely, your broker will automatically sell $800 worth of another holding in your portfolio—and charge you commission to do it. Congratulations! You've managed to lose 58 percent of your original investment on a 25 percent drop in your stock!

If you hadn't used margin and had just purchased 500 shares of the stock at $20, after it fell to $15 you would have retained $7,500 of your original $10,000. A 25 percent loss is, for you, just that.

The Dreaded Margin Call

Related to the magnification of losses attributable to margin is the harsh reality of the *margin call* (also sometimes referred to as a *maintenance call*). A margin call occurs when the value of the collateral you put up for the loan (that is, the marginable securities in your portfolio) falls below a predetermined minimum requirement. Usually, this requirement is about 30 percent of the loan, though it may run 50 percent for more volatile stocks.

That means that if the stocks in your portfolio (the collateral for the margin) fall to a level that is below 30 percent of the amount loaned to you by the broker, your broker will contact you, wanting more collateral. The equity in your account (that is, the market value of your securities, minus the amount loaned to you by your broker) must stay above this minimum requirement.

Let's use some numbers again to get a better grasp on this. Taking our 1,000 shares of the $20 stock bought on margin, imagine the price falls to $13 a share. At this point, the $20,000 investment is worth $13,000. Remember, you and your broker each put up 50 percent of the money, but you have to pay back what you borrowed. So, $10,000 of that $13,000 remains the broker's (plus interest).

Your measly $3,000 in equity is now 30 percent of the amount of the loan, about the level at which we earlier indicated you'll get a margin call. Thus, if this darned stock falls any more, you won't have to call them (as the old saw goes), because *they'll call you*. At this point, you'll have to send additional collateral to fulfill the minimum requirement. The additional collateral can be either cash or other fully marginable securities. Only a percentage of the market value of an added security can be used to meet your margin call, though.

Hmmmmm. What if you can't meet your margin call because you don't have additional cash or other securities to send? Your brokerage will then sell the margined securities in your account to cover what it's owed. You gave them this right when you signed the agreement to open a margin account.

Adding insult to injury, after such an obviously unexpected and disappointing drop, too often you'll find yourself exiting the stock (the firm pressing the button) at the worst possible time. You have few or no shares left yourself, you may even owe the brokerage some additional funds, and lookee there, your stock just recovered back to $20. Without you. Perhaps it is now somewhat clearer how the risks of margin might outweigh the benefits.

Investing with margin isn't a complete no-no automatically for all people in all situations—just for many, in most. If you already have been investing for a few years and decide to use margin, you should limit yourself to borrowing no more than 20 percent (at the very maximum) of your portfolio's value. Thus, on a $20,000 portfolio, you'd be borrowing a few thousand more (up to $4,000), putting $21,000–$24,000 to work for you. That's called leverage. A little of it can be a useful and not too risky thing if invested Foolishly in great companies over the long term.

We wrote that last paragraph somewhat reluctantly, stating our belief but doing so with the fear that some less experienced investors will think, *Oh yeah, okay, so I do get to borrow and invest. The Fools say so. Great!* and run out and go on margin. So again, if it is *ever* used, margin should be used with extreme caution and moderation, and only by those who fully understand what they're doing.

In no situation would we advocate anyone (experienced or otherwise) maxing out on margin, borrowing 50 percent of the value of their portfolio. If you ever feel tempted to use anything more than a modicum of margin, please sign online to Soapbox.com and search for an author named William Davis. Pay the $10 to buy and read his report entitled "Margin 101: From Rags to Riches (Or Vice-Versa)." See what we mean?

Benjamin Franklin said, "Experience is a dear teacher, but fools will learn at no other." Small-*f* fools perhaps, Old Ben, but not Fools. Help us settle the dispute. Don't wait until margin burns you to conclude that you've been using too much of the stuff, or that you shouldn't have been using it at all. Many of the best and most experienced investors we know have always steered completely clear of it. As of this writing, none of our real-money online portfolios at Fool.com have used margin, and they're all doing just fine.

Of course, there is *one* reason why, even if you're not interested in buying stocks on borrowed money, you still might want to open a margin account . . .

Shorting Stocks

• • • • •

In short, I deny nothing, but doubt everything.
—*Byron*

I f you've ever swaggered up to a craps table, cleared away the necessary elbow room, and slapped down a few candy-colored chips
on the Pass Line, you were doing what most of the people at a craps
table do. You were betting with the crowd.

Adjacent to the Pass Line, however, is a cheaper strip of real estate
(usually a vacant lot) known as the Don't Pass. It's virtually the opposite bet; you win when the Pass Line crowd loses, and lose when it
wins. The odds for Don't Pass are no worse than the Pass Line. (None
of these are good odds, of course!) But because you're betting *against*
the roller and most of the rest of the table, betting Don't Pass is considered bad form. Craps jargon for people like you is "wrong bettor." Many
other bettors will actually dislike you for doing it, a feeling that will be
reinforced whenever you smile at dice rolls that make them frown.

It's quite the same for those who habitually sell stock short.

A Short Lesson: How It Works

When you short stocks, you profit not when they rise but when they
fall; it's a neat idea that not everyone realizes is even possible. And of
those who do, most won't consider it. Some think it's un-American to
profit off the failure of corporations and other investors, giving hedge

investors a Don't Pass reputation. Many others have rightly heard that the stock market has been the best place to put your money in the twentieth century. These people don't want to short stocks, because they fear that the market's tendency to rise will pull their short up with it.

But prior to an intelligent consideration of the pros and cons, let's make like engineers and first learn how the thing works.

For starters, to short stocks you'll need a margin account, covered last chapter. You initiate a short by first borrowing shares from a current shareholder. This may sound difficult, but it isn't. In fact, you'll never notice it happening, because your broker does this for you automatically. In the very next breath, you *sell* these borrowed shares at the current market price. Then in the coming days and weeks you sit and wait, rooting for the stock to spiral downward. When you're ready to cash out of your investment—whether for profit or for loss—you close out the position by buying the stock back, so that you can return your borrowed shares to the lender (another thing your broker does for you automatically). That's it.

Let's look at a couple of examples.

You decide clandestinely to short 100 shares of the corporation you work for, Overrated Technologies (ticker: FALL), at $56.50. You just call up your broker and say, "Harry, I want to sell short 100 shares of Overrated." Harry will borrow 100 shares for you and then sell them immediately at $56.50. Three months later, when the stock has dropped to $46.50, you want to cash out. You'll place an order to buy 100 shares of FALL at the market price ($46.50), enabling Harry to return these newly bought shares to the lender.

So what have you made? Well, you sold 100 shares in the first place at $56.50, so your sale came to $5,650. Then, to close out, you bought 100 shares back at $46.50, or $4,650. Your profit was $1,000, minus commissions. Off the initial investment of $5,650 you've made $1,000, a three-month return of 18 percent. Snazzy.

Now let's reshuffle the cards and pretend things get ugly. You've sold your Overrated Tech shares short at $56.50 and alas, the stock begins to go up—$60, $65, $70. You keep holding, thinking, *My company is* so *overvalued now!* A year later it has surpassed $75, and you can't stand it any longer. You want out. With the price at $76.50, you call your broker. "Harry," you wheeze into the pay phone, "I've got to get outta this thing. Buy it back and get rid of it. And don't bother returning my call to confirm the trade; Ma Bell has cut me off for a couple of months. Just return those damned borrowed shares!"

So what have you lost? Tally up the damage and you see you sold 100 shares short at $56.50 ($5,650). You eventually bought back those shares at $76.50, for which you had to come up with $7,650. You lost $2,000, or 35 percent—and you must add in Harry's commission.

Now on the face of it, the technique would seem to require no cash at all. You're borrowing shares and selling them, right? That *creates* cash, adds bucks to your account. When you then decide to buy back, you're just paying out of your cash to reacquire the borrowed shares. However, if you're buying the stock back at a *higher* price than that at which you sold (the second example, above), you'll pay more than you initially received. In other words, you'll need additional money to cover your losing short position. It's for this reason that brokers require you to short the stock from a margin account and to have enough cash and stocks on deposit to meet the margin requirements. You should always check with your broker first and make sure you understand the firm's policies for margin requirements and shorting. Of course, we have helpful people who hang out in our area online answering questions on the subject, some of whom know more than you might ever *want* to know about the abstruse details of the subject.

A tidy way to summarize shorting is simply that the normal order of trading stocks is reversed: You sell first, *then* buy. Selling short is really no more difficult than that.

Why Bother Shorting?

In fine old Foolish style, we're first going to examine why *not* to short. After all, you really don't have to short. Stocks *do* go up over time, after all, so most people will do fine just owning a good index fund long. So why fight the tape *and also* have to spend any additional time at all with your investing? In fact, if you don't follow the market closely (that is, quote your stocks at least once a week), then you definitely should *not* short at all. Shorting requires an almost daily attentiveness to the stock market and should not be attempted by those unwilling or unable to pay the requisite attention.

Then there is the specter of the rising short. When a stock you short goes up, you have to fork up extra dollars to bail yourself out. It's the nature of the investment. You have what some people refer to as "unlimited upside risk." That sounds scary. Maybe even real scary. You can lose 200 or 300 percent of your original investment, while your best possible result is only a 100 percent gain.

If this makes you uncomfortable, or if you are at all uncomfortable about anything you read in this chapter, stay well away. *But* do at least familiarize yourself with it in this chapter. We're almost the only ones in the financial world who are going to teach it to you. The concept is anathema to the establishment—the very reason they won't teach it to you, the *very* reason we will.

Short People Do, in Point of Fact, Have Reasons to Live

Picking up right there, let's talk a bit more about why the shorting of stocks is underpracticed by the "professional" investment community at large. First of all, from a purely Foolish point of view, this makes shorting stock a little bit more compelling. As you well know by now, Fools relish a good swim against the tide. When most investors are trying to figure out how many more half-point gains they can squeeze out of their equities, you're looking the other way. You're regarding these same securities from the top down, assessing how far each might fall. The seldom-taken contrary view can be lucrative.

But let's fix on why exactly the establishment is so uninterested in shorting, why in some cases it is openly hostile to shorting. Not many brokers suggest short selling to their clients. Only a tiny fraction of mutual funds do any shorting. Probably an even smaller percentage of banks and pension funds short. Further, we live in a world in which Wall Street firms cannot even safely issue sell recommendations. How peculiar!

Not really, actually. Investment firms make millions by helping companies raise money to finance their growth, in addition to their reliance on access to corporate insiders for equity research. So let's say you own a company, and you take a Wall Street analyst out to a cushy lunch to share your whole business outlook with her: all about next year's growth prospects for hot dogs, how misunderstood hot dogs are by the conventional dietary press, how resilient the hot dog is as a traditional player at deli stands. She then goes back to New York and two weeks later issues a sell recommendation on your stock, dropping it several points in the process. How would you react? The answer is, not only would you skip sharing a hot dog with her next time but you'd probably never talk to her again. You wouldn't share your business plan with her firm, and you also wouldn't consider employing her to help you raise capital or float a bond.

That's why Wall Street never says, "Sell." It only says, "Buy," and, "Hold." "Buy" means a recommendation to buy your stock. "Hold" means a recommendation to sell your stock. What an unpleasant work environment! Deceit in the form of euphemism, institutionalized.

Given what you've just read, you can now clearly understand why the establishment may never say "Short." So pity Wall Street. In fact, do it one better: take advantage of its constraints. Short stocks.

We're constantly coming across establishment ideologues on CNBC or in the *Wall Street Journal* who make shorting stocks out to be incredibly risky. They love to play up this idea of unlimited upside risk. The idea, again, is that if you short a stock and it goes up, and just keeps going up, you'll *have* to cover one day. The stock could theoretically cause you to have to cover at infinity—a very high price. That's right, you just shorted Etter's ermines at $27 and whaddaya know, the fur retailer went to $infinity. You're out of luck. In fact, you're in jail, bankrupt. You've now felt the sting of unlimited upside risk.

Hmm. Is the concept of unlimited upside risk reasonable? Does anything go to infinity tomorrow? Do you spend long sleepless nights worrying about the potential threat of our planet getting clocked by a gigantic uncharted ice ball?

In the brief thirty-some years we've spent on this steadfast little rock in its unremarkable corner of the Milky Way, we have yet to meet the bloke who got victimized by unlimited upside risk. Oh sure, we've met people who've lost money shorting . . . in some cases, *lots* of money. We've also met people who've lost lots of money investing in all sorts of things: options, stocks, options, real estate, options, precious metals, even their own businesses. And options. (See Appendix E.) The world presents us hundreds of opportunities to lose money every day. But find us the guy who suffered the ultimate indignity of unlimited upside risk and we'll mail you back the cereal box tops you submitted to receive your copy of this book.

We use a very simple device to make sure that we won't lose a ton shorting. You see, we set a *quitting price* whenever we short a stock. The quitting price is typically 20 percent above the price at which we shorted. If our short sale rises to its quitting price, we throw up our hands, wave the white hanky, and make like a tree; we're outta there. Now, do we do this when we *buy* a stock? Nope. We have *no* downside sell rule with our purchases, and have been known to lose more than 20 percent on many a once-loved investment. We have lost more money, historically, on our losing longs than on our losing shorts. (We have also made more money on our winning longs than on our winning shorts, for obvious reasons. That's what we mean by low risk.)

If you, dear reader, concur with what you've just read, you now see how silly we find the pratings of the Wise, those who would have us avoid shorting altogether because it's so "dangerous." If you don't have time for shorting, we well understand—a perfectly acceptable excuse.

Or perhaps you've assessed the higher switching costs of this strategy, and decided it's not for you. After all, you'd be trading more frequently and thus paying more in short-term capital gains taxes and commissions. All good considerations. But if you're only letting fear hold you back, you're playing wallflower at your own wedding. (Okay, that's a little overstated, but these days you nearly have to shout obscenities if you want anyone to read printed material. Cut us some slack.)

If we believe we can identify undervalued stocks, it stands to reason that we can locate overvalued stocks as well. And once you've learned how to short, you can take advantage of these very situations to augment your bottom line.

We include shorting stocks in our Foolish investment approach primarily as a hedge. You're taking compensatory measures to counterbalance a potentially plummeting stock market. As it is a hedge, we short in moderation (no more than 20 percent of our portfolio), because although a good short seller will make consistent money on his shorts, he does well to keep the majority of his funds invested traditionally—long. The primary direction of the stock market is up. Accordingly, most of the short positions you take should last only a few months. (It should be easy to remember that *shorting* stock is best used as a *short-term* strategy.)

You can make money selling stocks short in almost any market environment, though. Ultimately, therefore, you should short stocks not because you think the market is going to crash, but simply because selling stocks short can lead to consistent profit. The whole idea is to make money both ways, simultaneously—long, as your growth stocks and the general market rise, *and* short, as the stocks you've identified as overpriced wither. When it works right, it's a gas! In fact, before we turned Foolish enough to short stocks, we didn't know just how much fun we were missing.

The Real Issue: What and What Not to Short

We use three primary tests to determine which stocks to short.

1. High debt-to-cash ratio combined with low cash flow.

If cash is the lifeblood of a company, debt is hemophilia. Once the skin is breached, it's tough to stem the outflow. Some small- and mid-cap companies will assume a lot of debt to grow their businesses quickly. At first, results look great—revenue and income are rising quickly, thanks to the rapid expansion, and the company's stock price follows upward. If expansion isn't coming from the existing business, or if that core business slips up, growth through debt becomes unsustainable. Interest payments can cripple the overextended company in no time flat. The bleeding, once it starts, instantly attracts the hyenas and the vultures—feeding time.

Keep in mind that large companies often will carry a sizable debt load that exceeds current cash. But they can handle this, because they have deep credit lines and high cash flow from existing operations.

You'll need to find situations where it's not cash flow but the debt itself that is funding the company's growth. This has been true of most of our best shorts.

2. Short "closed" situations; avoid "open" ones.

We like to draw a distinction between "open" and "closed" situations. Open (or open-ended) situations are those we never short. They're the companies that have the capacity to create a humongous surprise by crushing all earnings estimates in sight. Often, these companies have just introduced revolutionary products, have hit the groove of a tremendous growth period, or have industry peers who have recently reported consistently stellar earnings. Avoid shorting these companies, because they have the capacity to blow away the market's expectations. A good example of this was America Online (NYSE: AOL), a consistently popular and *killing* short all through the 1990s. The company demonstrated the capacity to beat every earnings estimate tossed its way, became the top online franchise over that period, and sat squarely at the center of the Internet craze that invaded the market beginning in 1995, which eventually sent everything even remotely linked to the Internet skyward. AOL was a classic open situation and carried with it the strong possibility all along that it might be acquired by a much larger suitor. You'd have had to be an imbecile to short it.

Closed situations are just the opposite, companies that have no real compelling product and little likelihood of dramatically surprising market expectations. They're typically in nothing-special industries, probably moving toward the end of their maximum growth phases. A good example here was Bed Bath & Beyond (Nasdaq: BBBY) back in the mid-1990s, a fine enough company whose stock happened to be beyond—way beyond—our expectations for its corporate growth. (The company's motto at the time, "Beyond any store of its kind," gave rise to many a wisecrack in the halls of Fool HQ.) Bed Bath operates national superstores that sell at bargain prices every color of household item imaginable. Was this a compelling industry? Nope. Was Bed Bath's "product" unique, life-changing, and capable of seizing the imagination of an entire generation? No. Was Bed Bath blowing away all its earnings estimates? Not really; it was hitting its targets or exceeding them by a penny or two. This was a classic closed situation, and having shorted it right about $30 in mid-1993, we waited slightly more than a year for the stock to eventually drop to $18, following an unimpressive earnings report.

Next time you ask yourself what a closed situation is, think of Bed Bath & Beyond. Next time you forget what an open situation is, click in to Yahoo!.

3. Short stocks with low short interest; definitely avoid those with high short interest.

Having now explained that you should short only high-flying closed-situation stocks with lots of debt and low cash flow, we have one more test left to apply before deciding to short. It's time to check the short interest.

Short interest is simply the total number of shares of a given security that have already been sold short. This figure is reported monthly in the *Wall Street Journal* and *Investor's Business Daily* and in a company's profile at Yahoo! Finance (finance.yahoo.com). Why do we bother checking it? Well, let's think for a second about what short interest represents.

On the one hand, it represents the amount of bearish sentiment in a stock. Let's take a Foolish example. *IBD* prints short interest of 4 million shares for Lunar Development Technologies (ticker: NEVR). The company has only 16 million shares outstanding and a float of 12 million; that means 25 percent of its total shares outstanding and 33 percent of its float have been borrowed and ditched. Hordes of bears are obviously skeptical about the company's efforts to terraform our satellite neighbor.

On the other hand, however, short interest represents latent buying power. That's because in the short-to-intermediate term almost every single share already sold short will be bought back. The irony is clear: While high short interest *looks* like a bearish sign, it's actually a bullish indicator.

Knowing this, you should typically *avoid* Lunar Development Tech as a short because too many others have already shorted before you. If the stock has resided at $18 to $19 per share for months, what's going to happen if it drops to $16.50 suddenly? *Finally,* many short sellers will say to themselves, it's fallen far enough. And a fair number of those holders of 4 million in short interest will buy back impatiently to earn the long-awaited small profit. Result? Stock goes right back to $18 to $19 again. You'll have a hard time ever earning the 20 percent profit you're shooting for.

Now, if Lunar Dev Tech happens to announce surprisingly good news—say, early indications that it has maintained plant life for more than four weeks in an airless atmosphere under a geodesic dome—*look out!* The stock suddenly jumps to $22 on the news and creates a panic among stunned short sellers. They start covering. The stock rises to $24 on volume of a million shares more, driven by fearful bears. That rise creates even more fear—wow, the thing's up over 30 percent in two days!—and so even more short sellers buy back at these higher prices, creating further upward spiraling in the share price. We have before us, ladies, gentlemen, and Fools, a "short squeeze."

As we've just demonstrated, stocks with high short interest are bad to short because (1) they're less likely to drop significantly due to short sellers impatient to take profits, and (2) they're ripe for the dreaded short squeeze. Conversely, stocks with a *low* short interest are just fine to short. Little short selling has taken place so far, with the likelihood of more occurring if the stock remains overvalued. When your fellow investors move in and begin to short this unshorted stock, they'll create downward pressure, increasing your returns.

The best way to measure short interest is actually the *short-interest ratio.* Above, we looked at the percentage of a company's total shares outstanding that are short. That's one sort of short-interest ratio and it's not bad. But we can go one better by comparing the stock's short interest to its *average daily volume.* This figure will reveal the number of days of normal trading volume that it would take short sellers to cover their positions completely. Blasting back off into outer space again, we find that NEVR shareholders are trading 200,000 shares of this stock on an average day. So let's take short interest (4 million) and divide it by the average daily volume (200,000), giving us a short-interest ratio of twenty days to cover. That is, as you may have expected, very high. We almost never short any stock with more than ten days to cover. We prefer to short stocks whose short-interest ratios are five days or less. You should too. Chances are you've found a good one, and you're *not* going to get squeezed.

A Few Pitfalls

All right, you're ready to take the dive, ready to root for something that will, you hope, take the dive with you. Before doing so, we need to catalog five annoying little things that can work against you as a short seller. Just so you'll be prepared.

First, you call up your broker, and you're told that the *shares aren't available.* What? Hmm. Well, that may be the case. It does happen sometimes with stocks that are either small-caps, or recently popular shorts, or both. In these situations, about all you can do is to ask your broker to put you on the waiting list, then call him back each day and plead. Seems like a raw deal, since no waiting list exists for those who want to buy. But that's one of the limitations to shorting stocks, and we all live with it. Fortunately, it doesn't occur too often.

You also may be tripped up by a second minor annoyance, the need to get an *uptick* before your trade goes through. In creating this rule, the exchanges have effectively said, "If you want to short a stock at $34, you'll have to wait for a trade at $34.13 before we can carry out your order." This really is a raw deal, because it's a completely artificial stumbling block put in place to prevent short sellers from piling onto a losing stock and sinking it. If a stock you want to short goes into sudden free fall after reporting bad earnings, you can't hop on the shorting bandwagon until some brave soul pushes the stock up. Does any rule prevent buyers from piling into an issue that is suddenly rising? No way, Josiah. Short sellers are hosed on this count.

Third, once in a blue moon your broker may be forced to *return your shorted shares* to the anonymous lender, usually because the lender wants to sell them and your broker can find no other shares to borrow. Forced into doing so, you may have to buy back the shares prematurely—whether you've made money or not. This happens only with very small stocks that have few shares outstanding (the sort that you probably shouldn't have shorted in the first place). In fact, despite having received "warning calls" from our broker in the past letting us know we may have to return the shares early, we've never once had to do it. Should the incident ever take place, however, we wouldn't sweat it. We'd just put the money somewhere else.

A fourth niggling little detail involves *no additional interest* on your short-sale-inflated account balance. To review, when you sell a stock short, your account's cash balance rises (as it does with any sale) to reflect the liquidation of the stock. However, what you'll find is that most brokers won't pay you *any* interest on this additional money. This compares with the close-to-100 percent interest that institutional investors typically receive on money raised by short sales. This is yet another minor drawback to the small-time short seller, who can now number the government, Wall Street, and his broker as hostile parties to his short sales. Fighting back, our online readership joined together to poll a slew of deep-discount brokers to determine whether any would be willing to offer individual investors interest paid on short sales. As it turned out, we discovered that Ameritrade, the Manhattan-based deep-discounter, *did* pay this interest. (Some new accounts were opened at

Ameritrade that day.) Meanwhile, a top-ranking officer of National Discount Brokerage, another deep-discount firm in New York City, stopped by our online area to make a special offer to pay interest to our readers for their short sales. All they had to do was to say they were from The Fool. The transforming powers of cyberspace . . .

Here's a fifth bee in your bonnet: If a stock you've sold short pays a dividend, *you pay that dividend.* No way around it. This is, in a way, a form of recompense for your borrowing these shares from your anonymous unsuspecting fellow investor. In most cases, however, the dividend amounts to less than 3 percent annually.

Despite this list of five lesser irritations, we still enjoy occasionally selling short. None of them is terribly consequential, and even all five taken together give us no pause. We just wanted you to know about them.

We'll close this section with an exhortation to follow your shorts carefully and respect the goals you set for them. If your stock dips 20 percent, for most of us that's a good enough goal to reach to buy back and cash out. Don't get greedy! If your stock instead rises 20 percent, you're going to think, *Now, more than ever, it's* really *overvalued!* The last thing on earth you're ever going to want to do is to have to buy the darned thing back. But you should. You've timed your investment ill-fatedly, whether your research was good or bad. Just admit you've been wrong and move on. Fact is, some really great short-busting news could be abrewin', and the stock's run-up may presage superlative (and unexpected) developments at the company.

A Short Conclusion

Is the Foolish way to short the *only* way to short? Of course not. Some people play sectors, concentrating their short selling in specific industries that they believe are either overloved or in trouble. Others short with everything they have, eschewing the Foolish notion that only a minority of one's portfolio should ever be short. Their records aren't too good, but they do represent another alternative and must make *some* money from time to time.

Understanding shorting stock is one telltale that separates the sophisticated investor from the novice, even though it's not terribly difficult to do or to understand. (Please note that not all sophisticates do much or even any shorting!) Related to this, believing that selling shares short is difficult and highly dangerous, some people pay oodles of money to enter "hedge funds," mutual fund partnerships whose managers short stock. Having read this far, you already know most of what these "pros" know, and you can do it yourself.

Having now graduated from the Fool's School on shorting, you've reached a fork in the road. Your choice. You may either seek to share with others the joy and happiness that comes of learning, living up to the words of Oliver Goldsmith more truly than ever before:

> *Cheerful at morn, he wakes from short repose,*
> *Breasts the keen air, and carols as he goes.*

Or you can play it the other way. Once your Pass Line friends find out you're shorting stocks, they may start to regard you as Darth Vader. That's the impression most people have of short sellers. So what the heck? Divest yourself of your motley, put on some dark clothes, sport a low visor, breathe loud, and milk it.

PART VIII

PUTTING IT ALL TOGETHER

·23·

Why Invest?

· · · · ·

No! I am not Prince Hamlet, nor was meant to be:
Am an attendant lord, one that will do
To swell a progress, start a scene or two, advise the prince.
—*T. S. Eliot*

Actually, if you sat down at your desk and looked at the hard numbers based on any average one-year investment performance, you'd have to conclude that there's no reason to put your money into the stock market. Consider this: If you have $10,000 to put away in stocks, the average market year (11 percent) will reward you with profits of $1,100, one-fifth of which you'd have to shell out to the federal government in taxes if you sold at the end of that year. The hassle of pulling together the funds, transferring them to a discount broker or moving them into an index fund, monitoring your monthly statements, and sending the documentation over to your accountant at year's end—all that effort and what do you get? Profits in the neighborhood of $800 a year. Divided out, in an oversimplified fashion, that would be about $67 a month, or $2.19 per day, or 9 cents per hour.

Less than 10 cents an hour just ain't inspiring. Take that same amount and run it out ten years and you'll have made a mere $7,000 on your initial $10,000 investment. Seventy percent growth per decade should have you asking yourself why you paid anything for this useless book. There simply must be better ways to put your savings to work for you.

How true all of the above would be if there weren't one great flaw to the analysis. Can you locate it? If your portfolio grows at a rate after taxes of 7 percent per year, you don't actually make $58 a month. The percentage growth might remain the same, but the dollar growth will *increase* each month. After all, 7 percent of $10,000 is less than 7 percent of $11,000. And in those numbers lies the simple beauty of compounded growth. Time builds wealth. You'll make more in the second month than in the first, and you'll make more still in month twelve. By the tenth year, you'll effectively be realizing over $180 in pure after-tax profit per month, and this assumes that you don't put away any additional money between now and then, an assumption that we hope will prove misguided.

But maybe $180 a month on a $10,000 investment ten years later doesn't inspire you either. That's equivalent to $1,800 a month pure profit off a $100,000 starting kitty, and $18,000 a month off a $1 million personal bank. Maybe those numbers don't move you, given what you think could be achieved by, for example, investing the capital in your own business. If you're, say, an architect, you probably believe that those monies put toward new projects and staff would reap far greater rewards over the decade. Oddly enough, given the focus of this manuscript, you'll find a Fool agreeing with you. In the short to intermediate term, the stock market pales in comparison to intelligent investments in your own small business.

But let's not oversimplify, here. Let's not make life all about a commitment to short- and intermediate-term profit. When you make fast money on your own, you usually work long, hard hours for it—building more homes, teaching more classes, fixing more engines, manufacturing more semiconductor wafers, selling more Foolcaps, whatever your business. This business of "more" takes a lot of effort. And since technology hasn't yet found a way to lengthen the twenty-four-hour day, there's only so much you can do professionally before your spouse and kids don't remember what it's like to hear your voice, can't recollect the last time you all went biking together on the weekend, don't recall whether you like blueberry or buckwheat pancakes.

The very opposite is true when you build a Foolish investment portfolio, letting compounded growth carry your savings forward generationally by investing in other people's efforts. Your capital grows without any herculean effort on your part, particularly as—in the least challenging strategy—you'll just be loading it into an index fund. Let the scientists at Johnson & Johnson, the salespeople at the Gap, the reporters at the *Chicago Tribune,* the technologists at Hewlett-Packard, and the bankers at Citigroup turn profits for you, as they will if you invest in an S&P 500 Index fund. By letting others build up your savings, you'll free up the hours for recreation that every Fool needs to live a spirited life.

Put your money into an index fund and $10,000 will turn into $28,400—before Uncle Sam takes his cut—at the end of a decade. And again, those numbers suppose that you won't be putting any savings away between now and then, a move that is *très* Wise. You can see that the initial dollar amounts don't mean much compared to the basic principle of compounded growth: You'll generate greater and greater returns with time. Investors who focus on that longer-term perspective, who can hammer together a vision of what their life will be like ten, fifteen, twenty years hence, and who recognize how much sweeter it'll be to have a larger and larger portfolio generating higher and higher dollar profits, *these* are the people who will successfully guide U.S. and global markets throughout the twenty-first century. Save, invest the dollars intelligently in stocks, and watch the portfolio grow.

Mixing Rule Breakers with Rule Makers

It is precisely this awesome potential for long-term profitability as part owners of businesses that encourages Fools to seek out extra percentage points of compounded annual returns. Remember our point earlier about every extra percentage point of annualized gains? Each of these points is lucrative. En route to attempting to land those points, you'll need to build a Foolish portfolio, one that is ideally constructed on the shoulders of giants and uses a few additional holdings in promising high-growth stocks to see further than the market's returns. Or take a pigskin analogy: When you've cobbled together an awesome offensive line in football, it's time to find yourself a couple of flashy running backs. Over the past decade, investors have seen players like America Online, Microsoft, Dell Computer, Starbucks, Oracle, Cisco Systems, eBay, and dozens of other smaller or mid-cap companies break away to all-star status in their respective industries. All of these companies have made their long-term shareholders extraordinarily happy, and all of them were sitting there right under growth stock investors' noses, waiting to be plucked up.

Of course, while you'll hear all sorts of talk about great growth stocks—quite a bit of it in these pages, since growth stocks have given us our greatest investment successes—you need to understand how to evaluate them. Because an ill-chosen small company's volatility will be your bane, not your boon. We hope our chapters explaining how to think about and select growth stocks of all sizes and how to read their financial statements went a long way toward helping you make your own decisions in this field, rather than relying on human fund managers to charge you a pretty penny for generally mediocre performance, instead.

Selecting your stocks isn't always an easy and is never an idle process. Whenever you think, *Ahh, I really like this one, I'll skip running the numbers this time,* just recall our presentation on Styles on Video, the company that burned a hole in our investment club portfolio. Everything looked terrific: tremendous growth, a compelling story, a stock on the rise. But sitting right there in full view on the balance sheet was the tale of an accounts receivable disaster. Apparently, they weren't much bothering to collect the monies owed them for their glamour systems. And the stock, six months later, was worthless.

One of the beauties of the U.S. market is that by law companies have to lay out their performance for all to see four times a year. That makes the mission of seeking and finding less onerous. And even though there are plenty of examples of creative bookkeeping out there, far more often than not, the cheap pages in the back of each annual report tell a clear story to investors willing to look in and listen. How much of a time commitment would it take to review the quarterly financials? We don't think there's any reason to spend more than a handful of hours each year on any one of your stocks. As we've noted, you'll want to examine the cash situation, understand the products, and have some sense of management's philosophy. Also, you'll want to consider the company in the context of its industry, comparing it to the competition and determining very broadly why its sector will or will not outperform in the years ahead.

Speaking of companies and growth stocks, prudent investors will look first at those that make the rules in their industries. You'll succeed much more often than not simply by using our Rule Maker criteria to identify the biggest and the best that corporate America has to offer. These companies have already proven that they have what it takes to dominate. Odds are they will continue to do so.

You'll see even better returns by keeping your eye out for the future Rule Makers, the companies that are blazing their own trails, leading new and important industries, and learning to rule them. Consider using a portion of your portfolio to take some chances on tomorrow's Coca-Cola, the future Yahoo!, the emerging Pfizer. Following the Rule Breaker criteria briefly presented in this book may lead you to some dogs, but the stallions you find will carry you well beyond the index fund's horizon.

(The book that follows this, *The Motley Fool's Rule Breakers, Rule Makers,* is the complete guide to our way of looking at the business world and the companies within it that we'd like to own.)

Picking long-term market-beating stocks isn't a great mystery, it isn't a random-walk process, and it isn't something only M.B.A. graduates can do—quite the opposite, actually. If you're going to invest in individual stocks, your aim must be to outperform index funds and their 11 percent annual growth. If you can pull it off, twenty years from now you won't be worrying much about your financial position, no matter how much money you have put away for investing today. And remember, always track your performance against the indices. If you aren't beating them, guess where you should reinvest your money? (Hint: Two words, first beginning with an *I,* and the second is the word "fund.")

Given that we spend so much of our time focusing on the long-term ramifications of investing in the stock market, be advised that we think your entry into stocks ought to be a cautious one. There's no rush. Why not enter into an index fund or some blue-chip stocks exclusively in your first year, while merely simulating growth stock investing? Then balance some of your savings on this, the second pillar of Folly, only when you've convinced yourself you can outdo index-fund investing. It doesn't seem like a bad plan.

Doing Good Business with the Right People

When Fools look around the financial world, spying dubious investment-product sales practices, hyped initial public offerings that only institutional investors can get their hands on, the steady spate of high-priced newsletters, and the burst of thousands of mutual funds onto an already overcrowded financial stage, we note a lot of bluster amidst an abundance of conveniently medieval, self-serving accounting. It's just the sort of bookkeeping that theater owners employed to beat up playwrights like our liege Shakespeare four hundred years past. Now we know well enough to hold strictly accountable anyone indirectly or directly tied to the management of our finances.

No doubt Fools for centuries have learned a lot of these lessons the hard way, but at least there's great strength in being a witness. As much as anything, belled-cap investors now are singing loud praises to Warren Buffett in our online forum. As you'll recall, it was Buffett who proclaimed: "You can't do good business with bad people." That's just a very simple, very plain, very Foolish fact. When someone's putting the heat on you in any business scenario, whether it's stocks, real estate, your own business, whatever, you can be certain that you're in the wrong conversation. Don't waste time on bad business, of which there are so many examples, they could fill the Library of Congress. We'll take one example here: If you spend enough time floating around the business world, you're bound to hear something like this: "So, we convinced him to pay X dollars when what we we're selling was only worth Y dollars. Just awesome, it was brilliant." That's bad business because it's a short-term win with no long-term viability. Creates bad blood, too. And it's the very sort of quote too frequently echoing through the halls of America's money managers, brokers, and financial advisers.

The key for you is to be so thorough in your accounting and so clear on your long-term expectations for growth that any meetings designed around the management of your money are studies in composure, patience, and logic. And anyone intent on creating a win-lose investment partnership, with you left holding the shorter stick, is merely fodder for a couple of good jokes among good friends.

Losing sight of your bottom-line expectations can create havoc in your portfolio; don't open the door on your own personal Barings, Orange County, or Long-Term Capital Management disaster, where some rogue trader you don't much know goes nuts leveraging your savings, trading options, dabbling in $3 stocks, playing the commodities game, and gracing you each month with an unreadably incomprehensible account statement. Remember that when you're investing *your* money, you're running *your* own business. Act like it. Keep as much of the knowledge and control on your side of the table as possible. It makes the future much clearer.

Sharing Information

The dark ages for the individual investor are, blessedly, coming to an end now that we've entered the digital world. With millions of investors linked by the World Wide Web, never again will you have to make tough investment decisions without guidance. We've spent the last decade on our site and off listening to countless tales of cold-calling brokers pressuring customers into buying the next great biotechnology company trading under $4 a share, or some such wonder. Access to capital has never been so easy for companies like our own disaster scenario examined earlier, the hypothetical Huge Fruits. But just as the regulatory pressure is easing and private investors are becoming more vulnerable, the Information Age is building momentum. Immediate distribution of accurate information is going to make the Huge Fruiting of individual investors less and less likely. Amen to that.

You should never find yourself denied access to the information necessary to making a levelheaded, well-informed decision about an investment. When a salesman is pushing an investment product on you and you don't have it in yourself to just walk away, at least take down the company name, ticker symbol, and stock price. Then post them all in our online financial forum, and you should get a prompt flow of analyses. Of course, we've heard of telephone salesmen pushing Dell Computer (Nasdaq: DELL) before its fantastic run in 1995 was over, so there are some fine investment opportunities presented. But unfortunately, more often than not it's $3 stocks with few prospects that telemarketers are hawking—just the ones that can devour your savings.

What you need to do is to get yourself into a research team of sorts with other investors where you'll be able to patiently sort through stocks and their valuations together. Year after year, investment clubs have outperformed the market, as private investors in groups have focused on keeping commissions down, building long-term wealth, and outperforming the market. The strengths of the club format are the sharing of research responsibilities and the broader range of expertise, bringing together individuals with experience in a variety of industries. If you're just starting out, the Fool thinks you ought to find other investors in your community with whom to compare notes. We've got an area of our site devoted to investment clubs (www.Fool.com/Investment Club/InvestmentClub.htm), where you can contact thousands of other Fools who are participating in investment clubs right now. We also have a book on the subject, *Investment Clubs: How to Start and Run One the Motley Fool Way,* written by Selena Maranjian. For more information, check out the National Association of Investors Corporation (NAIC) at their Web site, www.better-investing.com.

As you now already know, the accumulation of information and analysis online is unmatched by anything in the offline financial industry. If you have questions about 401(k) plans, tax strategies, dividend reinvestment plans, individual companies, industry analyses, Dow-stock investing, shorting stocks, you name it, the financial questions that float around in your head have been and are being addressed in our forum. Fool.com is, in essence, a national investment club and research firm with tens of thousands of daily participants. And in this context, it's not a surprise to us that our Fool Portfolio, now the Rule Breaker Portfolio, has posted annual returns over 50 percent versus S&P 500 growth of 22 percent. (Both are unsustainably high over the long term, of course, as that market return figure is approximately double its annualized average.) With ongoing, open, interactive research on thousands of stocks (and anything else concerning money) happening at Fool.com, we expect to continue to outperform the market averages. Collaboration, good business, and clearheadedness all packaged together have drubbed the market, and we expect that to continue in our forum in the decades ahead.

Avoid Bad Investment Approaches

It certainly can be tempting to free up some of your capital for more active trading, trying to speed the compounding of growth. After all, decades—that's a long time! Day traders get more involved in the stock market than Fools do, and they may even, on occasion, have more fun. Active trading makes money management more of a sporting challenge, serving up greater highs and lows, making the whole experience far more volatile and far more emotional. It can be more addictive than nicotine soup or heroin soufflé, and it can teach you a lot about market psychology, not to mention human psychology. No wonder so many investors become "traders" at some point in their lives.

But short-term trading features two punishing attributes often ignored by its proponents. The first, commissions, has dealt death blows to many an individual investor. Imagine making ten trades a day for the entire year at the bargain-basement rate of $7 a trade. With approximately 250 trading days gone by, you're looking at $18,000 in commission payments waved off into space.

At what point is it reasonable to partake in such active trading? Out of the kindness of our hearts, let's just imagine that the active trader can compound 30 percent in pretax, precommission growth per year over a matter of decades. We've never seen anything scientific that proves such returns attainable, but we'll run with it for the sake of this analysis. With $18,000 eaten up in commissions, a $50,000 portfolio with the most generous accounting standard (commissions deducted only at year end) would become worthless, would put you in *debt* by the seventh year. Now *that's* investing! A $100,000 portfolio afforded the same returns at the same bargain commission rate would compound 17.6 percent in annual growth. All of that return, however, would be subject to tax every year at the personal income rate (let's call it 25 percent per year, between state and federal), which knocks the annual growth rate down to 12.3 percent. That means that those seven years spent taking risks daily yielded results only slightly above those you would have gotten if you'd just put the money in an index fund and forgotten about it. Time is money, too; seven years represents quite a loss in earning potential. Anyone tackling the market this actively with anything less than $100,000 would do better to load the *denarii* into the S&P 500 and call it a day, even if they were extraordinarily good at it.

The second powerful objection to active trading revolves around quality-of-life matters. Can you actually imagine day trading stocks for two decades? Computers flashing charts at you, the phone on your shoulder, a handheld quoting device Scotch-taped to your forehead, ticker symbols flooding the unconscious, closed office windows, dusty books, dimly lit rooms, a moldy half-eaten bologna sandwich on the chair beside you. Day trading pretty much demands total dedication, and as noted above, it takes just an awful lot of capital and luck to make it worthwhile down on the bottom line.

Consider also that you're not the only one who'll suffer through dank rooms and reams of information; imagine your poor tax accountant, hunched over the record of trades for the year, sorting through cost bases and capital gains (you hope), and wincing. That work ain't going to come cheap! Factor in as well that when the tax estimates do come back, they'll reflect the higher short-term capital-gains rates, which can be twice as high as the long-term 20 percent rate. Ouch! Trading doesn't come dollar cheap, nor does it come inexpensive to the mind and spirit.

Oh, and did you just hear a Fool use the word "accountant"? Accounting is taboo in the circles of short-term traders. Our experience of the world may still reflect a youthful insufficiency, but we have yet to see a single active trader properly account for his bottom-line returns. Not one. It's to the point where Fools listen to short-term-trader victory stories with levels of enthusiasm and credulity they reserve for Vegas gamblers who always at least break even and scratch golfers who don't actually putt out.

Stack it all together—the high commissions, the low quality of life, higher and more frequent tax payments, and the difficulty in accounting—and you'll understand why Fools eschew active trading. We hold in low regard the strategy of entering the stock market looking for a quick buck, watching stock prices lift and fall, and trying to capitalize on that short-term volatility. It ain't worth it.

Measure More Than Twice

To end our recapitulation, we simply remind you that future profits aren't going to run and hide. If this book is your first foray into stock market investing, delay, dear Fool, delay. You needn't plunge your savings in before sorting back through this guide, building your own Foolish portfolio on paper, and reporting to quote.Fool.com to type in and follow your selections via an online portfolio. Enter with real money only when you're comfortable.

Too many individual investors jump in before understanding what they've gotten themselves into and what they ought to expect. In our minds, no one should invest money without an understanding of the concepts of market-average performance and earnings-growth analyses, complemented by the ability to assess the qualitative aspects of a business. Astonishingly, this limitation, imposed broadly, might put a large number of professional investors on the sidelines. The entry bar is still that low on the institutional side.

To repeat: The stock market isn't going anywhere. Your entry point isn't nearly so important as your commitment to invest for the long haul when you do enter, to save and invest portions of your future earnings, and to think in terms of decades, not days, weeks, or quarters. The market will rumble at times, and you should certainly expect cracks of thunder, bolts of lightning, and powerful corrections in the years ahead. But a portfolio bolstered by large-cap blue-chips, spread thick with well-chosen growth stocks, and maybe even shored up by a mechanical investment approach or even a short or two should survive the bad weather quite winningly. Your aim at all times, if you're going to invest in the stock market directly, is to beat it. And if the S&P 500 drops 15 percent and you fall a punishing 10 percent, drink a toast to perseverance, gong the celebratory bell, jangle the belled cap, and take even a few more vacation days than you did when the market and your portfolio both rose 30 percent in a year.

Putting It All Together

Just as with any business, higher returns open up new worlds for investors, whether that means a new career, extended travel abroad, a chance to buy some time for more creative, less profitable ventures, more hours to spend with the family, the opportunity to pursue charitable works, or just a chance to blow a lot of money buying up merchandise offered on late-night TV. Prosperity leads to opportunity, and opportunity to prosperity.

Just to prove that we believe it can't be overemphasized, we'll close the section by stating once *again* the importance of compounding long-term growth on your savings through investments in well-chosen stocks. The stock market, while volatile, has provided and will continue to provide the best annual returns of any investment vehicle, by a large margin. That's because it will always offer investors the best, most liquid opportunities at capitalizing on the greatest business growth opportunities available in the known galaxy. Taking advantage of these situations and committing yourself to long-term prosperity, come hell or high water in the near term—all of these will contribute to the great financial and emotional rewards associated with forsaking Wisdom.

PART IX

CONCLUSION

A Foolish Farewell

* * * * *

Even bad books are books and therefore sacred.
—*Günter Grass*

The Motley Fool Investment Guide has, from start to finish, shared the same aim of all our online financial undertakings: to educate, amuse, and enrich. It is our earnest hope that our guide has smashingly exceeded these goals, making it at least as influential as Mrs. Susswein, the kindergarten teacher who taught you how to read. (Failing that, we'll settle for matching the fifth-grade phys ed instructor who taught you to jump rope without breaking your nose.) If, saddest of all, you've read all the way to here and you still don't see how to make your money make more money, we hope you at least liked a few of our jokes. And, say, did you ever hear the one about the ingrate and the spontaneous human combustion?

We spent the better part of the last decade designing our investment approach and several months' worth of late nights to stuff it into this book. So as long as we have you here, we're going to run the Absolute Essentials at you one more time. The Absolute Essentials are simple because Foolishness is, and they work.

Manage Your Own Money

No one on the institutional side of the financial markets is going to suggest that you can consistently outperform the stock market without hard work and great effort. Money managers don't generate high commissions by telling their clients that equities investing is *easy*, that the stock market is fueled by logic, that any Fool can do better than the majority of the umpthousand mutual funds peddled today in newspapers, magazines, over telephones and online computer services, in banks, insurance agencies, and brokerage firms. *They* may not tell you, but now you know. Be a Fool: Manage your own money and beat the market and the experts without spending your every waking hour worrying about the investments somebody else picked for you that you know nothing about.

Further, if you can ignore the siren calls of hype stocks and the impassioned importunings of the "Have-I-got-a-stock-for-you" brokers and look instead to the examples of Philip Fisher, Warren Buffett, and Peter Lynch—the three most important investment instructors of the just-completed half century—you can see that the task is not impossible. Using a few simple principles easily duplicated by anyone with discipline, each of these paragons has crushed the stock market on an annualized basis.

With this goal in mind, we first showed you how to look for companies with solid financial statements and good growth prospects. From there, we talked about buying the bosses of their industries, the head Rule Makers. To spice up that portfolio, we suggested looking for the future Rule Makers, the Rule *Breakers* and also some Foolish Eight small-caps, and taking advantage of their hypergrowth years. Remember, if you can't beat the S&P 500, don't waste your time. The Motley Fool Investment Portfolio (now known as the Rule Breaker), from inception to final printing of this text, was in its six-year history up an annualized return of 50 percent versus S&P 500 returns (with all dividends reinvested) of 22 percent. How? We focused on growth, on potential, on internal cash generation, and on collaborative research in our forum. Can you do that too? Does the moon affect our tides?

Will we compound 50 percent–plus growth every year? Can you? Certainly not. Will we beat the S&P 500 *every* year? Unfortunately, no. Hall of Famer Cy Young didn't win every game he pitched, and neither will you. (In fact, Cy actually *lost* more games than any other pitcher.) The Foolish aim with stocks is to beat the market as soundly as we can with as little time and effort as possible. And making sure you're enjoying the hunt.

Be Aggressive, Too

You're not going to make a million overnight unless you start with *much* more than that. The investment strategies you've found here are for those willing to look to the future and wait while their money and the market do the work. The most attractive aspect of the long-term approach to investing in stocks is that it eliminates day-to-day risk and worry. If you're generating in excess of the market's annual growth on disposable income, sleeping peaceably, and reflexively saving money, you can *and should* constantly open up your model, challenging yourself to do better. Far too much of our nation's financial psyche is weighted down with thoughts merely of spending and saving, like a dieter who forgets that exercise is the key to staying in shape. Be aggressive in investing your money once you've learned how to run the numbers, how to weed out fabricated growth, how to account for your returns against the market overall, and how to be patient and disciplined.

We certainly don't think that 15 percent annualized growth is out of the realm of possibility for the individual investor. That's a few percentage points above the average annual returns of an index fund, a method that demands none of your time. The question, of course, is how much time it would take to achieve 15 percent gains, and how much it's worth to you.

Permit us then to run some numbers one last time. Let's take $25,000 as our nest egg. To that, we'll add $2,500 in new savings per year. And we'll compound out 15 percent in annual growth. How long until that initial $25,000 has turned into $1 million? Twenty-three years.

So, where are you going to be in 2024?

"But where am I going to get that kind of nest egg?" you ask. Well, if you concentrate on saving 10 percent of your salary each year, as well as working on nailing down other income alternatives, you should be able to put away $25,000 in seven years. This takes real preparation; saving 10 percent of annual income means fewer beers, compact discs, and new clothes, it means some home-cooked meals instead of elegant restaurant dining, and you and the family stick with the old jalopy instead of springing for a new car. It also might be worth your while to check out our popular Living Below Your Means area (just type LBYM into Fool.com's search engine to find it) for a host of additional tips and support. Finding the right investment strategy and the right stocks is probably easy compared to this first crucial task, but the journey can be enjoyable, and the final reward will be worth it.

To get there, you'll need to draft a plan for your savings goals. If you bring in $30,000 per year today, what's it going to take for you to save $3,000 per year? You might have to take on some contract work on the weekends to meet those targets. And if you're halfway through the year, it's June, and you haven't tucked away $1,000 yet, maybe it's time to drag out that lawn mower and float through the neighborhood. You've trailed your estimates, and the market doesn't like underperformers. Set to!

Once You Have It, Give It Away

Information, that is. When you have your saving and your investment strategies down cold, give 'em away. Share them with others like you. Join our gang online or form your own.

Giving information away is just what The Motley Fool has committed itself to doing into perpetuity: distributing financial information and analysis on the cheap. Without paying a dime, our readers can access some of the most sophisticated, most comprehensive, and most timely research on the stock market. In the multitrillion-dollar financial industry, it's a rather radical notion that you could actually spend no money at all to master stocks, nail down extraordinary growth for your savings, and actually enjoy the entire process. For the Wise to compete, they'll have to explain their models as we have, account for their returns without flaw, and convince us all that they can consistently outperform the S&P 500. If they do, amen to that. If not, heck, amen to that!

One Last Thing

You know, the market could actually tank this year. And you better believe that working as a group, our readership will locate some new undiscovered small-cap winners. In either of these cases, the book you hold in your hands does not offer the *latest* help you can get from friends and Fools online. But until you've mastered what's in here, the latest help probably wouldn't be much help at all. Let this book serve as your textbook; let the new medium be your life's continuing education.

One of the great paintings of the Italian High Renaissance came out of a commission from Pope Julius II, who hired a twenty-five-year-old man named Raphael Sanzio to redecorate certain of his rooms in the Vatican. Raphael went on to create for him his famous painting *The School of Athens,* depicting a crowd of philosophers from antiquity up to Raphael's time milling about outside the Academy in Athens. In the center are the two great philosophers of all time: Plato and Aristotle. Their two poses perfectly evoke the fundamental distinction in their beliefs . . . and in ours. Aristotle juts his right hand forward as if to say, "Look, this is the way things are." Practical man. He was the founder of the formal logic and proponent of the scientific method, which he applied to everything from natural science to poetics, breaking each into its component part. Plato, on the other hand, is pointing upward, in reference to his doctrine of perfect Forms, which proposes that there is an ideal that exists beyond the parts. He thought that we couldn't recognize truths by looking only at their parts. Examples are imperfect. He looked at the central concept.

We're with Plato because Plato, you see, was a Fool. He always looked askance at people who thought they had all the answers. Like him, we question the received Wisdom of the ages. We shall continue to look to the world around us to evaluate our investment decisions, using every means possible—annual reports, financial statements, product analysis, and the like. We don't think, however, that we can properly evaluate a company based solely on its parts. That's what the Aristotelian approach might tell us. That's the basis, too, for the Efficient Markets Theory, since everyone can look at those same parts and come to the same conclusions, once they have established a framework.

We reserve the right to an open mind; we must all be flexible and must welcome change, the proverbial "only constant." Plato encouraged us to question our assumptions, to doubt those who profess to know the truth, and—above all—to continue the process of learning through discussion our entire lives. Let the believers in Aristotle say that they can look at a chart and know whether an investment is good or not, and why you should probably just assume that reason cannot beat the market, that the market is going to crash anyway, that—we seem to be hearing—only a Fool would dare to think things out.

But being Foolish is not just about being prepared for change. It also means sticking to your guns. Even if the market bombs altogether this year or next, we'll be there buying right into the bottom, knowing that the market will always come back, and our stocks back stronger with it.

The Wise will continue to offer you their sophistical ramblings and their many-splendored mediocrities. The whole point of this book is to brush off the worldly wisdom, point up *and* out at the world around us, and find the next damn winner.

Folly forever.

APPENDIX A

· · · · ·

Stocks 101:
A Primer for Those
Who'll Admit They Need It

So, you've decided to do it, to get out of your mutual fund, strike out on your own, and buy some stocks. But what do you do *next*? There are hundreds, nay, thousands of self-proclaimed financial experts churning out newsletters telling you *what* stocks to buy, *why* to buy them, and always *when* to buy them (which often is right after they do). But these mavens rarely if ever tell you just *how* you might go about buying stocks.

Many investors plunge right into the stock market, using the first brokerage firm recommended to them or the first one to catch their eye with a cheesy advertisement in their financial daily. Taking the time to think about boring stuff like tax-deferred investment vehicles and commission schedules might seem like an unbearable tedium. And guess what? It is. But if you take time to familiarize yourself with some of these concepts, you may end up saving time, money, and heartache.

What *Is* a Share of Stock?

Funny how common it is for investors, individual *and* institutional, to jump into the equities markets without understanding why and how businesses are built, why they issue stock, and how they grow.

Growth: That's the first matter at hand; businesses are launched in expectation of growth. Tomorrow's profits will allow for higher salaries, more employees, increased opportunity, prosperity at work and home— all the good news we hope for. Of course, there are hoards of other reasons that businesses sprout, bud, and blossom; some aspire to serve customers, others to exploit them, others to serve a larger corporation, others to fund trips to Lake Tahoe. But one thing's true of 99 percent of them: They aim to expand.

How? Sometimes a company has a great new product, like a potential treatment for cancer. Other times it's recognized a niche for the provision of a great new service, like Internet-access companies. But often, whatever the driving force is—products, services, or whatever—the company lacks the money to drive the operation forward.

Let's cursorially examine FlubSoft, the brand-new software company that you and we just started together that specializes in virus-protection applications. Office space, phone services, networked computers, health insurance, salaries—kicking off this new operation is a costly undertaking. It's no wonder the vast majority of start-up businesses go belly-up within five years.

To survive these initial costs, FlubSoft has two traditional alternative sources for funding. First, it can ankle down to the nearest bank, lay out its financial statements and projections, and plead for a loan. Often, this may not work; the less established the company, the less likely a bank is to lend it money. And even when loans do come through, they can do more damage than good. How? Well, risky loans demand higher interest rates. And the higher the rate, the greater the possibility that our company won't be able to pay it down. Never a borrower be, some say.

FlubSoft could instead sell chunks of itself to investors willing to take a shot at a big payout down the road. Conveniently, we would thus avoid costly debt financing, while now sporting business partners who are cheering (to understate the situation) for our virus detection and defense software.

The best of start-up companies—and we wouldn't have started this baby, you and The Fool, if we didn't aspire to superiority—can generate millions of dollars by selling off 30 to 40 percent of their equity to venture capitalists. In this situation, we'd create shares of ownership in our company and sell them off. We could pick a number out of the sky and say that 100 shares of stock makes up FlubSoft in its entirety. The number is insignificant; the percentage of the company's total value is what matters. If we sold 40 percent of our company to VentYour Capital Inc. for $1 million, we'd keep 60 shares and VentYour would take 40 shares. Our company wouldn't be listed on any of the U.S. exchanges, like the

New York Stock Exchange, but we *would enjoy* the same sort of "shares of ownership" as Microsoft, Wal-Mart, or General Electric.

Now, how do we get from being anonymous little FlubSoft, with twelve employees, a decent infrastructure, and impressive sales growth, to gargantuan FlubSoft, with five hundred employees, a square block of office space, national and international distribution, and tens of millions in annual sales? *We go public,* again selling more ownership in our company. This time, however, we'll be selling shares to a base of millions of investors, and taking our spot on one of the major U.S. exchanges.

The Public Company

There are three main ways that shares of ownership in American corporations wind up in the hands of former nonowners. The first is the *initial public offering* (oft-abbreviated "IPO"). Companies aiming to go public work through a brokerage that does investment banking to sell their first batch of shares to investors. They become, for the first time, a publicly owned entity that trades every day on a stock exchange.

The second way is for those public companies that have already had an initial public offering to acquire *more* capital to fuel future growth. They make a *secondary offering.* No matter how many more times a company offers shares, the sale will be called a secondary offering. Issuing more shares dilutes the existing value of the shares held by the previous owners, as it creates more units of control, but for a growing company this is normally not a problem. If we at FlubSoft need another $5 million to finance a new venture into entertainment software, we could sell another load of ownership, believing that the growth from our new project would far outweigh the share dilution. Most of the companies with a couple of hundred million shares started out with only a few million. They kept going back to the well for more cash, though, and they split their stock.

The final way that stocks get issued is directly to employees, either officers of the corporation or workers, through various profit-sharing and compensation plans. The board of directors, which represents the shareholders, figures that paying the company's officers in stock and not just salary gives those people a little extra impetus to improve the stock price. Giving the employees stock instead of just a paycheck gives them an interest in making an extra effort as well. Plus, companies are able to lower their salary overhead by partially compensating employees with stock.

Splits

A stock split simply involves a company altering the number of its shares outstanding and proportionally adjusting the share price to compensate. This in *no way* affects the intrinsic value or past performance of your investment, if you happen to own shares that are splitting.

A typical example is a two-for-one stock split. A company will announce that it's splitting its stock two for one in one month. One month from that date, the company's shares (having traded the day before at, say, $30) will now be trading at half the price from the previous day (so they'll open at $15). The company, which had 10 million shares outstanding, now consequently has 20 million shares outstanding. The price has been halved in order to accommodate a doubling of the share total.

The most common splits are three for two, two for one, five for four, and three for one. But they can happen any which way: five for one, 10 for 9 . . . They can even happen in reverse: one for ten . . .

Why would a company do this? Excellent question. A few reasons. First, as a stock price skyrockets, some people will be psychologically unwilling to pay that high price, so a stock split brings the shares down to a more attractive level. Again, the intrinsic value has *not* changed, but the psychological effects may help the stock. Second, a stock split generally occurs in the face of new highs for the stock. Thus, it's an event dripping with positive connotations and associations . . . it makes bulls snort and roar to suddenly have "twice as many shares" as they started with, for example. Third and final, with lower-priced shares, a stock's liquidity increases, often reducing the bid/ask spread and making it easier to trade. This is always good.

The Principal Markets

Public stocks are traded in public markets, organizations that create outlets for trading equities. Each market has various requirements that a company must meet before it can be listed—minimum asset value, minimum annual sales, maximum management ownership limitations—all designed to prevent manipulation of a stock's price.

The three markets in the United States are the New York Stock Exchange (NYSE), the American Stock Exchange (AMEX or ASE), and the Nasdaq stock market (Nasdaq).

The New York is the oldest exchange and has the strictest requirements for listing. Its typical member is a more established company—

the giants that have been in business for decades. Many in the invest-ment community perceive it as a sign of status when a company "makes" the NYSE.

The American Stock Exchange contains smaller, more speculative companies than the NYSE and has less strict listing requirements. It is actually a leftover from the days before telephones and other rapid forms of communications. The AMEX has five supporting member ex-changes: the Pacific, Cincinnati, Boston, Philadelphia, and Chicago stock exchanges. It recently merged with the Nasdaq but maintains separate listings.

The Nasdaq is the youngest and most dynamic. It is best known for offering fast-growing technology companies, although it lists stocks in every industry. The market has no central location, but rather is a net-work of brokerages that move stocks to one another via a computer system. The brokerages that participate are called *market makers.* They sign up to fulfill orders for individual companies. Thus a certain brokerage might *make a market* in Microsoft, but not in Intel, which means that if you want to buy some Microsoft they'll find the shares in *their* inventory, but if you want to buy some Intel, they'll have to phone up another firm and borrow the shares. This has absolutely no effect on you as an investor; you'll probably never know who makes the market in your stocks.

Companies will switch exchanges from time to time. America Online started out on the Nasdaq trading under the symbol AMER but moved to the NYSE and adopted the more familiar AOL symbol. Microsoft and Intel, on the other hand, have stuck it out with the Nasdaq. It clearly has no bearing on the attractiveness of a stock.

Lastly, how do these market makers make money? They make it off of the bid/ask spread, or the difference in the prices at which individual investors can buy or sell a stock. They'll quote you one price to buy and another price for someone else to sell, and pocket the difference themselves. The Nasdaq has been criticized—and even investigated—in the past for setting its spreads too wide, thereby earning an unrea-sonable profit. Things have improved, however, and spreads will only get slimmer when the exchanges switch to a decimal system.

The Traditional Brokerage

Now that we have an idea of what stock is and how companies go about issuing it, we can talk about how you purchase shares of your own. The most common way that investors purchase stock is through a brokerage. A brokerage is an institution licensed by state and federal authorities to buy and sell securities (a fancy word for stocks). Brokerages join the various exchanges and are policed by them as well as by the Securities and Exchange Commission (SEC). Brokerages take many shapes and sizes. Knowing a little bit about how brokerages work can help a Fool decide which one is the "right" one. That's the spirit in which we proceed.

Although they might stress their uniqueness, the largest, most renowned *full-service* brokerages are by and large cut from the same mold. The traditional big-name brokerage is broken down into a retail division, a research division, and an investment banking division. These firms also have a *back office,* where all the number crunching for customer accounts is done, and a *trading desk,* where customer orders are processed and communicated to the various stock exchanges.

The retail part is the one with which you're—perhaps, unfortunately—already familiar, or about to become acquainted. This is the one with all those salesmen (brokers) who make nagging calls to individuals or institutional clients, trying to get them to buy or sell the firm's recommended stocks. They make money for themselves and their firms by generating commissions off trades. It's a little-known fact that most big-name brokerages actually *lose* money in their retail operations. "What?" you say. "Why have them at all?" We'll make that clear in a bit.

The research side is made up of all the analysts and their assistants who write reports evaluating individual companies. The firm recommends them as a "buy," a "hold," a "market performer," and so on. You'll almost never see a firm labeling a stock a "sell." Why? As we noted earlier in the book, research firms rely on their relationships with every company they follow; they don't want to jeopardize those ties by motivating investors to sell. We remember hearing an analyst at one of the big brokerages saying, on PBS's *Nightly Business Report:* "Banker's Trust has fallen from $75 to $50 in a matter of months. When the stock was at $72, we labeled it a hold. So we were right on this one." Right? To *hold* for a 30 percent loss? *Hold* in analystese usually means *sell*.

The investment banking side of a brokerage is the most important part for the big firms. This is where they make all of their money. When companies want to make initial public offerings (IPOs) or companies want to issue more shares as an alternative to borrowing money, it's the investment banking people that do the multimillion-dollar deals. And the firm will leverage its alternate businesses to their favor when they bring companies public. How? Read on.

Conflicts of Interest at
a Traditional Brokerage

As we noted above, an investment banking relationship with a company is a very lucrative one for a brokerage firm, one that it's loath to jeopardize. This relationship has a profound effect on a brokerage's retail and research divisions. Firms keep their retail operations—even if they're ostensibly losing money—to serve as a sales channel to push initial public offerings and secondary offerings. When Rydholm's Taxi Service, Inc. (ticker: LATE) issues 2.5 million additional shares, the firm that helped with the offering often puts LATE on its Hot Weekly Buy List. Nice research. Then legions of brokers call all their clients, asking if they want in on this Midwestern cost-cutter, Pinto-cab operation. So keep in mind, when a broker gives you a call recommending a stock, it's not always because he thinks it really is a great buy. Sometimes the firm needs him to sell it.

The research people are not immune to this pressure either. When a firm has an investment banking relationship with a company, instead of having its analysts issue that dreaded "sell" recommendation when they think the stock is overpriced, many firms tacitly persuade their analysts to mumble "hold" instead. All the professionals know it's Wall Street doublespeak, so that the company doesn't have its feelings hurt by that nasty "sell" word.

'Course, there may be interesting reversals where a "hold" actually might mean a buy, as the firm is looking to keep the price a bit deflated to get its clients in on the cheap. (Heck, a "hold" may even sometimes mean *hold!*) How pronounced a problem all of this is, is open for debate. We'll look for you at the Fool's Galactic Gathering for Debate on the planet Jupiter in 2020. Between now and then, though, we can all agree that *no Fool* should ever buy or sell stocks based on the qualitative parts of a brokerage recommendation. Keep your eyes on the numbers . . . who cares about the names?

Discount Brokerages:
A Revolution on Wall Street

Before the days of lightning-fast electronic communication, full-service brokerages and the brokers they employed were a fairly vital link between individual investors and Wall Street. When you needed to communicate to someone down on a stock exchange trading floor regarding which stocks you wanted to buy or sell, you needed an agent.

That's how the commission system, on which most brokers' pay is still based, evolved. Commissions are the fees that you pay to a broker in order to have your request to buy or sell a stock fulfilled. Because of the time and trouble that it took to place an order—sending a runner to the exchange to communicate to the brokerage's agent on the trading floor—compensation was pretty substantial.

But with the changes in technology, Wall Street has lost the stranglehold it once held on investors. Now with wireless and online communications, the balance of investing power has shifted toward Main Street. It is now as easy for an individual investor in Anchorage, Alaska, to send in an order to buy or sell a security as it is for a well-paid broker in the Big Apple. Yet the oldest brokerage firms on Wall Street still do business in much the same way they did one hundred years ago, charging substantial commissions.

What specifically happened to break the control that the traditional brokerages held over the investment world? The watershed moment occurred in May 1975, when the Securities and Exchange Commission, the federal agency that has been charged with policing the investment world, decreed that the traditional fixed system of commissions would be repealed and brokerages could charge whatever they wanted, within certain guidelines. Thus, with pricing variables, the price wars began and the so-called discount brokerage business was born.

A discount brokerage is one designed to serve the individual investor. The "discount" label means nothing other than that the brokerage doesn't act as an investment bank. It doesn't launch IPOs and generally doesn't have any in-house analysts. All it does is buy and sell stocks.

The hodgepodge of discount brokers offers varying fee schedules, benefits, and account minimums. The two main kinds of discount brokerages are a *normal discount brokerage,* which does the same retail-side stuff as a traditional brokerage—providing news, some research materials, and a few perks at low cost—and a *deep-discount brokerage,* which is essentially there only to take your order and execute it with the fewest possible frills.

It's difficult to generalize about deep-discounters, though, since each offers a different combination of services and features, including cheap commissions, services, locations, and hours. Some try to undercut the discount brokerages a bit and still try to offer as many services; others let you trade for free with a $100,000 or greater account; others give you great rates if you type in your trades over your computer rather than call them in; still others charge you very little to trade but are open only from 9 A.M. to 5 P.M.

Many people believe that discount brokerages are riskier than regular brokerages and might fold in a stock market crash, but that's mainly just full-service industry scare tactics. To the extent that they offer the same minimum account insurance that full-service brokers offer, discounters are just as secure. The government-sponsored Securities Investment Protection Corporation (SIPC) insures accounts up to $100,000 cash and up to $400,000 in other assets. (Obviously, double-check that your prospective broker is SIPC insured.) If your account is larger than $500,000, ask your discount broker how you can go about insuring it further. This shouldn't be a problem.

Boutique Brokerages and Money Management Firms

Most of us divide brokerages into two camps, so-called full-service brokerages and discount brokerages. Although this is definitely a useful distinction, there's a class of brokerage firms that falls somewhere between the full-service and discount flavors. These are the so-called *boutique brokerages,* or *money management firms.*

These are regional brokerages, licensed to trade securities that focus on certain regions or certain types of investors. These firms typically charge somewhere between what a full-service brokerage and a discount brokerage would cost, depending on their research, their individual service, and the convenience of their locale. Typically, these firms have in-house analysts and might even do some investment banking and market making but derive the majority of their money from the retail operations.

So, Which Brokerage?

The first major decision you need to make when investing is what kind of brokerage you want to use. The use of full-service brokers must be considered, under most circumstances, quite *un*-Foolish. Consigning your money to the houses of Merrill, or Salomon, or Morgan is as much as to say, "Do it for me yourself, Harry (or Janice, or Joey, or whatever your full-service broker's name might be). I think you can manage my money especially well, and I'm going to pay you extra to do it for me. In fact, I'm going to pay you a premium for *every* trade you make on my account, since you're going to be coming up with virtually all my investment ideas. Finally, I may further pay you an annual management fee as a kind of goodwill gesture acknowledging the fine job you're doing for me."

Basically, what you're saying is that you're willing to pay up for what might well be a market-underperforming portfolio, and what most probably will be an S&P 500–underperforming portfolio as well. That's not Foolish, that's dumb.

Some investors, due to time constraints and a fear of going it completely alone, find having their own broker very amenable to their needs when starting out. The assistance that the right dedicated broker provides can be a valuable commodity. The idea of having someone whose everyday duty is to watch the stocks in your account and call you whenever there is any news about them can be a real comfort to many a fledgling investor. Also, for busy people who have neither the time nor the inclination to do their own research, the notion of a broker giving you advice that comes from the firm's professional analysts can be downright exciting.

Typically, having a full-service brokerage means having a broker who is yours and yours alone, through whom you make all of your trades. This broker is supposed to know about you and your goals and to advise you about what stocks may or may not be appropriate. He or she will supply you with scads of research, newsletters, and model portfolios developed by the brokerage in order to give you some ideas about what you should invest in.

Most investors, however, mistakenly think that all this activity will lead to market outperformance. If you're going to use a full-service broker initially, be sure to stack her returns against the S&P 500—the no-research approach to the stock market. If she can't beat the S&P—after deducting all commission and research costs—you won't be needing her assistance.

Cautious, or Confident?

Depending on the amount of money you have, how often you plan to buy stocks, and how much of your own research you plan to do, you'll make a choice somewhere on the continuum between price and service when picking a brokerage. And there are two typical roles that a Fool plays at the start, the "cautious" and the "confident" investor.

If you're a cautious beginner who's concerned about going it alone and would like to start slow, you can find a lot of ways to do this without relying on the big-name, high-priced firms. The most satisfactory option is the regional or boutique brokerage that can offer you competitive commissions, low account minimums, solid advice, and accountability. The less involved they are with investment banking, the better. To find one of these, you simply need to talk to friends who invest, scour the discussion folders at Fool.com, and drop in at the Brokerage Center on our site (www.Fool.com/dbc). Remember, if you're going to take things this route, you have to expect your broker to outperform the S&P 500 by enough to make it worth your while. Setting expectations right from the start with your broker is essential.

Always remember: Any broker who gives advice is basically a salesman shopping around his brokerage house's stock or fund picks and getting paid a percentage (the commission) for every sale he makes. What's really at issue here is not how good the salesman is, but rather the quality of the wares. Do the ideas your broker is selling you make good money, or not? If you have a good full-service broker who is driving your account to market-beating returns, then clearly this person is earning you additional dollars. If your broker, after reckoning fees and taxes, beats what you could do on your own, celebrate him, deify him, pay for his Thanksgiving turkey.

The Confident Investor

Fools are most at ease when they have the opportunity to demonstrate their expertise by making their own investment decisions, using only a discount brokerage. However, even when you've decided that you need no advice from brokers and no analysts' reports, you should keep in mind that there is still a wide variety of options left to you.

Many investors believe that simply because they're paying the lowest amount for transactions at a trading center, they're doing well. It ain't necessarily so. If you can't get your order in on an active trading day, or if a brokerage is so understaffed it's putting your order in late, then you might well lose the monies you saved with the lower commission waiting to get your order executed while your stock is jumping up or falling down in price. Those fluctuations are unpredictable, but it's still maddening to watch them while your brokerage twiddles its thumbs.

Also, there are a number of premium services that a more expensive discount brokerage can provide, including checking accounts, credit cards, and *Motley Fool Research Reports* mailed to your doorstep. Although you might pay a little more per trade, sometimes these perks are enough to make an investor choose Charles Schwab or American Express over, say, National Discount Broker.

As convenience is always an issue, check to see if the brokerages you are looking at have a Touch-Tone service or an online trading service available. If they do, check it out and see how easy or difficult it is to use. Using these two little perks can often shave quite a bit off your commissions, as your orders are directly entered into the trading system sans any human involvement save yours.

The original Fool Portfolio was launched with Charles Schwab, as we enjoyed the convenience of being able to call a Schwab representative and ask what, if any, news there was on the stocks in our portfolio. For our $50,000 portfolio, however, the price of the Schwab commissions became a little ungainly, and we were getting most of the news we needed online. So we looked around for a deep-discount brokerage that had a reputation for giving timely executions with minimal mistakes. The Fool settled on a deeper-discounter that charged half the price of a Schwab trade, but with the loss of a representative to call and ask for news. The final deciding factor for this move was not price per commission, but rather what percentage of our portfolio was being used to pay commissions.

These days, however, commission prices have been falling, it seems inexorably, toward zero. Now you'll want to shop for a broker based not just on commissions, but on what services you'd like the broker to provide. It may be high interest rates on money market accounts, free IRAs, checking and ATM availability, low fees for transfers and stock certificate issuance, and so on. Figure out what services you want and look for them.

Finding Your Discount Broker

1. Advertisements can be misleading. When you read about an incredibly cheap rate to trade stocks, read the fine print. Often, you'll be reading only a sample detailing *one* sort of trade (like stocks over $50 purchased in 5,000-share lots), as opposed to *all* trades. Some brokers "forget" to mention their minimum charge, while others print out-of-date claims. "SMOKEY DON'S DISCOUNT BROKER HAS CHEAPEST RATES OF ALL, SAYS INDUSTRY STUDY," reads the ad, with a footnote. Locating the footnote text at the bottom of the circular, you see in five-point type: "As of 1/30/98." Read carefully. Also, hey, what sort of industry study is that . . . one carried out by Smokey Don's uncle, Smokey Dan?

2. Commission schedules vary considerably, depending on the trade. While deep-discounters' overall rates may look similar, individual trades may not look the same at all. The most Foolish way to go about this is to match your trading style with the broker who offers the best rates for it. So, what's your typical trade? If

you most typically buy 1,000 shares of stocks below $10 a share, use this typical trade as a test of your prospective brokers. See how much of a commission you'd pay for this hypothetical trade using each of your several prospects. If you trade a lot of bonds, check those. You get the idea.

3. If you trade foreign stocks, which we don't generally counsel doing, make sure your discounter is set up to trade them. That's because some deep-discount brokers, particularly those offering the least services, are very poorly equipped for handling such transactions. You'll be sorely disappointed if you've just transferred your account to an outfit that can't meet your needs.

4. If you want to use a margin account, which allows you to buy stocks with money borrowed from the brokerage, you're in luck, because discounters generally offer cheaper margin rates than full-service brokers. Make sure you inquire about the current margin rate of interest charged by each of your prospects. Keep in mind, this rate fluctuates from time to time and will probably be based on how much you're borrowing (the greater the amount borrowed, the lower your margin rate). Oh, and The Fool recommends never going more than 20 percent on margin. That amount of leverage is bad enough; beyond that, you're in the dragon's den.

5. If you like to keep up day-to-day with your own stocks, we highly recommend that you set up an online portfolio on Fool.com or Yahoo!, where you can practice various strategies and follow the daily happenings in your holdings. One nice feature of our Motley Fool Portolios area (quotes.Fool.com) is that we automatically track you against the market indices, so you can always see how you're doing with each individual holding, and overall.

Tax Deferment: IRAs and 401(k)s

Entire boring books can be written about the vagaries of tax-deferred retirement vehicles—why, The Motley Fool even publishes a tax guide (not so boring as the average fare, of course)! These are the accounts you can set up and trade on without paying any taxes until you're old enough (fifty-nine and a half) to withdraw and use the money. We can, however, make a couple of observations, which you can apply as your situation permits.

First, always try to avoid penalties for early withdrawal. If you want to stuff money in an individual retirement account (IRA), make sure it is money you are not going to need until you are fifty-nine and a half years old. All the tax deferment in the world does not help you if you have to remove the money early and pay a 10 percent penalty. The IRS has a fixed 10 percent penalty on *all* money withdrawn from tax-deferred accounts before retirement age, whether annuities, IRAs, or 401(k)s. The law provides exemptions on withdrawals for the purpose of paying for death or disability, higher education expenses, or buying a first house. Think about whether you are going to need the money for anything other than one of these purposes before you hit sixty before you tuck your money into one of these tax-advantaged beauties.

Incidentally, tax deferment is not the same as tax free. Tax-deferred investments allow you to pay the taxes on your investments at some future point, letting them grow without taxation until your retirement. This deferment can be a very powerful tool, especially if you continue to add more money on a regular basis. However, do not add anything beyond the stated limits to your IRA or other tax-deferred retirement account or you'll have a nasty little 6 percent excise tax taken off the top. And of course, if you have an IRA, don't think you have to use a mutual fund in order to have it in stocks. A self-directed IRA allows you to invest directly in stocks, making changes whenever you like. Almost all brokerages will set these up for you, some for free, some for an annual fee between $25 and $35 per year, depending on your account balance.

If your employer offers to match your contributions to a 401(k) or 403(b) plan, by all means, take the guaranteed 100 percent return. Free money is very difficult to pass up. Even if you do not plan to stay on the job until retirement, you can always simply roll over your 401(k) into a self-directed IRA at a brokerage firm and use that money to invest in common stocks as well through the tax-deferred instrument.

If you have a choice between putting into your self-directed IRA stocks that pay a dividend and stocks that do not pay a dividend, *always* go with the stocks that pay a dividend. As dividends are taxed at the rate of income and not subject to a maximum, long-term capital gains tax, you can gain the most advantage out of tax deferment if you use it to shelter dividend income until you retire.

Finally, if you decide to open an IRA (and we hope you do!) consider carefully which benefits you more, the Roth IRA or the traditional IRA. The basic difference is that the money you put into a Roth is taxed up front, but after that you don't pay *any more taxes whatsoever* on any gains your account incurs. (When you cash out, it all comes to you at face value.) On the other hand, you put funds in a traditional IRA *pre tax*, so that you pay less in taxes now and can reinvest that money, letting it compound until your retirement. Then, however, you pay taxes on the IRA distributions. That means that a large factor in your decision is going to be whether you think that your tax rate is higher now than it will be in retirement or vice versa. Also, the younger you are, the more you should tend to open a Roth. Paying taxes now in order to rack up decades' worth of compounded returns, eventually withdrawing *all* of it . . . that's a sweetheart deal. If you have more questions on this, check into Fool.com. In addition, several financial sites including Vanguard.com offer free worksheets to help you calculate which method is best for you. Give them a try before making your decision.

Investing on a Limited Budget: The Dividend Reinvestment Plan

For investors who don't have a lot of money and can't afford to open a brokerage account, there's still an alternative to your average underperforming mutual fund. *Direct purchase programs* (sometimes called optional cash purchase programs) are almost always offered as a feature of a company's *dividend reinvestment plan* (DRIP). These little gems provide shareholders with a simple and cheap way to purchase stock without incurring brokerage costs. You just buy stock directly from the company.

DRIPs arose for two reasons. First, most companies have employee stock purchase programs. Since these companies have already undertaken the necessary steps to sell stock in-house, they figured they might as well offer it for the benefit of shareholders (the nominal owners of the company). The second reason was an attempt to decrease the volatility of the stock. If investors own shares in their name rather than having brokers hold their shares, these investors have to jump through some hoops in order to sell.

When you own shares in your name through a DRIP, in order to sell you need to contact the DRIP plan administrator, mail in the certificates, and have them sold on the specific sell day set by the plan. Or you have to take your certificates down to a brokerage and have the broker do some paperwork. The structure of DRIP investing promotes long-term holding, very much in the companies' best interest . . . and in our minds, often very much in the interest of the individual investor, who ought to buy quality companies and hold on to them tight.

With direct purchase programs, you can put small amounts of money, as little as $25 or $50 at a time, into the common stocks of companies that you believe are superior long-term investments. Many Fortune 500 companies have these plans, and many, many of them have excellent long-term prospects. Nearly every high-yielding Dow stock has a DRIP plan. For a complete, up-to-date list, check out www.net-stockdirect.com. Read the terms of each DRIP plan carefully, since they vary wildly from one to the next.

It can be a little complicated to enroll in a DRIP plan sometimes. For many, you'll have to register a share of stock in your name before you can open a DRIP account. That means that your broker will have to send you one of your shares. Some brokers will charge you a pretty penny for this privilege, so make sure you check what fees will be involved (try not to pay more than $20 for the service). A good alternative that bypasses this process is to open a low-commission account with buyandhold.com or sharebuilder.com that will let you buy small lots and reinvest dividends much more cheaply than a normal brokerage.

The best place to go if you want to learn more about dividend reinvestment plans and direct purchase programs may be your local library. Or you can try Fool.com, where some of the leaders in the DRIP industry sit in, waiting to answer your questions. We sport a DRIP Portfolio, where you can watch DRIP investing in practice, and we have a wonderfully informative book, *Investing Without a Silver Spoon*, written by Jeff Fischer, the Drip Port's manager. We don't want to tout ourselves too much—we mean, of course, we want to tout ourselves! But while we don't want to overdo it, we have to close this chapter by emphasizing how well The Motley Fool and its hundreds of thousands of readers can answer your questions promptly, thoroughly, and without the tangled conflicts of interest that many in the industry are tied to for their survival.

Investing in the U.S. Market from Abroad

Why should the U.S. market be reserved for U.S. citizens alone? If you live outside of the U.S. but want to participate in the strongest stock market in the world, fret not! It can be done!

Say you're living in Manchester, England. You've just ordered *Hard Times* from Amazon.com, loved the service you got, and want to invest in the company. There are a few different approaches to getting your hands on some shares. First, you could phone up your U.K. broker and ask him to buy the stock for you, but you will pay through the nose for the privilege. A typical U.K. execution-only broker of our acquaintance deals in any overseas securities at a commission of 1.8 percent, with a minimum charge of £30 plus account charges of £2.50 per stock per half year. Now, this may be okay if you want to buy only a single stock, but what happens when you get addicted to the market, or you want to buy AOL, and then Coke, and Microsoft and . . . and . . . ? You will end up paying simply tooooooo much in commissions.

At that point, consider your second option: opening up a brokerage account with a U.S. Internet broker. It really is easy, and you will save yourself lots of money. Just review the various Internet brokers' charges listed in the Discount Brokerage Center at Fool.com/dbc, dream of the day that you can get such low costs for buying and selling shares in the U.K., choose your favorite, and set to.

The process for opening a brokerage account with a U.S. discount broker is the same for nonresidents as it is for citizens. You just print off the application forms online, fill them out, sign them, and send them by snail mail (they need a real signature) with a check from a U.S. bank, or else wire them the funds from your foreign bank account, which takes a few days. (Some brokers insist on sending you the forms first via snail mail to make sure you are who you say you are and are living where you say you do.) A few days later you will get confirmation that your account is open and you are up and running and able to trade directly in U.S. stocks from the comfort of your own computer, surrounded as it is by half-eaten tuna sandwiches, moldy cups of coffee, and three-week-old copies of the *Financial Times*. Oh yes, we can see you!

Of course, it's not all such plain sailing. You do have to put up with the disgrace of being termed a "nonresident alien" by the American tax authorities. There are certain formalities concerning the tax treatment of your U.S. shares, and these formalities must be clarified with the brokerage house when the account is opened. Most individuals who are not U.S. citizens must complete a W-8 form (downloadable from the Web site of the U.S. Internal Revenue Service—www.irs.gov), which is a certificate of foreign status, and return it to the broker.

The specific rules governing how these accounts are taxed are described in IRS Publication 515 (withholding of tax on nonresident aliens) and IRS Publication 901 (tax treaties). The tax treaty issue is especially important. You can view these publications online at the IRS Web site, http://www.irs.gov/forms_pubs/pubs.htm. If the individual's country of residence has an agreement (tax treaty) with the U.S. government, then those rules apply and certain forms of income may have tax withheld on them at source, notably dividend income.

If your country of residence has no agreement with the United States, then you should complete the 1001 form (exemption form), also usually available to print off at the online broker's Web site, and no tax will then be withheld.

Happy Foolin'!

APPENDIX B

· · · · ·

How Investment Publishers *Should* Report Their Numbers

To be honest, we entered the financial publishing world licking our chops. That's mainly because the status quo was so clearly crying out for reform, and Fools have always enjoyed affecting the reformer's lilting tone. Here was the crux of it: Not only was the available advice generally wanting, but also much of it was extremely poorly—and in some cases shadily—accounted for. The two are not unrelated. It stands to reason that those offering mediocre investment advice would do their best to obscure the consequences. So going in, we knew that even if Ye Olde Printed Foole offered just plain, run-o'-the-mill, baseless stock picks, we would instantly join an elite minority if we simply accounted fairly and straightforwardly for what we were doing. It doesn't take much to outdo the standard fare in this regard.

In this appendix, we would like to share briefly the accounting standard we have adopted and attempted to popularize.

We write here for two audiences. For readers, we encourage you first to learn and then expect—nay, *demand*—the accounting standards put forward below. Any newsletter or investment service that you come across that does *not* follow our Foolish principles is skimping . . . probably for reasons that favor *them* and put *you* at a disadvantage. If you encounter such situations, we encourage you to do the right thing: Walk in the opposite direction.

1. Use Real Money

We consider this a necessity. All of the portfolios at The Motley Fool contain our own money, giving the reader a very strong sense that ours is exactly where our mouth is. Every single trade ever made on the Fool Portfolio/Rule Breaker Portfolio was done with real bucks. Why would you, or we, or anyone else want to follow investment counsel that wasn't backed by the hard-earned greenbacks of the adviser?

This doesn't mean that the adviser should have bought before you did, however. If she has bought her own picks but traded in *advance* of making her recommendation public for the purpose of profiting off others' attempts to get in, she is guilty of *front-running*. Readers should make sure they get an explicit statement from any advice giver that that person does not, as a policy, front-run. Front-runners are effectively using you to boost their own portfolios.

2. Deduct Commissions

Okay, now that we know we're dealing with real money, we must accept—and *reflect*—the real costs that all investors face. Let's begin with commissions. Almost all investors pay their broker a fee for executing their trades. Our portfolios have always and will always reflect the expense of making each trade . . . we do not consider our portfolios exempt from something that everyone else has to deal with. The amazing thing is that we're about the only financial publishers we know of who deduct commission costs from our returns.

It's not hard to figure out why. By ignoring the cost of commissions, investment newsletters can make their returns look better than they actually are. When you consider that most investment newsletters aim to help you make good money in stocks and that they market themselves based on their performance numbers, every little bit helps. Who would notice a tiny little thing like the cost of trading, anyway?

Why, a Fool, of course.

Frequent trading incurs high commissions; high commissions can kill you. Anyone who takes the time to run a few numbers can see how true this is. Let's pretend that you have a $20,000 account and you hold a balanced list of ten stocks, with $2,000 in each. Further, let's assume that you wish to day trade this account, because you think day trading is a good idea. (You're wrong; it's a bad idea. Hope you will read "Appendix E, The Carnival of Freakish Delights," where we run numbers very similar to these.)

For our purposes here we'll assume that you average two switches per day . . . two old sell and two new buy, which would mean that you hold each of your ten stocks, on average, for five days (many day traders hold them for something more like five hours, not five days). Anyway, two switches a day makes about a thousand trades a year, give or take. Let's continue to try to make your case look as good as possible by saying you're trading through a deep-discount broker, at only $7 a pop (an extremely good rate). Time to do some math. You're paying $7 a trade and making a thousand trades a year: That looks like $7,000 you're spending in commissions. After one year, the cost of trading will have eaten up 35 percent ($7,000 divided by $20,000) of your original investment! That's horrible! Good luck ever trying to beat the market on a consistent basis when you're "playing" like this. Maybe it works with big sums for institutional shareholders—doubtful, but maybe—but for average investors it's a real waste of cash (to say nothing of time!). You'll have to earn a return on your stocks of 46 percent a year just to equal the annualized market-average return of 11 percent. And don't even get us started on how much you'll pay in short-term capital gains taxes!

It is the above scenario that makes "Hot! Hot! Hot!" 900-number day trading hotlines ("Just $3.95 a minute!") so costly . . . and here we do not refer to your phone bills—which will be bad enough—but to your overall investment performance, which will be worse. These sorts of services are generally the most blatant violators of responsible accounting. Most don't show any overall numbers for their performance at all, let alone actually publish returns with commissions deducted. Fax 900-number services generally appeal to people who feel they need a new investment idea to trade in and out of every day; many of them are not smart or experienced enough to recognize that this sort of investing done over any intermediate- to long-term commitment should be considered their worst enemy. They get caught up in the adrenaline of the BIG DAILY TRADE and pay $7.90 for the privilege of dialing 1-900-HOTLUCKY to hear the two-minute report on Lucky's Hot Stock of the Day. This is sucker money . . . these are the same people who are just handing away money to their state government for the privilege of losing the daily lottery. Only in this case, the money isn't getting plowed back directly (supposedly, anyway) into public works.

All average investors who trade real money in the stock market face the natural consequences of their actions: a commission of typically $20 or more on every buy and every sell. Any investment service that conveniently neglects to account for these costs is working against—

not for—you. Of course, it's especially easy for them to hide these costs when they're not dealing in real money. (See item 1 above.)

We hope that some investment newsletters and services will join us in acknowledging the realistic costs of trading. It's awfully lonely right now.

3. Account for Spreads

Ah, but we can't leave off right there. Commissions are not the only cost of buying and selling. A second hidden cost, which can often exceed the amount paid in one commission, is the bid/ask spread elaborated upon earlier in the book.

To summarize, every stock actually has two prices, not one. Most people see just the "last trade" in their newspapers and figure that stocks have only one price. Nope. Every stock has a *bid price* and an *ask price*. As we explained earlier, the bid is the price you get when you sell a stock; the ask is the price you pay when you buy a stock. The asking price, for reasons that will become obvious to those who spend five seconds thinking about it, is always higher than the bid. (For those who couldn't spare the five seconds, imagine what life would be like if the price you paid for a stock—the ask—were lower than the price you could turn right around and sell it at—the bid. Instant money!) The reason that two prices exist is that the guy who matches buy and sell orders, the person who is effectively "making the market" in a stock, pockets the difference for his salary. He's the middleman, no different from any furniture salesman or bookie. He deserves to be compensated for the time and the risk that he is taking in holding an "inventory" of shares and orders waiting to be matched and executed.

Stocks trading on the Nasdaq have historically featured higher spreads. That's because these securities have typically been more thinly traded, requiring fewer market makers. Fewer market makers mean less competition between market makers, which equates to wider spreads. After all, when there's only one guy matching orders, you can bet he's going to skim more off the top than when he has four other competitors to worry about. Let's take an example of a typical Nasdaq situation: We'll call it Acme Thingamajigs Corp. (ticker: STUF), a stock that bids $10 and asks $10.25. Let's say you want to buy some 'jigs . . . you can expect to get the stock at $10.25 when you put in your immediate market buy order. The moment after it's executed, STUF will now be worth $10 to you—that's the bid, what you'd get when you sell it. In other words, you've just given away 2.4 percent of your money ($0.25

divided by $10.25 equals .0244). That's steep . . . for many trades, that 2.4 percent will come out to more than you gave away in commission.

Given what we learned in item 2 above—that investment newsletters try to sell copies by publishing attractive-looking returns—do you think the same guys who ignore commissions will actually account for spreads? Of course not. If they're going to blow off the 2 to 4 percent that commissions typically represent for a trade, they're certainly going to ignore the additional 2 to 5 percent paid on spreads, as well. Whether you wish to call this flat-out dishonest is up to you; it is certainly intellectually dishonest, at the very least.

The various Motley Fool portfolios, as they are *real money* moving in *real trades,* always account for the spread. We buy at the ask, and sell at the bid . . . there's no other way around it! Contrast this with newsletters that will claim, using the above example of Acme Thingamajigs, to have *bought* at $10, at the bid—as if you could buy at the bid. They'll point to a "last trade" in the newspaper of $10, and hey, that may well have been the last trade; the person who got $10 on that last trade was a seller, however, not a buyer. You simply cannot *buy* STUF at its bid. For investment publishers to use the "last trade" figure to suggest they entered a new long position at $10 demonstrates what a fantasy world they're living in . . . a fantasy that they hope *you'll* make-believe in too, when you consider subscribing to their stuff.

Ignoring spreads (and commissions) is cheating. It is also currently rampant among newsletter "gooroos." It may take a Fool to spoil this party, but then again, who would feel safe masquerading with these people?

4. Compare Performance Numbers to S&P 500 and Nasdaq, Daily

Above, we solved the Case of the Missing Expenses. Now it's time to turn our magnifying glasses onto the ever-sinister Case of the Failure to Compare One's Returns to the Market. The game's afoot!

It may seem obvious that the performance of any investment should be placed in the context of the overall market's. But it's clearly not obvious to financial publishers, most of whom would rather that you *not* compare their numbers to the general market's return. In fact, financial newsletters were so loath to make themselves accountable that an entire new *business* sprang up undertaking to track and report on their performance, since in many cases they wouldn't. We refer to the *Hulbert Financial Digest,* a newsletter that tracks how other newsletters do. The *Hulbert Financial Digest* has consistently demonstrated just how few investment rags even *equal* the market. That's not surprising, given that the vast majority of mutual funds underperform the averages. It is surprising, though, looked at in light of the grotesquely inflated claims that some investment newsletters make.

Mark Hulbert qualifies as one of the mavericks of money publishing for his lone efforts to match the *actual* returns of investment newsletters to those that they *claim*. In the process, Hulbert has ended up one of the financial world's more beloved figures to individual investors and one of the more hated to financial publishers. (He must be doing something right.) We love and admire Mark's efforts to keep up with the shenanigans of some whose advertisements would have you believe they earned a "100 percent–plus Annual Return!!!" when in fact they had just one great month and then annualized that figure to produce the fictional 100 percent figure. This sort of chicanery is too typical, brought to you by the sophists of our modern era.

We report on our portfolios' progress *daily*, posting not just our numbers but a full written recap of goings-on with our stocks, exploring potential investments, and expounding and expanding our strategies. Our numerical report includes the portfolio's performance as of market close every day, measured against two key market benchmarks, the widely followed S&P 500 and the Nasdaq., This comparison of investment returns to the market averages on a daily basis should become standard practice for any publication or service trying to solicit subscribers looking for investment information and stock-picking advice. The model here is mutual funds, which update their value and performance at the end of every market day (though they conveniently often do *not* offer comparisons between their performance and the S&P). Mutual fund companies use computers to run their numbers; so do we; so do many newsletter publishers . . . in fact, who would trust one that didn't? If we're all using these computers every day, why not appoint them to track our investment performance and report accurate numbers (expenses deducted) contemporaneous with the close of market business every day?

The answer, for too many, has been that such exposure would make their poor performance relative to the averages so glaringly obvious that they might have to go out of business. Right.

5. Report Longs at the Bid; Report Shorts at the Ask

And while we're on the subject of reporting numbers and accounting for bid/ask spreads, our portfolios report their prices each reporting period (each day, in our case) in the most conservative manner possible. That means that we represent our long holdings at their bid price, since that's what we'd get for selling them. And we report our short-sale holdings (when we have any) at the ask, since that's what we'd have to pay to cover our short. To report one's prices (and therefore performance) any other way would be unrealistic. However, we once again have thought and thought of who else out there in the big, wide world *also* reports their numbers this way; perhaps we have a limited imagination, however, since we could think of no one.

6. Make Trades When Your Readers Do

The next charge relates not to how numbers should be presented but to how a business should be run: namely, that those who pick stocks publicly should make their trades *at the same time,* not before, their readers do. We got into this a bit earlier, when we mentioned front-running. The subjects are related, but different.

Have you ever subscribed to an investment newsletter that gave you stock picks in the mail . . . one week *after* the newsletter writer had already published and *acted upon* his picks? You may have found that the hot new stock up for recommendation had already risen a point or more. Is that useful to you? If you find this a regular event with a rag that you currently take, you'll also no doubt find the publisher claiming significantly better returns than you, the subscriber, could ever expect. That's neither useful nor fair.

The Motley Fool makes a strong point of announcing all its trades publicly at least one night before the trades are made. Once a trade is announced to our readers, we'll make the trade within the next five business days.

7. Refrain from Ridiculous, Misleading Advertisements

The final Foolish standard of accountability regards the advertisements that publishers draw up to market their products. We want to see good, accurate ones. (We know, we know, we're hopelessly naive . . . but then we're just wet-behind-the-ears kids in our thirties.) Of the existing lot of financial ads on TV and in print, many violate common standards of accountability and respectability, and to anyone who knows investing, are also very, very lame. Of course, these ads aren't composed for anyone who knows investing. Quite the opposite. They're written for suckers unable to recognize any of the following: artificially annualized returns, Mickey Mouse investment approaches invented to exploit back-testing, unrealistic "one-shot-deal" investment bonanzas, and much, much more.

Let's look at these.

How about artificially annualized returns? We've already referred to one such typical scheme above. What happens is that an unprincipled stock picker has a great month or quarter, then begins to advertise that performance by projecting it out over a time period far beyond that month or quarter. Let's say you yourself, dear reader, just finished a *great* first quarter, your investments returning you 24.6 percent. It was a bull market—the Dow was up 12 percent—and your stocks stampeded over the market averages and made you a very happy Fool. Okay . . . now let's pretend you're the typical unprincipled financial publisher. What you might well do, if temptation overcame you, is to publish an ad with the following garish headline:

ARE *YOU* MAKING
141 PERCENT ANNUALLY?

What an eye grabber. Of course, all you've done—you sly devil—is to *annualize* that quarterly return; you've projected a 24.6 percent return on an annual basis, as if this were realistic or fair. Would *anyone* be well advised to search you out for 141 percent investment returns in *any* year? Not you, and not us either. Not anyone, actually; anyone with this sort of consistent performance would own most of the world's GNP after one investing lifetime.

So, what do you think of an operation that would do this? We don't think much of it, either. The only ones who do are the ones who can't figure out what's going on. As usual, ignorance is vulnerability.

Then there's always the magic of back-tested returns. "You would have turned $10,000 into $39,160,394 since 1980 by using Dr. Stephen Leeb's Master Key (trading strategy)," the fateful ad read. We say "fateful" because it was this advertisement that led to an SEC investigation of the otherwise uninteresting investing career of Stephen Leeb, editor of the financial newsletters the *Big Picture* and *Personal Wealth*.

How was this "Master Key" invented? Back-testing. In other words, using past results, somebody essayed to develop a formula that succeeded in identifying the optimal times to buy and sell stocks over the past history of the market. Beginning with a basic premise for when to buy and when to sell, the resulting formula would then be tweaked anytime it didn't work. Let's say the back-tester formulated things this way: Buy on Mondays, sell on Tuesdays. He would then begin back-testing until he hit a snag in which it was actually better to buy on Tuesday and then sell on Monday. Let's say that first snag came in August 1994. The back-tester would then tweak the back-tested formula to say, "Buy on Mondays and sell on Tuesdays, *except* in August 1994, when you buy on Tuesdays and sell on Mondays." And so on. Once you go back far enough and invent enough exceptions, you can end up devising a perfect market-timing formula. Unfortunately, you would have wasted your time; such a formula has no predictive value or useful application (other than to unscrupulous advertisement copywriters).

Let's sample a bit more of Leeb's text: "The information in this letter can make you rich in five years, starting with a small stake. False modesty aside, I've discovered the secret to forecasting the stock market."

Ironic use of the word "false."

The third and final example we'll include of bad financial ads intending to hoodwink the novice and the unwary comes to us from the Wall Street headquarters of Data Broadcasting Corporation. Publishers of a real-time quote service called eSignal, Data Broadcasting is notorious at Fool HQ for cranking out ads like this one:

> "I made an average 78 percent return using Signal!" says David Baluh, Oklahoma Signal User. "I support my family—5 kids under the age of 7—with the money I make in the stock market. I'm a day trader and in the year I've had Signal, I'd say a conservative estimate of my return would be over 78 percent."

How did the esteemed Mr. Baluh earn this return? Who knows? One suspects options, and anyone can have a good year in options, then lose twice as much the year later . . . the year the ads never tell us about. This is a classic example of unrealistic one-shot-deal investment bonanzas trying to grab your eye with sensational claims. But when we look more closely at the claim, it's even lamer than we first noticed: "I'd say a conservative estimate of my return would be over 78 percent."

It's clear from this text that Mr. Baluh probably does not have any precise idea of how his investments are performing. He's having to give an estimate, qualifying it with "I'd say." That Data Broadcasting has to tout someone about whose returns they can make no claim for accuracy suggests a certain paucity of candidates. The selection of the non-round number "78 percent" is a very nice touch; it attempts to imply an accuracy possibly lacking from the statement itself.

You know, it continually miffs us that more newspapers and magazines don't play watchdog and make a big point of exposing the trumpery of this tripe. But then we conk ourselves on the head and roll our eyes . . . how could we be so silly? These are the very same newspapers and magazines whose businesses rely on taking in these advertising dollars. Geez, what were we thinking?

◆   ◆   ◆

One aim at Fool HQ has always been to make our numbers duplicable by *anyone*. Everyone has to pay commissions and spreads—we do too—so we account for them. And hey, because we interact with our readers online every single day, we couldn't get away with anything less. Getting away with much less has been a commonplace for the past several decades of "one-way publishing," where publishers could impose their own standards and conventions—legitimate or otherwise—without fear of retribution. Welcome to the new millennium, where your readership has now become its own community, able to communicate and organize itself with the ardor and coherence of a grassroots political party. Subterfuge just became that much more difficult.

That's all right with us: We're all for rectitude in the first place.

APPENDIX C

* * * * *

A Tale of Two Stocks: Iomega and AOL

Iomega Revisited

We wrote about Iomega in our foreword to this book in the summer of 1995. The reason we wrote about Iomega is that our online readership had discovered the stock well before anyone else—including (most interesting of all) Wall Street. Within our readership were many "early adopters," who had purchased the Zip drive the first few weeks it hit the shelves; these people were happy and extremely enthusiastic owners of the product and urged us to take a look at the financials. From that point on, we found more information about Iomega in our online area than in any other source on earth. We were getting hundreds of postings about it per day! That was the reason for our fascination—a new way of accessing real-time national information about a company. People were driving to the factory on weekends to see if the parking lot was full and were calling every computer store in their city to find out inventory numbers and how fast the Zip drive was selling.

The discussions took place on The Motley Fool and all the detailed analysis of the community caught our attention. We did more research on the company (almost all of it online and in message boards), and in May of 1995 we bought shares in Iomega for the real-money Fool Portfolio (since renamed the Rule Breaker). The shares represented less than 10 percent of the portfolio's holdings upon purchase.

Within thirteen months, the Fool's Iomega investment represented nearly half the portfolio's total value after having risen over 1,500 percent. The Zip drive became the best-selling computer peripheral device in history (a rank it still holds), with a million being sold every several weeks. Most major PC makers began to offer Zip drives in their "boxes." The possibility for a new data storage standard held strong. But not strong enough.

At its 1997 business peak, Iomega earned $1.7 billion in revenue and $0.41 per share in earnings, with a net profit margin of 6.6 percent. The market value of the company had soared from 1995's $300 million to nearly $7 billion at the stock's high in May of 1996. Afterward, the stock began its long descent in the summer of 1996, months before (you'll note) its business performance actually peaked. Profitability levels are rarely high in the cutthroat data storage industry, and new technology is a continuous threat. In Iomega's case, however, management seemed to make the biggest missteps.

For one, in 1998, management launched an expensive ad campaign to boost declining revenues following price cuts that were. in part brought on by competition. With profit margins falling to nil and shrinking, the strangely timed ad campaign (Q1) helped push the company into the red for most of 1998 despite the fact that management had thinned production staff (again) and had long before closed a U.S. plant in favor of cheaper labor overseas.

Revenue declined in 1998 and again in 1999. A net loss in 1998 stands to forever tell the story of the harsh transition from the company's best year, 1997, to one of its most disappointing—until 1999 served up even bigger losses. At last count, the company had burned through two CEOs since 1998, and despite gallant efforts, has failed to produce another consumer-wide product hit despite its best efforts with Clik. It is difficult to continually reinvent your business, especially when it is focused on consumer technology products.

Iomega Annual Results (in millions)

Year	Sales	Net Income	Profit Margin
1999	$1,525.1	(103.5)	—
1998	1,694.4	(54.2)	—
1997	1,740.0	115.4	6.6%
1996	1,212.8	57.3	4.7%
1995	326.2	8.5	2.6%
1994	141.4	(1.9)	—
1993	147.1	(14.6)	—

A few lessons. First, in the euphoria of May 1996, a whole bunch of people bought Iomega near its top. Some of these borrowed goodly amounts on margin to do that (very un-Foolish), while others traded options on the stock (even less Foolish). They lost their shirts, as will gamblers in most arenas. Their story remains with us today, and is worth mentioning over and over. Don't get caught borrowing in periods of market volatility; it can break your heart.

Second, the whole nature of the stock market is that in the short term, prices are volatile and unpredictable, and move on the basis of hundreds of factors that simply can't be simplified down to one reason or one source. To simplify in that way is to engage in reductionistic thinking of the most vulgar sort, something that too many of us bring to market analysis in particular. But in the long term, the stock market rewards great brand names and consistently strong growth in profits. That's what we invest for, and all we've ever invested for in the case of Iomega.

Brand names can be short-lived, however. Iomega occupied a niche that was very important for a brief time, but it soon became redundant as more companies created private networks. The storage capacity of personal computer hard drives, too, soon became so large that home PC users no longer needed very much backup space. Suddenly storage devices lost a big part of their raison d'etre. Iomega's subsequent product lines never realized the popularity that the Zip drive had. Which leads us to a third lesson: Brand names matter only when they reside in an important, growing industry.

A few months into 1997, we sold a portion of our holding in order to lessen the overweighting in the Fool Portfolio of Iomega stock. Some of the proceeds were used to buy another great brand name, Amazon.com. Still, the amount that remained after that sale kept Iomega the biggest holding in the Fool Portfolio. That was entirely appropriate, given our thinking at the time, which continued to be that Iomega is a great stock to own for as long as it looks like the company will be a world beater. We love to invest in companies that have the power almost to create their own industries.

In December 1999, however, we concluded finally that Iomega had lost its edge. Its brand name no longer inspired thoughts of innovation, but of stagnation. Competition had increased, new product lines were not revolutionary, and profits had evaporated in the heat of increased advertising costs and shrinking margins. Meanwhile, we'd found another company that captured our imagination much more: Celera Genomics. It, too, came to us through the research efforts of thousands of people online and offered a new technology capable of turning the world on its head. We decided that Celera held more potential than Iomega, so we sold the rest of our Iomega position and bought into Celera.

Most ways you cut it, Iomega was a great investment for The Motley Fool. The first half of our Iomega holding was sold about four years ago for a 700 percent gain. The remainder, sold more recently, was up virtually exactly the same amount as the market overall during that time it was held. Yes, we did lose much of our advantage over the S&P 500 with the second half of the investment. There are *many* Foolish lessons that can be taken away from this, none of them cut and dried or simply stated.

Aside from the investment offering both success and a qualified failure at the same time, and therefore a multitude of lessons, Iomega will go down in the history books as one of the first stocks to undergo consumer research en masse online. Fools recognized Iomega's huge potential for sales growth (and a ramp-up from losses to over $100 million in net income three years later) long before the Street did. To the Street, Iomega was a total joke all the way through.

But not so, online. Many 1994 and 1995 Iomega investors participated in something that no investor had ever had before: global real-time research shared Foolishly in one place by many.

The Golden Child

On the other side of the Channel is America Online (NYSE: AOL), the tool that allowed investors to communicate in the first place. We added AOL to our Fool Portfolio the very first day that we went online, August 4, 1994, seven months before we bought Iomega. The two stocks soon came to dominate our portfolio.

The two stocks shared many apparent similarities in those early days. Both had risen sharply in the preceding year; both stood at the forefront of significant technological developments that had almost universal application; both were maligned for offering commodity products, even though they each had trouble meeting the huge demand for their products. That last commonality was the most important, since it meant that the companies had each branded their product as special and superior to those of other companies.

And together they appreciated. In April 1997, these two brothers combined represented 45 percent of the Fool Portfolio, both having risen about 600 percent since we bought them. We sold portions of both in order to diversify. By December, it began to look like we had forfeited some big gains by making these sales, after both Iomega and AOL almost doubled from the point at which we'd sold them.

That's when AOL and Iomega began to diverge. As Iomega saw its sales slump, AOL continued to imbibe human growth hormone. Far from becoming an obsolete industry, the Internet continued to boom. People all over the world signed up for AOL's service in record numbers. It had become the most trusted name in one of the most important businesses on earth. That led to premium prices for its stock.

Hindsight tells us that we missed out on a 2,000 percent gain on the portion of AOL that we sold. The lesson of Iomega tells us, however, that it's important not to let your portfolio become too sensitive to the movements of a particular stock. If we had counted on Iomega to lead our portfolio for the next twenty years, we would have met with a very unpleasant fate after its technology became less valuable. AOL was vulnerable to the same forces. If a technology had come along and made it redundant in 1998, it too could have fallen to Iomega's level. Now that AOL is set to merge with Time Warner (at the time of this writing), that's not as likely anymore, but the company still faces new competitive pressures from cable, satellite, and DSL Internet service providers. That's why we don't like to let one stock become too, *too* dominant in our portfolios.

Another lesson that we took away from the AOL/Iomega bifurcation is that big winners will far outweigh big losers in an investment portfolio. We may have proceeded to lose 60 percent of our gains in Iomega before we finally sold it, but we made 2,000 percent in our remaining AOL. That translates into about a $5,500 drop in our Iomega stock, but a $224,000 gain in AOL. Suddenly the loss in Iomega seems less significant, no?

We take our best shots at choosing stocks with great brands in important, emerging industries. Sometimes we don't back the right horse—hey, we're only human! If we can get a few big winners among our picks, however, we can handily beat the market. That eases the pain quite a bit.

APPENDIX D

. . . . .

Zeigletics:
The Penny Stock
That Never Was

Long before we launched *The Motley Fool* (a.k.a. Ye Olde Printed Foole)—a printed publication that had us throwing down dollars to lay out, print, and mail off our rag, burning the leftover loads of inventory afterward—long before this, we learned age-old lessons from our grandparents and parents about wolves and lambs, lions and antelope, snakes and individual investors. No matter how much we wanted to believe that everyone out in the field was there to assist us, to improve our investment returns, to serve our financial needs, the fact remained that not everyone was looking out for our best interest. And they're still not. Not ours and not yours.

Just as evolution taught the antelope to run in herds to survive the attack of a lioness, individual investors have been forming investment clubs around the country to help them keep a tight hold on their capital. Places like Fool.com offer that opportunity for collaboration, only now it's a twenty-four-hour operation, and it's nationwide.

But we didn't just start talking up survivalism and herding after getting online. We spoke of it back in the days of Ye Olde Printed Foole: The best investors pool their informational resources and their analytical expertise to wallop the market average. As has been noted in this guide, many investment clubs have outperformed the S&P 500 for years running.

But the lions are never far away, offering up expensive financial information that often hurts portfolios more than it helps them. We ran into scenarios that were, in fact, far more grisly than the provision of overpriced information. Some outfits were actually profiting by *misleading* individual investors in the offline and online world. Whole businesses that were fashioned to hype and manipulate the value of nickel-and-dime stocks were taking their operations from the analog to the digital world, where they could reach large audiences instantly. Of course, unfortunately for these schemers, online communications also allowed the herd of Foolish investors to assemble, and then assess and speak out against this sort of nonsense in the forum—an option none of us had had as individuals on the other end of brokerage cold calls.

What follows now, though, is an abridged version of a parody we did on penny-stock hyping. We conducted this parody on a national online service. It wound up in our 1994 April Fool's edition, for which we invented our own hypester, complete with an imaginary penny stock to hype. Below is our account of the creation, success, and demise of the legendary Joey Roman. We begin with an overview of the process.

THE COMPLEAT HYPESTER, REVEALED

"By right means, if you can, but by any means make
money."
—*Horace (65–8 B.C.)*

Customarily, the companies promoted by the Compleat Hypester—online *and* offline—are bantam operations with insufficient prospects to qualify them for any of the major U.S. exchanges. The potential reasons include grim financial statements, a stock that is too thinly traded, a share price that is too low, and a management team that owns too large a chunk of the company.

These disqualifiers are used by the major U.S. exchanges in part to complicate any efforts to manipulate share prices. For example, a company with 1 million total shares that trade at $0.10 per stub will have a hard time getting listed on an American exchange. The entire value of its stock—the value of the company, therefore—is a mere $100,000 (1 million shares times $0.10 per share equals $100,000).

Imagine the push that can be exerted on the share price by a hypester who manages to induce five hundred online acquaintances to each buy $1,000 worth of the stock. This $500,000—equivalent to five times the market's value of the *entire* company—will quickly and dramatically push up the share price, whatever the actual merits of the stock or the company. It's just such situations that can prove so lucrative to those interested in using the power of a new medium—online computer communication. For the first time ever, a single person can get the attention of thousands of others merely by posting a message on a public forum (anonymously, if desired) with the click of a button.

The operation is simple. First, the Hypester purchases thousands of shares for himself at a bargain price (usually a few dimes). Next he signs on to one or more online services and writes rhapsodically (though, in practice, illiterately) of the company's outstanding prospects. Some novices are swayed to buy, pushing the price up. The hypester shouts, *"Buy!"* louder. More people buy, the trading volume goes through the roof, and the price follows in tow. At some confidential point in time, the Hypester simply parts with his shares, selling them to the very people he'd duped into buying. That he could actually foist off his shares on someone else at such a dear price is a testament to the power of the imagination, since it's the sensationalized, often exotic story that so dependably attracts these novice investors.

What sort of profits could be turned? A $5,000 investment in a stock that moves from 25 cents to $1.50 in a month would net the investor a tidy profit of $25,000. Now, compound that monthly. Yes, that sort of stock price appreciation *was* happening. Incidentally, $5,000 compounded at 500 percent monthly turns into pretax profits of over $78 million in six months. No wonder these guys were fired up!

'Course, it was all highly unethical and a fine example of poor business. But they went on flipping in and out, buying and selling stocks, and would have continued ad nauseam absent some interruptive Foolishness. To run interference, though, we had to deconstruct the system piece by piece.

The Fairy Tale—Hyping the Company

The Grimmsian accounts of company operations that one can read in online hype necessitates, even from the dimwitted, a mild (sometimes *wild*) suspension of disbelief. More often than not, the stocks trade on wildcat Canadian exchanges, and the "corporations" (which may be nothing more than two- or three-man operations) are doing business primarily in countries that the average American citizen couldn't place on a map, making the business story that much harder to follow (a bonus for the Hypester). Invariably, at least one Hypester claims both to have flown to the distant country to view operations *and* to be in communication with management on a twice-daily basis. This go-between speaks confidently of his access to inside information, and drops hints (sometimes even correctly) regarding the timing of upcoming news announcements.

And what types of business are these companies doing abroad? Well, take Wye Resources, the Canadian owner of a Zairean diamond mine. Despite, to our knowledge, its failure to secure enough crystallized carbon to inlay a single diamond hairpin, Wye—a "hot issue" that was promoted on several online services and broadly across the Internet— witnessed a 500 percent gain in its stock in less than one month before regulators stepped in and halted trading.

And consider March 1994's "hot stock," Interlock Consolidated Enterprises (ILS), a company said to be providing materials for prefabricated housing to the "exciting" Russian market. The excitement largely surrounded an announcement of multimillion-dollar contracts with Russia for unbuilt houses planned for returning Red Army soldiers. Whatever. A quick buzz over to ILS headquarters turned up only this: Interlock received no money up front and would not comment on the pending contracts. So, what was the name of the Russian company involved? That too had to be kept secret. And each of ILS's press releases ended with a disclaimer never seen on those of listed U.S. companies: "This press release has neither been approved or [sic] disapproved by any Exchange or Regulatory body."

Hmmm . . . convenient.

Hype: Buy Now! Now! Buy!

But that won't stop a Hypester! Exclamation and exaggeration are the twin pillars of stock manipulation, and any news—the less verifiable, the better—that he can scrounge up provides the framework for his tale. He routinely hops from one online service to the next, posting semiliterate, fully exaggerated growth claims for each chosen peewee company. With millions of people now online—many of them looking for help on how to invest their money—it doesn't take too much noise to rally a profitable group of inexperienced investors.

ILS, the apparent home builder in the former Soviet Union, like many other hyped stocks, had a half dozen bulletin boards on the Prodigy online service where investors posted hourly quotes. Therein they dreamed aloud about the stock's prospects as the company crept across central Russia, and then the potential for monstrous profits once ILS began supplying the components for millions of prefab homes in Africa—though no such deal had materialized. Oh, and had any such deal been announced, investors would've been greeted with that standard disavowal:

"This press release has neither been approved or [sic] *disapproved by any Exchange or Regulatory body."*

Hmm.

Buy Zeigletics! (Hurry?):
Our Foolish Hoax Recap

Into this online arena stepped our man Joey Roman, penny stock superman, walking April Fool's joke, and full-fledged parody. He launched a massive national online propaganda blitz, just like all the other penny-stock hypesters, only the company he celebrated didn't exist, nor did the exchange on which it purportedly traded. But Roman was better than all of his competitors, even if he didn't have a real company to hype. Roman had always bought all of the competing hypesters' stocks for a dime less, always pushed them up a few nickels higher, and he claimed to enjoy the gushing admiration of the entire penny-stock world. Roman was a disgusting extreme.

The fifty-some-odd messages published by The Fool on Prodigy over a one-week period were read by thousands of investors. And the notes occasioned a couple of hundred responses in just a few days. Told in the voices that created it, what follows is a dozen of Joey Roman's online notes, which detail his brief but meteoric rise and fall. Likewise, we provide a full description of his hotcakes, sugar-dumpling recommendation: Zeigletics—Canadian manufacturer of linked sewage-disposal systems for the Central African nation of Chad, trading on the most conservative of Canadian stock exchanges, our cloud-built Halifax Exchange. Zeigletics made Roman, and Roman made ZEIG.H.

The Story (As Told by Mr. Joey Roman
in Online Postings)

Post #1: Roman Emerges

Zeigletics (ZEIG.H) trades on the Halifax Canadian Exchange at $0.37 x $0.39—a HUGE bargain!

That's because the company has introduced portable toilets (*Zeig-Lo-Pots*), bathroom deodorants, and other septic accessories to Central Africa, specifically Chad. Sounds pretty unusual, huh? But Central Africa is just introducing linked-sewage disposal. So this is a

MAJOR growth industry; cleanliness is next to godliness. It's a sizzling market, and Zeigletics, based out of Ludlum, Canada, is capitalizing on the possibilities.

Just between Roman and you, there *are* no other septic-accessory suppliers currently in Chad, or neighboring Sudan. Management is right now in N'Djamena, the capital of Chad, installing the first few hundred thousand Zeig-Lo-Pots, complete with bathroom deodorants. Roman spoke with the chief financial officer yesterday—collect call—and the day before, and the installations are beating all company estimates!!!! The Zeig-Lo-Pot is the envy of the Central African region. Why do you think the stock has six-bagged in a week!?

But the real kicker is plungers. Last autumn's streamlined installation of portable toilets in Libya did not include plungers. The recent sewage debacle in southern Libya was the direct result of inadequate declogulation apparatuses. (Basically, they needed plungers, and they had none.) The African infrastructure is so dated in these areas that more clogulation crises will definitely continue to occur at alarming rates. It's happening right now in Zaire, where (Tip, Tip!) Zeigletics has even now shipped (get this!) over a million plungers. BIG BUCKS that you don't have to wait for! This one has been going up, up, up, and will keep at it all the way to $5. Roman's taking it to 5. *Routine for Roman.*

According to the president of ZEIG.H, in Africa the name Zeigletics is virtually synonymous with toilets. The company recently sponsored the Sudanese equivalent of the Boston Marathon, where hundreds of fans were waving plungers at the finish line!!! Chad is at the dawn of its Septic Age, and Zeigletics is the only player in the region.

You want numbers?!

How 'bout 700 percent sales growth in the last six months? Our conversations with management (insider info) suggest a CONSERVATIVE estimate of $1.22 per share (Canadian) by fiscal year ended July. THE STOCK IS AT 37 CENTS RIGHT NOW!!!!!!!!!!!!!!!!!!!!!!!!!!!

Where does it trade? On the Halifax Canadian Exchange, one of the smallest and most conservative of the Canadian exchanges. It has stricter reporting requirements than any U.S. market, rejecting nine out of ten listing applications.

You gotta get in on this thing right NOW. The Canadians don't even know about it yet! The only people who know are Roman and the few others who've ALREADY made 600 percent in one week. Roman knows management, and management loves Roman.

This company is an overnight Canadian success story, and you're getting it just after twilight. Hurry! Hot, Hot, Hot! Sizzle. Hotter than an egg on the roof of my new Porsche in mid-August, when it's at $7. (My third new one.)

I already have seen the buy-side volume premarket Monday, and it's pushing the ask envelope on this one past 53 cents. Stochastics have it oscillating in the 80-cent region (no joke!) by midday. Stochastics don't always work; they can err too high or too low. But they have NEVER erred on the low side for one of Roman's stocks in his seventeen years of penny stock brilliance. 'Nuff said.

Post #2: Roman Hypes the Issue

BUY ZEIGLETICS!!! MAJOR HEAT! A special one just for you, folks! Up from $0.06 to $0.37 just this week!

People on this service brag about five-baggers in a month . . . Bah! How about a six-bagger in a week? That's Routine for Roman (the name of my newsletter as well). I have to laugh at these other investors. What did ILS do on Friday? Bah! My picks go up and KEEP GOING UP!!!!!

Nobody EVER sells my stocks until I've made my sextuple! I've made my players a bundle. Did you see the coverage on me and my letter in *Penny Stock Player* last month, entitled PINK SHEET SUPERMAN!?

Routine for Roman: "Most successful penny stock investor of the decade."—Roman

Post #3: Inside Info

Management report expected at about noon on toilet salts deal with Central African Republic. This one's DEFINITE. Just got off phone with Lars Saah, the president of Zeigletics!!!!!!!!!!!!!!—Roman

Post #4: Roman's Reach

Routine for Roman is the most successful publication BY FAR in the penny-player industry. I'm the only one to have earned regular CABLE TV time nationally, on local-access cable. My players are going public with the approach, finding little-known conservative exchanges with HOT HOT HOT companies, like Zeigletics, the African toilet products manufacturer. ROMAN HAS COME TO PRODIGY. When with Roman, do as Roman does—Roman, *Penny Stock Superman*

Post #5: FDA Approval!

Just got off the phone with Lars Saah, Zeigletics's president and also a petty-office holder in the government of Chad. Guess what? News is great!!!

Here's the scoop: Zeigletics has received permission from the federal Food & Drug Administration of Chad to sell its Zeig-Lo-Pots directly to the market!!! Previously, the Zeig-Lo-Pots were sold through middlemen who charged stiff commissions for distribution outside the Lake Chad region. What this means is hundreds of thousands of savings in Chad francs, the country's currency. This justifies Roman's write-up in the March 15 issue (six days ago) of *Routine for Roman*:

"Look for Chad's eventual permission for the direct marketing of Zeig-Lo-Pots throughout the country on or about March 21st."

This is a stock that our readers bought at 6 cents at the beginning of last week; it closed Friday at 37 cents!!—Roman

[Editor's Note: Over the next three days, Roman led the multitudes down the primrose path, while desperately trying to keep the gag alive.]

Post #6: ZEIG.H—Monday's Action

$1.12 x $1.14!!!! Up $0.75 today!!!!

This baby just tripled, in ONE DAY!!! Roman's now taken this one up from 6 cents last Monday to $1.12 now! Thanks to all online Prodigy readers for your support . . .

Routine for Roman: Nobody sells. Our stocks never go down. If you haven't bought Zeigletics yet (Halifax Canadian Exchange, symbol: ZEIG.H), you're no player at all.—Joseph Roman, Investor

Post #7: ZEIG.H—Tuesday's Action

Zeigletics, quote as of 12:21 P.M., Tuesday: $1.74 x $1.76. Whew!!!! Roman's made big money once again! *Routine for Roman*: The shorts have been squeezed like an orange on a strainer, and Roman's the one who's squeezin' 'em.

To anyone who hasn't bought yet: Isn't it time you listened to the player, superman penny-stock picker of the decade?—Roman

Zeigletics closed Tuesday at $1.92 x $1.93, UP $0.80 on the day! Thanks to all for hurrying into this one! I'll keep you posted; meeting with Lars Saah here in Manassas tomorrow. Big announcement about Madagascar should come tomorrow at about 1:56 P.M. Buy more, if you want to make more.—Roman

Post #8: Zeigletics—Wednesday's Action

At the open, $1.55 x $1.57, DOWN $0.37.

What's up here, people? Let's keep the shorts on the run. Roman's stocks *never* go down. We all need to stay in to get this to work. BIG NEWS coming soon! The Madagascar deal should be announced today. Keep your eyes peeled on Reuters. You just watch. ROMAN SAYS BUY!!! BUY!!! BUY!!!

Looking for it to go back over $2 today. I think $3 is reasonable by the end of the week. $$$$$$$$—Roman

(Two hours later . . .)

Post #9: Ssshhh! SELL!

Joey Roman and *Routine for Roman* put out a sell order on this one this morning. The stock right now is down $1 to $0.92 x $0.94. We told you to get out at $1.92 [yesterday's close], and if you did you made big money on this one . . . you did better than ten times your money in ten days. Zeigletics is a good company; we'll keep our eye on this one. Meanwhile, buy RUMR.H on the same exchange. That's where a lot of *Routine for Roman* readers are moving their money for the next few days.

We made big money, people! $$$$$

I'm lookin' out for ya.—Roman

Post #10: ZEIG.H—Wednesday's Closing Comment

Zeigletics had a bad day, closing at $0.68 x $0.70. If you got out when we told you to, you made a bundle on this one. We sold at $1.92, and moved the money into our new pick, RUMR.H. We bought it this afternoon at 0.12. Closing quote? 0.23, on 1.4 million shares (average daily volume: 2,000 shares). ROMAN STRIKES AGAIN!!!! $$$$$$$—Roman, Superman

Fly and Swatter

Along the way, Mr. Roman received loads of fan and hate mail. Below we publish some of the notes sent to Roman, as well as his responses, all in our Foolish fly and swatter format.

Fly

Hype has been taken to a totally new level. Roman, if you have been having this type of success for seventeen years, you would be the richest man on earth.—Geaty

Swatter

Sure, but there's no reason on earth why I shouldn't keep working. *Routine for Roman*.

Hey, did you just ask about my newsletter? *Routine for Roman*—the premier penny-stock player letter!!! Most people can't afford it, because subscription is $2,000/year. We do that on purpose, to price out nonplayers. We have a lot of BIG players, trust me, but we never reveal the names. We have a couple of people you routinely see on national network television, a couple of professional athletes, a couple hundred mutual fund managers (of international hedge funds mostly), and some average Joes too.

Our readers don't care about the subscription cost, especially when they make $20,000 in a month. They thank Roman for his tips, and we get several invitations to Christmas dinners every year!

Routine for Roman has been called "the Penny Stock Bible" by the MAJOR movers and shakers in pink sheets. And that doesn't mean small-time online service players. We're talking NAMES, people you see in the newspaper and on TV. Thanks for your interest.—Roman

Fly

Roman, if you really are legit, I will issue a public apology on this board. But PCFN, the discount broker, had never heard of the Halifax Exchange either. So first, you need to give us some phone numbers. What's the phone number for this company? How does one go about trading on the Halifax Exchange if one's broker has never heard of it?

Since you're new to Prodigy, you will have to excuse our skepticism.

If you really are legit, then it will be great to have you on board. There are a lot of nice people here. But, first, some phone numbers, please.—Juanita

Swatter

Roman is in constant (everyday) contact with the half dozen companies featured in *Routine for Roman*. Our one stipulation is that they deal with Roman, and Roman *only*. We don't work with anyone who won't work with Roman exclusively. WE HATE P.R. FIRMS AND 800 NUMBERS, and Roman doesn't need pipsqueaks to move these stocks UP UP AND AWAY. A lot of companies won't work with us, because we demand exclusive access to the story and numbers.

That's fine with Roman. *Routine for Roman* only picks one maybe two hotcakes an issue, and again, WE HAVE EXCLUSIVE AC-CESS TO OUR COMPANIES. Their phone numbers are UNLISTED; they DElist their phone numbers when Roman initiates coverage of their stock. So only Roman has the phone number. It's the best arrangement for *Routine for Roman and* its players. All news gets forwarded through Roman before the market catches wind of it. . . . It's all part of the deal.

Would you complain about Leaf Tectonics if YOU'D bought it at 15 cents (like Roman players did) last November and it was $3.43 at Friday's close? Roman doesn't think so. We laugh (hahahaha) at people who invest in other penny-stock companies that don't offer exclusive access to one individual. That's the best way to make money in stocks. But you have to know the right people, big-time money managers who gain exclusive access to company stories and numbers. Like Roman.—Roman

Threats and Insults

Then, in the succeeding days, Roman's mailbox and posts in the folders were deluged with follow-up responses. Some came to praise him, many more to bury him. Why many more? Because, as online services allow more than one screen name per account, angry penny-stock hype-sters logged on under multiple aliases and beat up our poor promoter and his newsletter. After a while, it was time for Roman to answer his detractors. Many of them had taken to tossing out vile threats, even di-aling into Fool HQ with strings of invective and threats. We've chosen not to reprint them here. Not worth your time. Roman's reply is, though.

Roman Responds

It's sad that some people invest large portions of their time trying to knock down Roman. Some of the saddest cases actually become *consumed* by it. But that's the price of greatness. Check it out in the history books: Every beloved figure over the course of human his-tory has had some mosquitoes buzzing around his ears. Heck, George Washington had an entire country out for his head!

Roman on Roman—Let me ask all of you this: Is your broker able to quote securities off the venerable Halifax Canadian Exchange? Has he ever heard of Zeigletics (Halifax: ZEIG.H), which was up over

3,000 percent in eight days??!!! Can he come up with shares of ZEIG.H at 2-cent spreads in any lot you request? Roman's guess is that your answer to these questions is an emphatic no.

But that doesn't surprise Roman, because long ago he came to accept his own superiority to *all other investment advisers*. And Zeigletics is just the latest in a fifteen-year-long litany of MONSTER stocks that Team Roman has taken up to stratospheric heights in a matter of days.

The respected industry publication *Penny Stock Player*—that seasoned observer of pinks and pennies—wouldn't have given its Lifetime Service Award to Roman haphazardly, would it? And hey, Roman can't help it if *Micro-Stock* magazine insists on calling him (February 1993 issue) ". . . the Minnesota Fats of micro-cap, thinly traded foreign stocks with large spreads. He calls the shots and then he sinks 'em." These ARE NOT paid advertisements, just unsolicited praise for a great investment technique, and a great man.

Roman will keep to his brilliant, can't-lose investment formula, keep making disgusting amounts of money for his loyal followers, and will keep giving away 75 percent of it to charity (this past year saw the erection of the Joseph Roman Empire Library at Roman's alma mater). The way my life is going, I don't think it'll take very long for a larger-than-life-size statue of Roman to be erected in Roman's hometown.

And probably in yours, too.
—*Joseph Lincoln Roman, Sr., American*

The Illuminati

We've decided to share the wrap-up commentary on the Zeigletics April Fool's joke that we thought the most eloquent. We have no idea who Mr. Hughes is but, to our ears, his note pretty well and Foolishly summarized the one-week plunge into the squash of online penny-stock manipulation.

This is the funniest exchange I have ever seen on this board. Come on, people, think! Toilet seat exports? Clogulation? Crowds of cheering plunger wavers?

The point Joey Roman is making is pretty clear: It is so easy for a fast-talking hypester to establish a position in a low-volume stock, rattle off a bunch of crap that sounds plausible enough to convince a novice, let the price pop due to uninformed amateurs flying in, and sell into the rise, laughing all the way to the bank.

Dear people, learn to evaluate and think for yourselves. There are some legit stock pickers on this board, and good ones at that, but please check their records and do your own research before buying someone's rec. The risk/reward ratio of buying something you haven't checked yourself will get you torn to pieces, so don't buy into hype. Intelligent investors (and prudent speculators) can and do get rich. But patience is critical, and risk must be calculated and limited as much as possible, and that only comes through knowledge and education. Read Peter Lynch, Warren Buffett, and Ben Graham.—Hughes

Wrap-Up: Shakedown

And there you have it: a condensed report of our Foolish send-up of on- and offline pyramid schemes tied to foreign-listed penny stocks. It didn't take any great stroke of genius to peer into and see through the system—a pretty transparent promotional strategy, no?

The Motley Fool was then featured in the *Wall Street Journal* and *Forbes* magazine in the weeks ahead, and many other traditional media operations have since taken an interest in the story. What is, unfortunately, not oft reported is that this sort of racket has and will continue to thrive over the telephone for many years to come. It isn't merely an online phenomenon.

In fact, not only is the online world not the breeding ground for penny-ante scamsters, it's their graveyard. The Motley Fool continues to work with state securities regulators in the months succeeding this Folly, and we believe that greater scrutiny is now tied to online financial services than any other mode of communication. We love it! When individual investors by the tens of thousands can gather to share information and advice about full-service brokers, discount brokers, mutual funds, aggressive bank salesmen, insurance salesmen, car salesmen, realtors, and the rest, the information is going to be the commodity; the service is going to be the distinguishing factor. Foolish investors like the sound of that!

In the meantime, the Foolish catchword is *patience*. Any investment vehicle with which you're not entirely comfortable or familiar is an "opportunity" to let slide by. Remember that rogue traders bring down multibillion-dollar banks *because* the banks aren't familiar with the rogue's investment approach. The same happens right down the food chain, with individuals watching their money evaporate in the hands of a financial manager whose strategy they did not understand and whose accounting system they couldn't untangle.

We hope our *Investment Guide* has well taught Fools to understand what they've invested in, to account for investment returns professionally, and to compare overall growth to the S&P 500. Stick to those concepts, and Joey Roman and his fellow Hypesters will make for nothing more than a couple good laughs around the barbecue.

APPENDIX E

· · · · ·

The Carnival of Freakish Delights: Investment Approaches to Avoid

Abandon all hope, you who enter here!
—*Dante*

Some people do subsist on an intellectual diet of just the facts, ma'am, the sand-and-sawdust, hammer-and-nails reality of a situation. They can glance at the numbers and hear the story they tell. They understand that here be the dragons of fiscal demise while over there lie the Elysian Fields of profit and prosperity. Others, particularly newcomers, tend to want a peek at the meat and marvels of a situation before deciding to stay or flee. So, rather than simply post a series of WATCH OUT FOR FALLING ROCKS signs to caution you against the most dangerous ways a Fool can be parted from his money, we much prefer to invite you to a carnival, the Carnival of Freakish Delights.

Welcome to the Carnival of Freakish Delights

Please, please, take your seat, have a little cotton candy, and relax. The ringleader will take the spotlight in a minute or two. We're here to entertain you! You're going to have lots and lots of fun. Lots of fun. For a while.

Hey, you! Yeah, you. You gotta pay to enter this establishment, Mac. And of course, we hasten to add that this entertainment won't come cheap. You think carnivals just show up in your hometown and let you ogle the Bearded Lady for free? Forget it. In fact, you'll find that our delights may cost you more than you'd ever have imagined. Sorry if you misunderstood before you walked in.

Well our delights are now waiting in the wings, and our ringleader is ready, so we'll keep our fingers crossed that you'll *love* the show. The popcorn is, of course, free.

◆　◆　◆

Ladieeeeeeeees and gentlemen, welcome to our carnival! My name is Malbowges, I am indeed the ringleader—note my bright suit and my gold cane—and I have the pleasure of welcoming you to the most dangerous show on earth. Now, let us begin.

Your State Lottery

Bring in the Fat Man! Oops, I mean *roll* in the Fat Man, please! Roll him in.

Ah yes, here he is. The Fat Man, ladies and gentlemen. The Fattest Man in the World! Right here in our carnival, playing right now in your home state—in almost *all* your home states, ladies and gents. What a load! Give him a hand.

Okay, I'll need a volunteer. Preferably, if I may, someone not very well educated. You, sir! Thank you. Very good. Now, come right down here, and if you would please, sir, extract a dollar bill from your wallet. Yes, that's right. *Very* good. Okay, now if you would just insert it in the Fat Man's mouth. Right in there, if you will. Oh no, I'm quite serious. Right in his mouth. Thank you! And . . . well, of *course* he's eating it! Yes, that's his act. Oh, don't worry, there's something in it for you. Don't you see, sir, what he's holding out in his pudgy paw? Indeed yes, a ticket. *Your* ticket, sir. Please accept it with the Fat Man's compliments.

Yes. Yes it is. A very pretty ticket, sir . . . glossy as can be. I see you're very happy with it. Feeding the Fat Man does have its little pleasures, doesn't it?

Oh no! No, you can't return to your seat yet, sir. The very next thing you need to do is to extract another dollar bill from your wallet. Well of *course* you'll get another ticket, sir . . . we wouldn't *shortchange* you. But first you must feed the Fat Man. Good. And now there's another nice shiny ticket for you.

My, ladies and gentlemen, just look at that Fat Man eat! His appetite knows no bounds; don't worry about him. Yes sir, another dollar bill gets you another wonderfully glossy ticket! And another. Another dollar bill, sir. Yes, sir. And another ticket. A bill, a ticket. Why, of course you *must* empty your wallet of one-dollar bills! Yes, just exhaust the supply but please do make *sure* you get all your tickets, sir.

You say you'd now like to redeem your tickets? Actually cash them in, eh? Okay, sure. Alecto, if you would please present this nice man with 50 *cents* per ticket. Yes, indeed, ladies and gentlemen . . . say hello to my beautiful assistant, Alecto!

Why of course, that's exactly the way it works. Every single one of them: 50 cents. Well, 50 cents is 50 cents, sir . . . not a penny more and *not* a penny less. Why, you're quite welcome! And we hope you enjoyed it! Yes, it's a very simple little act . . .

And for the rest of the show, the Fat Man will be right here so that all others who'd like to get their own pretty tickets may do so at their discretion . . . I'm sorry, madam? Ho-ho, bite your tongue, madam! Of course it's all legal!

Okay, now, back to you, sir. All out of one-dollar bills, yes, I see. Would you happen to have a twenty or a hundred?

Vegas

Next, ladies and gentlemen, I'd simply like to reintroduce my lovely assistant, Alecto. Wave hello, Alecto! We met her briefly during the Fat Man act, but now I'm introducing her more formally. As you can see, Alecto is beautiful and looks great in a bunny suit, but you may not have known that she is also an inexhaustible source of free drinks for customers. Needless to say, we have no problems filling the seats every night. Which is really what this business is all about.

But above all, Alecto is a killer card player who plays for money. And she plays with a few advantages. For one, she won't let you count cards . . . that's illegal. And if your score ties hers in blackjack, she always wins by default. Additionally, some people think she stacks the deck, but I must confide to the audience my own belief that she does not. Every game she plays offers her opponents worse-than-even odds, so why bother?

Alecto is eager to play cards with you and will be circulating through the crowd throughout our carnival.

Finally, before we move on to our next act, a brief lesson for the budding entrepreneurs among the young members of our audience. Note if you will, kids, the importance of both filling our seats every night *and* fixing all the odds against our gracious guests. With a combo like that, you'll do some very good business in life. The whole key here is that we've created a very attractive *environment* in which to lose money, and I can see that despite my admission that that's what it's all about, many of you are *still* itching to lose money to Alecto tonight. A further sign of our success is our ability to attract out-of-town visitors in huge numbers who come to us for the very same purpose. This mingling of glamour with inevitable failure appears to be somehow seductive, and uncannily successful . . . a freakish delight in its own right. That's my assistant, ladies and gentlemen: Alecto. She's in a major growth industry, and we're looking to hire more of her.

Day Trading

Now, if the house manager will kindly dim the lights, we can bid a proud welcome to the many-veiled, mysterious fortune-teller Commissionia. For $7 she'll tell your fortune. Seven dollars for a fortune, anyone? If you're interested in the stock market—and who isn't?—for a mere $7 our soothsayer will gaze deep into her crystal ball and tell you exactly where the market will go tomorrow or an hour from now or even sixty seconds in the future.

She's even right some of the time.

Seven dollars, here!

Of course, right or wrong doesn't matter that much . . . what matters is the conviction on *your* part, my friends, that with Commissionia's help—for a measly $7 per consultation—you too can figure it all out. Every stock in your portfolio . . . $7 will tell you your destiny! Where will your high-flying telecommunications stock be at 11 A.M. tomorrow morning? Commissionia—a wealthy woman in her own right—may know. Should you discard that dog you bought yesterday, now that it's off half a point? If you have $7, why not indulge yourself in a freakish delight?

Let us transport ourselves back to ancient Greece briefly, where we meet Cassandra, Commissionia's illustrious direct ancestor. Daughter of the king of Troy, Cassandra was blessed with the gift of prophecy but cursed by the god Apollo never to be believed. A somber plight. Ladies and gentlemen, in yet another ironic instance suggesting that history is out to have a bit of fun with us all, a hundred generations later our own Commissionia possesses virtually the opposite gift: She'll never ever make consistently accurate short-term predictions, but she's still fated to be believed by too many.

Seven dollars, my friends!

Perish all thoughts of accountability. When you spend this much money and energy on making your picks every day, you can't afford to look backward. In fact, you can't afford to do anything else, period.

Forethought is too dear a luxury; tallying, valuing, and accounting are out of the question. If you don't like the result of her predictions, just pay another $7 to change it back! Then toss in another $7 and get a second great tip!

Before concluding, boys and girls, please indulge your ringleader once more for a brief lesson in accounting so that we may learn a finer appreciation of Commissionia's superb business sense. At $70 a weekday for five predictions and five retractions, her active clients will pay some $18,000 per annum for the privilege of playing the trading game. Any client with less than $360,000 to invest is therefore spending more than 5 percent of his entire nest egg on Commissionia alone! Small wonder that cynics have called her the Prophetess of the Profitless.

But $7, dear audience, $7 is all for every single consultation!

Options and Futures

I'd like to take this opportunity now to mention a feature of our carnival that is simply too big to fit underneath our tent. What might I be referring to? The Ferris wheel! I want to draw your attention to it because of its uncommon relevance to our Carnival of Freakish Delights, as it's just another way that we can induce *you* to support *us*. Hope you good people will give the wheel a try.

A few things you should know first, of course. The first is that this wheel costs lots. You have to buy a package of expensive tickets for the ride, though the actual number of tickets you wind up with will be well below the number you paid for. Before an attack of sudden outrage overcomes you, my friends, let me explain! The difference is pocketed by a middleman, and in the case of our Ferris wheel, the middleman just takes a lot.

Let me make this amply clear with an apt analogy. Um, how about the financial markets? Every stock has two prices, as most of you probably know by now: the bid and the ask. When you buy a stock, you pay the asking price; as soon as your buy order has been filled, your investment is now valued at the bid price (the lower price), because it is the bid price that investors receive when they eventually sell. The reason for having two prices rather than just one is that the "market maker," the middleman who's matching buy and sell orders, needs to get paid for his work. So he sets two different prices and pockets the difference for every trade.

The more liquid an investment, the more people are trading it (and the more easily it is disposed of). Liquid investments typically feature narrower spreads than illiquid ones. The huge volume of shares traded in a stock like IBM, my friends, means that the spread will be very low;

there is little penalty involved in purchasing that stock. When you take a separate sort of investment like, say, options, for example, you're dealing with a very illiquid investment. The amount an investor might pay in spreads can be 10 percent or *higher* for some options. It goes without saying that spreads of that magnitude will kill *most* investors' returns.

Purely coincidentally, I suppose, the spread on ticket sales for our Ferris wheel are right about at that level. "Why?!" you ask. Simple, because we have only one person selling the tickets and not many more than that buying them. It's not because our Ferris wheel isn't any good! On the contrary, our Ferris wheel is extremely *exciting* . . . too exciting, it seems, for most people. It probably has something to do with the "jump-off point," which I haven't told you about yet. Anyway, suffice it to say that riding our wheel is an expensive proposition.

Okay, it is now high time that we spoke of this jump-off point. Our Ferris wheel, you see, never stops running. It spins and spins, and you rise and fall and rise and fall with it in a most volatile manner. Don't think, good people, that our wheel runs at a predictable, rhythmic speed. On the contrary! Our wheel operates in an unpredictable herky-jerky motion designed for thrills. (Creates a lot of spills, too, but to maintain our gay carnival atmosphere, we instinctively accentuate the positive!)

So when you want to stop riding, you must jump off. If you jump off too early, we will of course have succeeded in ripping you off on the ticket purchase. But if you jump off too late, you'll lose it all . . . as in "kill yourself." Again, I refuse to get into the negative, nitty-gritty details here, so, dear friends, suffice it to say that when riding our wheel you'll need to time your jump *expertly*. Very little room for error if you want your investment to pay off.

When I think about it, that's probably why few people ride our wheel for very long. They either grow discouraged because they keep jumping off early, or they jump off late . . . and it generally takes only once. Of course, we'll always have a steady flow of new customers looking for a thrill, and there's nothing quite like the excitement of going up the wheel—*way* up—your first time.

Anyway, I hope you'll all ride our Carnival of Freakish Delights' Ferris wheel before you go! I haven't ridden myself, of course—never would—but I definitely think that once is *not* enough.

Technical Analysis

Next, put your hands together for the *amazing* Phyrum—magician to princes, wizard of the North, prestidigitator extraordinaire! Observe the sleight of hand, the sheer hocus-pocus, the hypnotic influence that this master of mummery exerts over millions. . . .

If I may just interrupt Phyrum for a few moments, I'd like to mention that I have spent no small time observing the sorcerer at practice, and right now, right here, I will *share* with you the secrets of his art. Yep, folks, let us start with an example.

Let us say you, my investor friends, come across a stock at $17. That stock rises to $21 in the course of a month, then loses 4 points back to $17 over some indefinite time period. From there, it rockets back to $21 in three days, only to fall back again.

Presto!

Did you not see it? The magic! Did you not see Phyrum waving his diamond wand, seemingly enslaving the stock, bending it to his will? When Phyrum pronounced, "Support!" the stock magically levitates just *before* dropping below the $17 level, while when he intones, "Hssst! Resistance!" the stock instantly retreats from $21.

Resistance and Support are Phyrum's twin towers of delusion, the foundations of his legerdemain. And while I admire a great magician as much as any man, my admiration doesn't prevent me from revealing his tricks. You see, in the example you just saw before your very eyes, Phyrum looks at a graph of the stock and notices that recent history shows that twice the line rose above $17 without going below, and twice the line fell from $21 without rising above. Phyrum's sorcery is completely predicated on the notion that those magical "price levels" will hold power over the future. The stock will not drop below $17 because of Support; the stock will not rise above $21 because of Resistance.

In your utter mundaneness you, my dear audience of investors, probably study financial reports, plod through long write-ups about company products, and calculate numbers until your eyes glaze over . . . *all* in the quest for value, I presume. How Phyrum's followers would shake their heads, bemoaning this sorry waste of time! You see, technowizards like Phyrum can make money hand over fist without ever referring to a company's financial statements. Promise! (Can we brighten the spotlight on him, Vinny?) Yes, indeed, a good sorcerer need not even know a company's *product,* or in fact the company name at all! Give the astounding Phyrum a ticker symbol and a stock chart, and he *shall* make gold appear.

We cannot, of course, return your money if he's wrong.

Phyrum scorns the tedious reality to which you are bound, inventing instead entirely artificial schemes of perception. A most precarious craft but highly profitable to him who manages to induce others to go along with it! And that, in the end, may be his greatest magic of all . . . the mass hypnosis that mighty Phyrum has practiced upon his minions.

One more thing I'll say about Phyrum before we whisk the great man off the stage. Ah, but listen closely, because this is the most important thing, the deepest secret of all: You *must* believe in Phyrum for his magic to work. And I don't mean just *you,* sir, or *you,* madam, no . . . I mean *all* of you. *Everyone* must believe in Resistance and Support for them to work.

Some Fool once said, "I never met a 'resistance' or 'support' level that wasn't broken." Scoundrel! We have no room or patience for dissenters. Another writes, "It rained two Fridays ago, and last Friday. And in both cases, it cleared up on Saturday. Should I therefore conclude it will rain *this* Friday and clear up on Saturday?" What bad faith. If there are any skeptics in our midst, do not spoil the delights for the rest of us. Begone, Fools!

Meantime, I ask the rest of you now to continue to suspend your disbelief and view the mighty Phyrum with awe and wonder. Close your eyes, ladies and gentlemen, boys and girls. Close them! Now, picture yourself throwing away all your financial reports, your ratios and your cash flows, your calculators, and your common sense, and believe only in Support and Resistance, Resistance and Support. And now repeat after me, "The stock hit $17 twice and bounced back. Resistance is at $17, so it can't go below . . ."

Penny Stocks

Ladies and gentlemen, we have a special guest in attendance this very night. Introducing Mister . . . Joey . . . ROMAN!

[Editor's Note: Refer back to Appendix D for his antics.]

Software That Makes Investment Decisions

Ladies and gentlemen, if you will, please, a *first* at our hallowed carnival, and a moment of great private satisfaction: I'm about to activate a robotic replacement for myself! Allow me a minute or so to explain the rationale behind, and advantages of, this grand development.

The robot that will soon take my place is reputed to be able to perform in the role of ringleader *better* than I do on my own. The robot will operate completely independent of me, using a neural-network artificial intelligence, much of which was designed by our friend the *amazing* Phyrum. The machine has been programmed by a score of brilliant techies to match my every gesticulation, my every speech pattern, my instincts, my emotions, my intellect . . . all of it ingeniously synchronized.

The advantages are obvious. In opting to use the robot, I free myself from the burden of decision making, turning over my performance and reputation to a highly competent, highly skilled machine. Meanwhile, I'll be able to take advantage of the "body double" to spend more leisure time doing the things I really enjoy doing: going to Club Med perhaps, or re-reading *Marat/Sade*. The replacement will take care of everything!

And from your point of view, my friends, there should be no noticeable difference. Just the same charming emcee you're used to.

Technology has come so far! Its ability now to relieve us of the burdens of duty and personal challenge is truly wondrous; we live in an incredible age. I just hope I don't get addicted to using this thing. Just think: Soon you can do the same—turn your money or your life over to your very own robot.

Okay, friends . . . I hope you have enjoyed our show tonight, and if any of you are still at the carnival next week, I think I'll be back from vacation then.

Robot—*activate!*

Ladies and gentlemen, welcome to the Carnival of Freakish Delightss! My name is Malbowges, and I'll be your ringleder this evenig . . . evenig or morng???????? System resrouces checking . . . 5:17 reporting incorrecting date terminalerror 3.14169. Beware the Jub-Jub bird and the Bandersnatch terminalerror system. Shuttttttttdowwwnn.

APPENDIX F

. . . . .

The Leibniz Preharmonic Oscillator

Fools are my theme, let satire be my song.
—*Byron*

We've already written of our affection for technical analysis, that catchall term for investment approaches founded on the collective suspension of disbelief in superstition, pseudohistory, and the "insights" afforded by price-performance graphs. Drawing on such fundamentally misleading concepts as Resistance and Support, technical analysis is for many the way to "play the market." It also represents almost everything anathema to Foolishness, which we hope our dear carnival made amply clear.

But it isn't enough just to sit back and criticize. That's too easy. We have to have some fun parodying, as well. What better time, therefore, to introduce you to the one technical analysis tool that we *do* advocate?

It's time for the Leibniz Preharmonic Oscillator (LPHO).

The first thing to notice about this most ingenious device is that its name denies even the discerning reader any possibility of comprehending its function or meaning. How terribly technical! Like the McClellan Oscillator, the Elliott Wave Theory, the Chaotic Energy Flow Indicator, Bollinger Bands, and a hundred other techie gimcracks, the name "Leibniz Preharmonic Oscillator" stingily refuses to provide any real clues as to what it's all about. All the better to impress your unsuspecting listeners!

Take a moment to chant these choice words a few times. Anyone who can pronounce "Leibniz Preharmonic Oscillator" quickly and confidently will be sure to win over admirers, readers, subscribers, you name it. Instantly.

Leibniz (correctly pronounced *LIPE-nits*, and the speaker should always affect a faint generic European lilt) was, of course, the eighteenth-century German philosopher who proposed the metaphysical theory that we live in "the best of all possible worlds." The good baron's views were resoundingly mocked by Voltaire in his superb work of 1759, *Candide*. Little did either of them know that two hundred forty-two years later "the best of all possible worlds" would dramatically return to the world's stage, right here in *The Motley Fool Investment Guide*.

Leibniz used his concept of *preharmony* to describe the perfect state of existence preceding the creation. (In other words, our world was perfect even before you and I got here to make it so. Go figure.) Leibniz also created the notion of *monads,* which he described as the units that make up all living matter. Monads were alive, in contrast to atoms, which were dead. Infinite in number and variety, monads have no material form. The particular description of monad we're using here appears in the current edition of *The American Heritage Dictionary* as definition numero uno. Without Baron Gottfried Wilhelm von Leibniz, that is, "monad" might today refer only to single-celled microorganisms.

Naturally, none of this has the faintest application to the matter of analyzing finances and valuing stocks. But neither has technical analysis had anything to do with analyzing finances and valuing stocks, so we're working in the best spirit of the tradition, here. And a concept like monads could not be more perfect for our new technical device.

Okay, you've met Leibniz. And now you have some vague fleeting sense of what the "Preharmonic" part might mean. Time to look at "Oscillator."

Here again, we've latched on to a term that means very little to most people. In the case of "oscillator," of course, it's also a term whose use is rampant among tech talkers. That's not surprising, given that "to oscillate" means to swing back and forth. Because many technical indicators are focused on the ignis fatuus of predicting short-term price movements, "oscillate" is a perfect choice, with its suggestion of prices twitching spasmodically higher and lower. We couldn't resist, therefore, making our own technical indicator an oscillator.

By now, we hope our motive is becoming clearer. You see, we believe that technical investing has rendered unto the world a useless noise. Lots of them, in fact. (Anything from "So, John, what are your Bollinger Bands telling you?" to "We expect some overhead resistance at the

$30.25 level due to an overbought condition combined with a break-down in the thirty-week moving average" to the simpler, equally useless "Where's the market headed next week?") And so what better way to fight it than to create our own indicator based on the same premises: gaudiness, pretension, uselessness, obscurity, and lack of accountability?

And by propagating the Leibniz, you too can join the revolution. In our crusade against blather, help us fight it all with *more* blather. Perhaps we can even drown out the old noise.

Here's how this works. The next time someone at a cocktail party asks you where you think the market is headed, and you're bored of stating (Foolishly) that you don't care, that it doesn't matter to your long-term investment approach, answer instead: "Well, of course the Leibniz Preharmonic Oscillator is showing very strong sentiment readings—" (Pause lengthily at this point to let that sink in, hoping to elicit some vague gesture of affirmation from your listener. Then switch gears.)

"—which is, of course, bearish as usual, since it's a classic contrarian indicator." (This to be accompanied by a very, very knowing look, something like the chess master executing a checkmate.)

You'll get one of three responses at this point. In many cases, you'll earn a pseudonod, a smile, or some other gesticulation intended to imply that your listener understood and agreed with you, even though in actuality he hasn't the faintest idea what your little speech means. Our recommended reaction here is just to go start another conversation with someone less superficial. You've accomplished your mission: One more piece of techie misinformation has been loosed on the world and seems likely to spread. The other two responses are the honest one (a blank stare) or the inquisitive one (asking what the LPHO actually is). In these situations, you now have the amusing opportunity of elaborating further upon a technical investing concept that, like its forebears, has nothing real behind it.

"Well, have you heard of monads?" you'll begin, and then launch into a brief, digressive biography of Leibniz. (A few notes: He wrote *Monadology* in 1714, he was an ardent opponent of Locke's notion of tabula rasa, and he is now considered—FYI—the founder of symbolic logic.) Completing your tour of Leibniz, you'll return to a discussion of monads—a subject by which you'll appear to be unduly fascinated, though without ever offering any genuinely useful or educated knowledge about it—and you'll suggest, vaguely again (vaguely, always vaguely), that the oscillator relies on counting the swinging to and fro of monads as a way of gauging market sentiment. "It's all about whether we're in the best of all possible market environments," you'll allow, reiterating, "and it's contrarian too, of course, so that a high degree of monadic oscillation means sure trouble, as usual." At this point, it's probably appropriate to leave it all go with the simple sign-off line that our marketers dreamt up: "Well, have you read *The Motley Fool Investment Guide*? You can read all about this in there!"

Actually, although we said above that you'll encounter three separate responses to your cocktail-party explication of the Leibniz, a fourth response is possible: complete understanding from your conversation mate, who's in on the game. Congrats, you just discovered an attractive new friend! To indicate that she is in on the joke, she should give the standard response: "Well, I've always favored Voltaire over Leibniz, but then I'm a sucker for irony."

Readers detecting similarities between *Candide*'s Pangloss and our modern-day technicians, as regards the vacuous optimism of their philosophical systems, may do so at their own risk, and may not necessarily *not* be hounds on the right scent.

We'll end this section exhorting all true Fools everywhere to join us, join the revolution, and talk Leibniz! We particularly need you on our side if you're a well-placed Fool, one of the "higher-ups" with access to airtime on a financial television show. *You need to introduce the LPHO.* As always, a quick and oblique reference will suffice: "We're hitting some seasonal highs now—the advance/decline line makes that obvious—and the Leibniz confirms it." That's all we ask . . . we get enough people doing this and financial television will suddenly become fun to watch!

Of course, if you're feeling cocksure, we invite you to consider something more elaborate. If you pull it off, expect rave reviews online; you'll be the toast of an entire Foolish world. "Where do *I* think the market is going?" you might ask, greeting the interviewer with an irrepressible grin. "Oh, well, I just keep my ear pressed to the Leibniz Preharmonic Oscillator, a dandy little device that perfectly epitomizes market-timing gadgets. And the Leibniz is, of course, bearish right now, since everyone thinks this is the best of all possible markets." Your gaze must positively shine with good humor, but without *ever* giving anything away, as you trail on, ". . . the Leibniz being, of course, a contrarian sentiment indicator, measured in monads . . ."

Acknowledgments

One thing we've learned in this whole messy process is that creating a book requires a tremendous team effort. We have many to thank, but we'll keep this short and sweet.

Suzanne Gluck, the turbo-high-powered Manhattan agent with spikes on her gauntlets, who cut this original deal, receives Foolish kudos for thoroughly squeezing the New York publishing world for everything it's worth. She's a great agent, and has an even better sense of humor.

Then there's Bob Mecoy, our original editor at Simon & Schuster, the guy who first described himself to us over the phone with the felicitous words, "I have big hair and little glasses." Would that every editor were so easygoing, humorous, and patient; the world would be so much more . . . er . . . easygoing and humorous (and patient)!

Thanks also go to our editor for this revised edition, the very pleasant Doris Cooper, who brings charm and persistence to any project she's managing. Also at Simon & Schuster, Isolde C. Sauer has copyedited virtually every one of our books, and we challenge the publishing world to put forth anyone better skilled at this sometimes thankless, always critical task. We count our blessings, and Isolde is near the top!

Closer to home, we'd like to thank Selena Maranjian and Brian Lund for taking hours and hours out of their summer to, respectively, locate and initally tackle all portions of the book that needed updating. They were overseen at various points by long-time Fool Gabrielle Loperfido and then by the unflappable Alissa Territo, who was tasked with organizing the efforts of myriad Fools. They included Jeff Fischer and Matt Richey, respective comanagers of the Rule Breaker and Rule Maker portfolios, who contributed to those sections of the book. Ann Coleman, who worked on the "Mechanical Investing" section of the book and our Fool.com site; Mona Sharma and Amanda Adams, who did the fact checking; Roy Lewis and David Braze, who helped us with taxes and REITs; and Fools Brian Bauer and Richard McCaffery, who made sure that the updated creature that was wrought cohered.

Heading down the home stretch, we thank our families—the one that got us started, and the ones that we started (David, at least, so far)—for providing incredibly attractive, fruitful, and loving households that so strongly account for why we're able to do stuff like this in the first place.

And now finally, to our online readers, thank you for teaching us more than we ever taught you. Pulling a line from an old movie set in 2001, we are (now in 2001) together creating "something wonderful."

Index

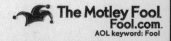